25TH ANNIVERSARY EDITION

Neil Somerville

What the Year of the Dragon holds in store for you

Your Chinese Horoscope 2012

HARPER
element

ISBN 978-1-4351-3907-7

Manufactured in Great Britain by Clays Ltd, St Ives plc.

2 4 6 8 10 9 7 5 3 1

CONTENTS

ABOUT THE AUTHOR

Neil Somerville is one of the leading writers in the West on Chinese horoscopes. He has been interested in Eastern forms of divination for many years and believes that much can be learned from the ancient wisdom of the East. His annual book on Chinese horoscopes has built up an international following and he is also the author of *What's your Chinese Love Sign?* (Thorsons, 2000), *Chinese Success Signs* (Thorsons, 2001) and *The Answers* (Element, 2004).

Neil Somerville was born in the year of the Water Snake. His wife was born under the sign of the Monkey, his son is an Ox and daughter a Horse.

AND A SPECIAL NOTE FROM THE AUTHOR
This year marks the twenty-fifth anniversary of *Your Chinese Horoscope*, and not only does this represent a personal milestone for me, but it is also a chance to convey my gratitude to many. Not only have those I have worked with at HarperCollins always been helpful, but for a great many years Liz Hutchins has carefully assisted with the editing, and so, Liz, and all at HarperCollins, a special thank you.

I have also been impressed by the quality of the many foreign language editions produced and would like to thank the publishers for the care they have taken, as well as for helping to make *Your Chinese Horoscope* so widely available.

The messages I have received from readers over the years have meant a great deal to me and I am especially grateful to those who buy my book every year for their wonderful support. To all readers, whether new to this series or regular, I wish every good fortune.

I hope to continue writing *Your Chinese Horoscope* for many more years. The first 25 years have been interesting … and just a prelude to the possibilities that lie ahead.

With thanks and best wishes,

Neil Somerville

ACKNOWLEDGEMENTS

In writing *Your Chinese Horoscope 2012* I am grateful for the assistance and invaluable support that those around me have given.

I would also like to acknowledge Theodora Lau's *The Handbook of Chinese Horoscopes* (Harper & Row, 1979; Arrow, 1981), which was particularly useful to me in my research.

In addition to Ms Lau's work, I commend the following books to those who wish to find out more about Chinese horoscopes: Kristyna Arcarti, *Chinese Horoscopes for Beginners* (Headway, 1995); Catherine Aubier, *Chinese Zodiac Signs* (Arrow, 1984), series of 12 books; E. A. Crawford and Teresa Kennedy, *Chinese Elemental Astrology* (Piatkus Books, 1992); Paula Delsol, *Chinese Horoscopes* (Pan, 1973); Barry Fantoni, *Barry Fantoni's Chinese Horoscopes* (Warner, 1994); Bridget Giles and the Diagram Group, *Chinese Astrology* (HarperCollins*Publishers*, 1996); Kwok Man-Ho, *Complete Chinese Horoscopes* (Sunburst Books, 1995); Lori Reid, *The Complete Book of Chinese Horoscopes* (Element Books, 1997); Paul Rigby and Harvey Bean, *Chinese Astrologics* (Publications Division, South China Morning Post Ltd, 1981); Ruth Q. Sun, *The Asian Animal Zodiac* (Charles E. Tuttle Company, Inc., 1996); Derek Walters, *Ming Shu* (Pagoda Books, 1987) and

The Chinese Astrology Workbook (The Aquarian Press, 1988); Suzanne White, *The New Astrology* (Pan, 1987), *The New Chinese Astrology* (Pan, 1994) and *Chinese Astrology Plain and Simple* (Eden Grove Editions, 1998).

———◆◆◆———

As we march into a new year
we each have our hopes, our ambitions and our dreams.

Sometimes fate and circumstance will assist us,
sometimes we will struggle and despair,
but march we must.

For it is those who keep going,
and who keep their aspirations alive,
who stand the greatest chance of securing what they want.

March determinedly,
and your determination will, in some way, be rewarded.

Neil Somerville

———◆◆◆———

INTRODUCTION

The origins of Chinese horoscopes have been lost in the mists of time. It is known, however, that oriental astrologers practised their art many thousands of years ago and even today Chinese astrology continues to fascinate and intrigue.

In Chinese astrology there are 12 signs named after 12 different animals. No one quite knows how the signs acquired their names, but there is one legend that offers an explanation. According to this legend, one Chinese new year the Buddha invited all the animals in his kingdom to come before him. Unfortunately, for reasons best known to the animals, only 12 turned up. The first to arrive was the Rat, followed by the Ox, Tiger, Rabbit, Dragon, Snake, Horse, Goat, Monkey, Rooster, Dog and finally Pig. In gratitude, the Buddha decided to name a year after each of the animals and that those born during that year would inherit some of the personality of that animal. Therefore those born in the Year of the Ox would be hardworking, resolute and stubborn, just like the Ox, while those born in the Year of the Dog would be loyal and faithful, just like the Dog. While it is not possible that everyone born in a particular year can have all the characteristics of the sign, it is incredible what similarities do occur, and this is partly where the fascination of Chinese horoscopes lies.

In addition to the 12 signs of the Chinese zodiac there are five elements and these have a strengthening or moderating influence upon the signs. Details about the effects of the elements are given in each of the chapters on the signs.

To find out which sign you were born under, refer to the tables on the following pages. As the Chinese year is based on the lunar year and does not start until late January or early February, it is particularly important for anyone born in those two months to check carefully the dates of the Chinese year in which they were born.

Also included, in the appendix, are two charts showing the compatibility between the signs for personal and business relationships and details about the signs ruling the different hours of the day. From this it is possible to locate your ascendant and, as in Western astrology, this has a significant influence on your personality.

In writing this book I have taken the unusual step of combining the intriguing nature of Chinese horoscopes with the Western desire to know what the future holds, and have based my interpretations upon various factors relating to each of the signs. Over the years in which *Your Chinese Horoscope* has been published I have been pleased that so many have found the sections on the forthcoming year of interest and hope that the horoscope has been constructive and useful. Remember, though, that at all times you are master of your own destiny.

I sincerely hope that *Your Chinese Horoscope 2012* will prove interesting and helpful for the year ahead.

THE CHINESE YEARS

Rat	18 February	1912	to	5 February	1913
Ox	6 February	1913	to	25 January	1914
Tiger	26 January	1914	to	13 February	1915
Rabbit	14 February	1915	to	2 February	1916
Dragon	3 February	1916	to	22 January	1917
Snake	23 January	1917	to	10 February	1918
Horse	11 February	1918	to	31 January	1919
Goat	1 February	1919	to	19 February	1920
Monkey	20 February	1920	to	7 February	1921
Rooster	8 February	1921	to	27 January	1922
Dog	28 January	1922	to	15 February	1923
Pig	16 February	1923	to	4 February	1924
Rat	5 February	1924	to	23 January	1925
Ox	24 January	1925	to	12 February	1926
Tiger	13 February	1926	to	1 February	1927
Rabbit	2 February	1927	to	22 January	1928
Dragon	23 January	1928	to	9 February	1929
Snake	10 February	1929	to	29 January	1930
Horse	30 January	1930	to	16 February	1931
Goat	17 February	1931	to	5 February	1932
Monkey	6 February	1932	to	25 January	1933
Rooster	26 January	1933	to	13 February	1934
Dog	14 February	1934	to	3 February	1935
Pig	4 February	1935	to	23 January	1936

Rat	24 January	1936	to	10 February	1937
Ox	11 February	1937	to	30 January	1938
Tiger	31 January	1938	to	18 February	1939
Rabbit	19 February	1939	to	7 February	1940
Dragon	8 February	1940	to	26 January	1941
Snake	27 January	1941	to	14 February	1942
Horse	15 February	1942	to	4 February	1943
Goat	5 February	1943	to	24 January	1944
Monkey	25 January	1944	to	12 February	1945
Rooster	13 February	1945	to	1 February	1946
Dog	2 February	1946	to	21 January	1947
Pig	22 January	1947	to	9 February	1948
Rat	10 February	1948	to	28 January	1949
Ox	29 January	1949	to	16 February	1950
Tiger	17 February	1950	to	5 February	1951
Rabbit	6 February	1951	to	26 January	1952
Dragon	27 January	1952	to	13 February	1953
Snake	14 February	1953	to	2 February	1954
Horse	3 February	1954	to	23 January	1955
Goat	24 January	1955	to	11 February	1956
Monkey	12 February	1956	to	30 January	1957
Rooster	31 January	1957	to	17 February	1958
Dog	18 February	1958	to	7 February	1959
Pig	8 February	1959	to	27 January	1960
Rat	28 January	1960	to	14 February	1961
Ox	15 February	1961	to	4 February	1962
Tiger	5 February	1962	to	24 January	1963
Rabbit	25 January	1963	to	12 February	1964
Dragon	13 February	1964	to	1 February	1965
Snake	2 February	1965	to	20 January	1966
Horse	21 January	1966	to	8 February	1967

Goat	9 February	1967	to	29 January	1968
Monkey	30 January	1968	to	16 February	1969
Rooster	17 February	1969	to	5 February	1970
Dog	6 February	1970	to	26 January	1971
Pig	27 January	1971	to	14 February	1972
Rat	15 February	1972	to	2 February	1973
Ox	3 February	1973	to	22 January	1974
Tiger	23 January	1974	to	10 February	1975
Rabbit	11 February	1975	to	30 January	1976
Dragon	31 January	1976	to	17 February	1977
Snake	18 February	1977	to	6 February	1978
Horse	7 February	1978	to	27 January	1979
Goat	28 January	1979	to	15 February	1980
Monkey	16 February	1980	to	4 February	1981
Rooster	5 February	1981	to	24 January	1982
Dog	25 January	1982	to	12 February	1983
Pig	13 February	1983	to	1 February	1984
Rat	2 February	1984	to	19 February	1985
Ox	20 February	1985	to	8 February	1986
Tiger	9 February	1986	to	28 January	1987
Rabbit	29 January	1987	to	16 February	1988
Dragon	17 February	1988	to	5 February	1989
Snake	6 February	1989	to	26 January	1990
Horse	27 January	1990	to	14 February	1991
Goat	15 February	1991	to	3 February	1992
Monkey	4 February	1992	to	22 January	1993
Rooster	23 January	1993	to	9 February	1994
Dog	10 February	1994	to	30 January	1995
Pig	31 January	1995	to	18 February	1996
Rat	19 February	1996	to	6 February	1997
Ox	7 February	1997	to	27 January	1998

Tiger	28 January	1998	to	15 February	1999
Rabbit	16 February	1999	to	4 February	2000
Dragon	5 February	2000	to	23 January	2001
Snake	24 January	2001	to	11 February	2002
Horse	12 February	2002	to	31 January	2003
Goat	1 February	2003	to	21 January	2004
Monkey	22 January	2004	to	8 February	2005
Rooster	9 February	2005	to	28 January	2006
Dog	29 January	2006	to	17 February	2007
Pig	18 February	2007	to	6 February	2008
Rat	7 February	2008	to	25 January	2009
Ox	26 January	2009	to	13 February	2010
Tiger	14 February	2010	to	2 February	2011
Rabbit	3 February	2011	to	22 January	2012
Dragon	23 January	2012	to	9 February	2013

NOTE

The names of the signs in the Chinese zodiac occasionally differ, although the characteristics of the signs remain the same. In some books the Ox is referred to as the Buffalo or Bull, the Rabbit as the Hare or Cat, the Goat as the Sheep and the Pig as the Boar.

For the sake of convenience, the male gender is used throughout this book. Unless otherwise stated, the characteristics of the signs apply to both sexes.

WELCOME TO THE
YEAR OF THE DRAGON

Vibrant, exciting and colourful, the Dragon heads many a carnival. Amid cheers and much rejoicing, it weaves back and forth, enchanting the crowds. It is bold and flamboyant, and in 2012 few will remain untouched by its influence. This is no ordinary year and no ordinary time.

Dragon years are action driven and times for major initiatives. As the Chinese proverb states, 'Better to do it than to miss it.'

This year, in view of some of the economic difficulties that have been experienced in recent years, many governments and organizations will be concentrating their efforts on encouraging growth and stimulating industry and investment. Major incentives will be offered to help the situation and in many countries projects will be announced to create new jobs and additional funding will be given to education and training. Dragon years favour progress, but opportunities *do* need to be taken when they arise. In this fast-moving year, there is no time to waste.

Elections will be held in several countries this year, with the economy featuring strongly in many a campaign. In the American election in particular, much of the year will be spent in considering the way forward. There will be controversy, surprise and drama. This election, as with others held in 2012, will be a driving force for change and ambitious new initiatives.

Another factor which will be important will be the question of national identity, with many people feeling concerned about their nation's role in the world. Some countries could see nationwide campaigns giving voice to certain issues, with minorities and smaller parties active and frequently influential. This proved the case with the Polish Solidarity movement in the Dragon year of 1988, and its strikes led to monumental change in Eastern Europe. The voices of some factions in this Year of the Dragon will be equally telling.

In addition to the incentive and investment schemes launched during the year, there will be important developments in many other areas. In building and infrastructure, some large-scale projects will be started which will bring considerable improvement to some regions, while in science and medicine, exciting advances will be made. Penicillin was just one of the major discoveries made in a previous Dragon year.

In 2012 the solar system is also likely to open up more of its secrets. The last Dragon year saw the identification of two new planets, and this year again some exciting new finds will be made. For astronomers, this can be a highly significant year.

There will also be major developments in the area of transport, especially in the creation of high-speed links and the manufacture of environmentally friendly vehicles. Green technology will feature strongly during the year, with Expo 2012, held in South Korea, being a showcase for some truly innovative thinking.

A feature of Dragon years is that they favour expression, and in the world of fashion, new styles are likely to catch the imagination, while in music, artists will be keen to experiment and promote new sounds, with some new bands attracting a worldwide following. Interestingly, it was in a Dragon year that Beatlemania became such a global phenomenon, with the Beatles being the first band to sell a million copies of a record before its release.

The film industry, too, will enjoy some major successes, not only with some spectacular blockbusters but also in furthering cinematography.

The internet will continue to have a great impact, with popular new sites and exciting advances in home entertainment. As is the way with Dragon years, certain ideas will take root and develop into something major. This was the case with Wikipedia, launched in the last Dragon year, which has now grown into a vast resource.

There will be an undeniable buzz to the year and many will find it inspiring and exciting. This will be especially true of the summer Olympics, held in London. People around the world will follow the fortunes of top sportsmen and women and see some spectacular achievements. The excitement will help generate a feel-good factor that, for a time, will be a welcome distraction from more worldly concerns.

The British royal family is never far from the news and 2012 promises to be an eventful year. It was in 1952, 60 years ago, that the young Princess Elizabeth came to the throne, and this Dragon year will again see considerable pageantry and celebration, as well as some surprises.

Dragon years have considerable positive energy, but sadly can also bring disaster. This year will again be marked by natural catastrophe, perhaps very early on. Not only could there be earthquakes in various parts of the world and volcanoes erupting, but the vagaries of the weather system may well play havoc in certain regions. However, when tragedy strikes, many nations will rally and provide support. Some wonderful gestures will be made, as with the Race Against Time, a charity event raising money to fight children's diseases which took place in a previous Dragon year, which had 50 million people participating worldwide.

As leader of the carnival, the Dragon energizes proceedings, and many will find that this is a year for action. The Chinese consider the Dragon year a time of good fortune and one favouring marriage and starting a family or business. Whatever your plans, this is a time to move forward.

Although some signs will fare better than others, the Dragon year will offer opportunities for us all. Do make the most of these 12 months, for your actions will in some way make a difference.

I wish you every success and good fortune.

YOUR CHINESE
HOROSCOPE 2012

18 FEBRUARY 1912 ∼ 5 FEBRUARY 1913	*Water Rat*
5 FEBRUARY 1924 ∼ 23 JANUARY 1925	*Wood Rat*
24 JANUARY 1936 ∼ 10 FEBRUARY 1937	*Fire Rat*
10 FEBRUARY 1948 ∼ 28 JANUARY 1949	*Earth Rat*
28 JANUARY 1960 ∼ 14 FEBRUARY 1961	*Metal Rat*
15 FEBRUARY 1972 ∼ 2 FEBRUARY 1973	*Water Rat*
2 FEBRUARY 1984 ∼ 19 FEBRUARY 1985	*Wood Rat*
19 FEBRUARY 1996 ∼ 6 FEBRUARY 1997	*Fire Rat*
7 FEBRUARY 2008 ∼ 25 JANUARY 2009	*Earth Rat*

THE
RAT

THE PERSONALITY OF THE RAT

To see,
and to see what others do not see.
That is true vision.

The Rat is born under the sign of charm. He is intelligent, popular and loves attending parties and large social gatherings. He is able to establish friendships with remarkable ease and people generally feel relaxed in his company. He is a very social creature and is genuinely interested in the welfare and activities of others. He has a good understanding of human nature and his advice and opinions are often sought.

The Rat is a hard and diligent worker. He is also very imaginative and is never short of ideas. However, he does sometimes lack the confidence to promote his ideas and this can often prevent him from securing the recognition he deserves.

The Rat is very observant and many Rats have made excellent writers and journalists. The Rat also excels at personnel and PR work and any job that brings him into contact with people and the media. His skills are particularly appreciated in times of crisis, for the Rat has an incredibly strong sense of self-preservation. When it comes to finding a way out of an awkward situation, he is certain to be the one who comes up with a solution.

The Rat loves to be where there is a lot of action, but should he ever find himself in a very bureaucratic or restrictive environment he can become a stickler for discipline and routine. He is also something of an opportunist and is constantly on the lookout for ways in which he can improve his wealth and lifestyle. He rarely lets an opportunity go by and can become involved in so many plans and schemes that he sometimes squanders his energies and achieves very little as a result. He is also rather gullible and can be taken in by those less scrupulous than himself.

Another characteristic of the Rat is his attitude towards money. He is very thrifty and to some he may appear a little mean. The reason for this is purely that he likes to keep his money within his family. He can be most generous to his partner, his children and close friends and relatives. He can also be generous to himself, for he often finds it impossible to deprive himself of any luxury or object he fancies. He is very acquisitive and can be a notorious hoarder. He also hates waste and is rarely prepared to throw anything away. He can be rather greedy and will rarely refuse an invitation to a free meal or a complimentary ticket to a lavish function.

The Rat is a good conversationalist, although he can occasionally be a little indiscreet. He can be highly critical of others – for an honest and unbiased opinion, the Rat is a superb critic – and will sometimes use confidential information to his own advantage. However, as he has such a bright and irresistible nature, most people are prepared to forgive him his slight indiscretions.

Throughout his long and eventful life the Rat will make many friends and will find that he is especially well suited to those born under his own sign and those of the Ox, Dragon and Monkey. He can also get on well with those born under the signs of the Tiger, Snake, Rooster, Dog and Pig, but the rather sensitive Rabbit and Goat will find him a little too critical and blunt for their liking. The Horse and Rat will also find it difficult to get on with each other – the Rat craves security and will find the Horse's changeable moods and rather independent nature a little unsettling.

The Rat is very family orientated and will do anything to please his nearest and dearest. He is exceptionally loyal to his parents and can himself be a very caring and loving parent. He will take an interest in all his children's activities and see that they want for nothing. He usually has a large family.

The female Rat has a kindly, outgoing nature and involves herself in a multitude of different activities. She has a wide circle of friends, enjoys entertaining and is an attentive hostess. She is also conscientious about the upkeep of her home and has good taste in home furnishings. She is most supportive to the other members of her family and, due to her resourceful, friendly and persevering nature, can do well in practically any career she chooses.

Although the Rat is essentially outgoing, he is also a very private individual. He tends to keep his feelings to himself and while he is not averse to learning what other people are doing, he resents anyone prying too closely into his own affairs. He also does not like solitude and if he is alone for any length of time he can easily get depressed.

The Rat is undoubtedly very talented, but he does sometimes fail to capitalize on his many abilities. He has a tendency to become involved in too many schemes and chase after too many opportunities at once. If he can slow down and concentrate on one thing at a time, he can become very successful. If not, success and wealth can elude him. But, with his tremendous ability to charm, he will rarely, if ever, be without friends.

THE FIVE DIFFERENT TYPES OF RAT

In addition to the 12 signs of the Chinese zodiac there are five elements and these have a strengthening or moderating influence on the signs. The effects of the five elements on the Rat are described below, together with the years in which they were exercising their influence. Therefore Rats born in 1960 are Metal Rats, those born in 1912 and 1972 are Water Rats, and so on.

Metal Rat: 1960
This Rat has excellent taste and certainly knows how to appreciate the finer things in life. His home is comfortable and nicely decorated and he likes to entertain and mix in fashionable circles. He has considerable financial acumen and invests his money well. On the surface he appears cheerful and confident, but deep down he can be troubled by worries that are quite often of his own making. He is exceptionally loyal to his family and friends.

Water Rat: 1912, 1972
The Water Rat is intelligent and very astute. He is a deep thinker and can express his thoughts clearly and persuasively. He is always eager to learn and is talented in many different areas. He is usually very popular, but his fear of

loneliness can sometimes lead him into mixing with the wrong sort of company. He is a particularly skilful writer, but he can get sidetracked very easily and should try to concentrate on just one thing at a time.

Wood Rat: 1924, 1984

The Wood Rat has a friendly, outgoing personality and is popular with his colleagues and friends. He has a quick, agile brain and likes to turn his hand to anything he thinks may be useful. His one fear is insecurity, but given his intelligence and capabilities, this fear is usually unfounded. He has a good sense of humour, enjoys travel and, due to his highly imaginative nature, can be a gifted writer or artist.

Fire Rat: 1936, 1996

The Fire Rat is rarely still and seems to have a never-ending supply of energy and enthusiasm. He loves being involved in some form of action, be it travel, following up new ideas or campaigning for a cause in which he fervently believes. He is an original thinker and hates being bound by petty restrictions or the dictates of others. He can be forthright in his views but can sometimes get carried away in the excitement of the moment and commit himself to various undertakings without thinking through all the implications. Yet he has a resilient nature and with the right support can go far in life.

Earth Rat: 1948, 2008
This Rat is astute and very level-headed. He rarely takes unnecessary chances and while he is constantly trying to improve his financial status, he is prepared to proceed slowly and leave nothing to chance. He is probably not as adventurous as the other types of Rat and prefers to remain in familiar territory rather than rush headlong into something he knows little about. He is talented, conscientious and caring towards his loved ones, but at the same time can be self-conscious and worry a little too much about the image he is trying to project.

PROSPECTS FOR THE RAT IN 2012

The Rat has a keen nature and likes to see quick results. However, the Rabbit year (3 February 2011–22 January 2012) is often a slow-moving one and there will have been times during it when the Rat will have felt frustrated. Patience is not one of his strong points, but he can take heart, as his fortunes are set to improve, with the closing months of the Rabbit year offering more possibilities.

One of the Rat's strengths is his ability to relate to other people, and in the remaining Rabbit months he should make the most of his opportunities to meet others. If seeking work or keen to advance his career, he will find that by speaking to those who may be able to help, he can benefit from some important advice and assistance. September and November may see some particularly significant developments.

The Rat will also value the support of family and friends in the closing Rabbit months and will see an increase in social activity at this time. It is important that he liaises well with others, discusses his plans and, at busy times, is flexible over arrangements. There could be some surprises in store for him, including travel possibilities or the chance to meet some people he has not seen for some while. In addition, someone close to him could have interesting news to share.

Rabbit years can be expensive, however, and with a lot likely to happen in the closing months, the Rat will need to be disciplined in his spending and, where possible, make advance provision for end of year expenses.

Overall, although the Rat may have found parts of the Rabbit year frustrating, he will have added to his experience, enjoyed some fine times with others and, in some cases, seen an addition to his family. As 2012 approaches, many a Rat will sense the tide is turning, with brighter times ahead.

The Year of the Dragon starts on 23 January and is a highly favourable one for the Rat. During it he will be able to put his strengths to good use and see some fine results.

For any Rat who is starting the Dragon year in low spirits, this is a time to seize the initiative rather than feel hindered by what has gone before. With resolve and determination, progress can now be made.

Almost all areas of the Rat's life can see positive developments, but his work prospects are particularly favourable. This is very much a year for moving forward and taking on more rewarding responsibilities.

For Rats who are well established in a company or a particular profession, there will be opportunities to take their career to a new level. Sometimes vacancies and promotion opportunities could arise suddenly, and if they are quick to put themselves forward, many Rats will benefit. Events can move swiftly in the Dragon year and here the Rat's sense of opportunity and timing can serve him well.

For Rats who feel prospects are limited where they are, this is a year to keep alert and make enquiries. Sometimes contacts could prove helpful in alerting them to new possibilities to consider. In this fast-moving and favourable year, many Rats will be able to move to a more satisfying and remunerative position.

Rats seeking work can also find new possibilities opening up. Again, if they are quick in following up vacancies that interest them, they may well be given the chance to prove themselves in a new capacity. This is no year to hold back. January (especially around the start of the Dragon year), February, September and October could see some particularly good possibilities, but such is the nature of the year that opportunities could arise at almost any moment. Time is of the essence in 2012 and for those who seize the moment, the rewards can be substantial. In particular, Rats who take on a new position early in the year could find further opportunities coming their way later in 2012 or very early in 2013.

The progress the Rat enjoys at work will also help him financially. However, he should still keep a watchful eye on spending, ideally setting money aside for specific purchases and plans. This way he can enjoy what he is able to do all the more. When possible, he should also consider taking advantage of tax incentives to save, add to a pension policy or reduce borrowings. With good financial management, he can help both his present and future position this year.

A feature of the Dragon year is that it sees the introduction of many new ideas and products. The Rat likes to keep up to date with developments and this will be another reason why he will fare so well in this interesting and fast-moving year.

On a personal level, he will find himself in demand. He will also be in fine form this year and will impress many. For the unattached, Cupid's arrow could strike unexpectedly at almost any time. The Dragon year has an exciting element to it and can mark a substantial change in fortune, particularly for Rats who have had recent disappointments to bear. Mid-April to June, November and December could see the most social activity, but at most times of the year the Rat will have things to do and look forward to.

The Rat attaches great importance to his home life and once again this year he will be active and involved, whether suggesting improvements, embarking on projects or assisting his loved ones in some way. Throughout the year, however, it is important that he is also open and forthcoming and consults others about his ideas and plans. Making assumptions could lead to some awkward moments or misunderstandings.

Also, while the Rat is always keen to help those around him, he will need to be careful that others do not take advantage of his willing nature or place too many demands upon him. If he feels under strain or has concerns at any time, he should speak up for himself. This not only applies to his domestic life but also to his relationships with new friends and some work colleagues. This may be a favourable time, but the Rat will sometimes need to stand his ground.

The Dragon year can bring some good travel opportunities and all Rats should take advantage of their chances to go away, whether for a holiday, for a short break or to stay with others. Here again the Dragon year offers the Rat considerable scope and quite a lot may happen quickly.

The Rat has a keen and curious nature and this year will give him an excellent chance to improve his situation as well as develop his ideas and interests. It is a time for seizing the initiative and making his talents count. Throughout the Rat will value the support of those around him and his personal life is favourably aspected. Overall, this will be a good and satisfying year for him, with his personality and skills serving him well.

The Metal Rat

This is a time of considerable opportunity for the Metal Rat. In particular, those Metal Rats who have been disappointed with recent progress will find the Dragon year providing the chances they have been hoping for.

At work the aspects are particularly encouraging. Metal Rats who are already established in a particular organization will often have the chance to take their career to a new level, perhaps through promotion or taking on specialist duties or being given the opportunity to use their skills in other ways. What opens up over the year may not only be an interesting change for the Metal Rat but also give him the challenge and incentive he may have lacked in recent years.

Metal Rats who feel limited where they are should explore possibilities. This is a time for action, and with resolve and resourcefulness, many will succeed in finding a new type of work that is ideal for them.

This also applies to those Metal Rats seeking work. Although the job-seeking process may be disheartening, the Metal Rat knows he has much to offer and ultimately his patience, self-belief and determination *will* prevail. The Dragon year holds great possibility and many Metal Rats will be able to make some important career moves.

With the Metal Rat's alert nature, he could identify possibilities to pursue at almost any time, but when he sees something that appeals to him, he should act quickly. January, February, September and October could see some particularly interesting developments. Also, for Metal Rats who see change in the first few months of the year, other possibilities could arise later in 2012. A lot is set to happen this year.

The Metal Rat's progress at work will also help him financially and in addition there could be an element of luck to enjoy, perhaps through an investment, policy, gift or bonus. However, while the Metal Rat's finances are favourably aspected this year, he would do well to use any upturn to help both his present and future situation. This includes looking to reduce borrowings and setting sums aside for specific plans and purchases. He may well come to be grateful for his discipline and prudence in times to come.

With work and other commitments, it is also important that the Metal Rat gives some consideration to his well-being, including making sure he has regular exercise and a healthy diet. At pressured times it is also important he gives himself the chance to unwind rather than feel he always has to be driving himself forward. This may be a positive year, but to make the most of it the Metal Rat needs to keep his lifestyle in balance.

He can look forward to some important developments in his home life, and the achievements of some of those who are very close to him are likely to be a source of considerable pride. This is a year favouring openness and good communication, and everyone in the Metal Rat's household can benefit from the encouragement and advice they can give one another. Here again the Metal Rat's ability to empathize will be so effective and he will appreciate spending time with his loved ones. The Dragon year can also have an element of spontaneity to it, and the Metal Rat will often enjoy occasions which just seem to happen or are arranged quickly, including breaks or weekends away. Domestically, this will be an active and interesting year.

With his social and engaging nature, the Metal Rat knows a great many people and over the year will again find himself in demand. His work and interests are likely to bring him into contact with new people with whom he will enjoy a particularly good rapport, and his social circle is set to widen even further. Mid-April to June and November to early January 2013 could see the most social activity.

For Metal Rats who are alone and would like new friendships or perhaps romance, the Dragon year can see a considerable brightening in their situation. By pursuing their interests and setting about their everyday activities, many will get to meet an important new person or group of friends who will become special. The Dragon year is well aspected for both romance and a richer and more meaningful social life, and can bring a transformation in the lives of many Metal Rats who currently feel dispirited.

Overall, the Year of the Dragon can be an exciting one for the Metal Rat. Whether personally or professionally, this is a time of important possibility, and by seizing his opportunities, the Metal Rat can look forward to making important headway and enjoying some well-deserved success.

TIP FOR THE YEAR

Be determined. With resolve and self-belief, you can find a lot opening up for you. Fortune will favour the bold and enterprising.

The Water Rat

This will be a significant year for the Water Rat. Not only does it mark the start of a new decade in his life, but some of the decisions he takes will have far-reaching implications.

To get the year off to a positive start, the Water Rat would find it helpful to give some consideration to his present situation and what he would like to see happen over the next 12 months. Having something definite in mind will not only give him something to work towards but also more chance to benefit from the opportunities that are soon to open up for him. In his planning, he should also draw on the advice of those close to him. Their input and encouragement can often strengthen his ideas and lead to improved results.

Some of the Water Rat's decision-making will concern his work situation. For any Water Rat who is feeling staid, bored and unfulfilled, this would be an excellent time to consider making a change. By looking at possibilities and obtaining advice, many Water Rats could be alerted to a new type of work which could use their strengths in other ways. Although this may involve retraining and some adjustment, these Water Rats will often feel more encouraged about their prospects than they have for some time.

This also applies to Water Rats seeking work. If they are eligible for training or refresher courses, they would do well to consider taking them up. With willingness, they can find opportunities can open up for them. Over the year, quite a few Water Rats will secure positions that are very different from what they have done before and set their career off on a rewarding new path. The Dragon year offers scope and possibility, but it is very much a case of the Water Rat persisting, adapting and putting himself forward.

For Water Rats who are well established in their career, this is also a time of important developments. With the experience they have behind them, many will now feel ready to move their career forward. Often opportunities will arise in the company or organization they currently work for, and their reputation and in-house knowledge will make them ideal candidates for a greater role. The responsibilities many take on will also give them the chance to learn about other aspects of their industry and mark an important step in their career development.

Those Water Rats who feel they could improve their situation by moving to another employer should remain active and alert in their quest. By making enquiries, talking to contacts and putting in applications, they will find their experience and resolve often bringing the position they want. Opportunities can arise suddenly and at almost any time, but January to early March, September and October could see important developments.

The Water Rat can also look forward to an improvement in his financial situation over the year. However, he will need to manage his finances carefully, including making provision for existing commitments as well as setting sufficient funds aside for forthcoming plans. Quite a few Water Rats may decide to mark their fortieth year in a special way, and it could be helpful to make early allowance for this, especially if travel is involved. This is a year when careful planning can lead to more being achieved.

Another beneficial aspect of the year will be the opportunities that it will bring, especially concerning the Water Rat's interests and recreational pursuits. He could be invited to take part in activities, decide to join a local group, find out about a new interest or take up a form of exercise that intrigues him. By making the most of such chances, he can derive considerable pleasure from his activities. For any Water Rat who feels unfulfilled, this is an excellent year to consider taking up a new interest or hobby. What is started in 2012 can have present *and* future value.

With his outgoing nature, the Water Rat places great importance on his social life and over the year will add to his circle of friends and acquaintances. For any Water Rat who would welcome new friends or perhaps romance, the Dragon year holds great promise. Mid-April to June, November and December could see some particularly good chances to meet others as well as be active times socially.

The Water Rat's home life is also set to be busy, with many calls upon his time. In view of all the activity, this is a year for joint planning and a willingness to share household tasks. In quite a few Water Rat homes some ambitious projects will be started, particularly concerning home improvements, and some Water Rats may also move. Whatever the Water Rat has in mind, home plans do need to be carefully costed and ample time allowed.

The Dragon year will also contain some special domestic moments and many Water Rats will be particularly heartened by the love and affection shown to them as they mark their fortieth birthday. In many a Water Rat household there will also be some family news to enjoy.

In general, the Dragon year holds considerable promise for the Water Rat. With his ability to seek out and make the most of opportunity, together with his willingness to move forward, he is set to do well this year. The support and advice of those around him, together with his strengths and personable nature, will enable him to accomplish a great deal and benefit from the opportunities that will open up for him. And what he achieves this year can have important long-term value.

TIP FOR THE YEAR

This is an excellent year for personal growth. Use your opportunities to develop your skills as well as learn new ones. What you do now can be an investment both in yourself and in your future.

The Wood Rat

This will be a busy year for the Wood Rat with some personally important developments.

Work prospects are especially encouraging, and for those Wood Rats who are languishing in their present position or seeking work, the Dragon year can bring the chance they need to move forward. However, to benefit, these Wood Rats should seek advice on the options available to them and explore possibilities. By being open to the advice, instruction and help available, many Wood Rats will be able to secure a new position, and often one with the potential for future development. With willingness and initiative, many Wood Rats will indeed find new doors opening.

Events can move quickly in the Dragon year and some Wood Rats could find themselves being offered a new position and asked to start almost immediately. Opportunities do need to be followed up the moment they arise.

The prospects are also positive for Wood Rats who are well established in a particular career. Over the year many will be encouraged to take on a greater role, often as a result of recent achievements. Although this may entail additional training and there may be a lot to learn, by rising to the challenge these Wood Rats will not only be advancing their career and increasing their income but also gaining valuable new experience. What is achieved this year can be an important step in their overall career development.

For all Wood Rats, January, February and September to early November are likely to be busy and eventful months for work matters.

The progress the Wood Rat makes at work can also help financially. Not only will many Wood Rats enjoy an improved income but, with their enterprising streak, some could also find a hobby or interest supplementing this in some way. However, while the aspects are encouraging, the Wood Rat needs to remain disciplined in his spending and budget carefully, especially if making sizeable deposits or involved in large transactions. And when entering into any important agreement, he does need to be thorough and check the terms and implications.

Another important consideration for the Wood Rat this year will be his general lifestyle. With the demands of his work, including, for some, a long commute, he does need to give thought to his well-being and allow sufficient time for rest and recreation. To be at his best, he needs to keep his lifestyle well balanced and not skimp on exercise, sleep or healthy food.

Also, while he will have many demands on his time, the Wood Rat will benefit from joining others in certain interests and recreational pursuits. Not only will he enjoy the social aspects of these activities, including the chance to form new friendships, but he could also be encouraged to take a particular interest or skill further. Life can work in curious ways in the Dragon year, with chance events sometimes opening up significant possibilities.

Throughout the year the Wood Rat will also value the support and camaraderie of his close friends. For the unattached, romantic possibilities are excellent, with a chance meeting – chance does play an important part this year – transforming their situation. Mid-April to early July, November and December could see the most social activity, but throughout the year the Wood Rat will find himself in demand.

This can also be an exciting year domestically. For Wood Rats who are parents or who become parents this year, this can be a special although sometimes tiring time. However, even though some days and nights may be exasperating, these Wood Rats will delight in watching their children's development and much fun can be had.

For others, this can also be a full and personally rewarding year. There will be decisions to take, purchases to be made and pleasures to be shared. Those with a partner will find that by doing a lot together, they can achieve a great deal. Accommodation plans will often be prominent and, as the Dragon year can have some surprises in store, synchronicity may come into play and exciting possibilities suddenly open up. For the Wood Rat, this is very much a year when his ability to sense opportunities will bring benefits.

Overall, the Year of the Dragon has great potential for the Wood Rat, particularly in the way it will allow him to further his skills and strengths. Over the year he should remain open to opportunity and be prepared to adapt. He will benefit from the support of those around him and a combined approach will often help get plans underway. This will be a busy year, but an often lucky one too.

TIP FOR THE YEAR
Seize any chances to develop your skills. What you achieve now can often improve your prospects later. Also, value those around you. Their love, support and advice may be significant and help in ways you may not anticipate.

The Fire Rat

The Dragon year will contain many interesting developments for the Fire Rat and, with willingness and good use of his time and opportunities, he can both prosper and derive a good deal of satisfaction from his activities.

For Fire Rats born in 1996 this will be a busy and sometimes demanding year, but it will have far-reaching value. The young Fire Rat will be faced with an almost bewildering range of subjects to study, as well as exams to prepare for. Although there may be times when he feels overwhelmed by the amount he has to do, with a positive approach he will learn a great deal and discover strengths it would be worth taking further.

Another positive feature of the year will be the new possibilities it will open up, including ways in which the Fire Rat can advance certain interests or become involved in something new. Again, a willing attitude is key to making the most of these opportunities.

A further benefit of the year will be the support the Fire Rat is offered by those around him. Throughout the year he will find that if he is open and forthcoming about his ideas and activities, including any concerns or doubts he may have, they will be better able to understand and help. Sometimes just mentioning something may result in others assisting the Fire Rat in ways he had not anticipated or making suggestions that could help his situation. To benefit fully, though, he does need to let others know what is happening.

The young Fire Rat will once again appreciate the company of his close friends over the year. With his outgoing nature, he usually gets on well with people, and he will find his friends especially helpful to him this year. Any Fire Rat who has to move, finds himself in a new environment or has been feeling dispirited and alone recently will find the Dragon year can be a time of important change. Although these Fire Rats may initially feel uncomfortable in their new situation, by making the most of it they will quickly be able to meet others and establish a new set of friends. The Dragon year is supportive of the young Fire Rat and will give him the opportunity to make more of himself as well as grow in confidence.

With all his various interests, there will often be things the Fire Rat will want to do and buy, and here the Dragon year can have an element of good fortune about it. By waiting and saving towards specific items, he could benefit from some favourable buying opportunities, especially involving equipment he may need.

Although the young Fire Rat will often be involved in studying and his own personal interests, he should also aim to contribute to home life, and any household tasks he can do will be appreciated. An older relation could be particularly grateful for his assistance in some matter and the bond between them will often be special. Playing a full part in home life can reward the Fire Rat, and those around him, particularly well in this busy year.

For Fire Rats born in 1936, this can be a pleasing year. Family and friends will be especially important, and the Fire Rat will value the support and affection shown him. Again the rapport between the Fire Rat and other generations can be special, and the encouragement and advice the Fire Rat is able to give will often mean more than he may realize. In turn, if he himself needs assistance or a second opinion on any matter, he should ask. Those around him will be pleased to offer support in return.

The Fire Rat will also derive much pleasure from his various interests this year and there could be a surprise in store. If he enjoys creative pursuits, he should consider putting forward his work or entering a competition. He could be encouraged by the response he receives or the way certain ideas develop over the year. The Dragon year will reward the enterprising.

The Fire Rat will also be keen to go ahead with certain ideas he has, and whether these involve adding comforts to his home, taking a holiday or some other venture, by planning carefully and budgeting ahead, he will be pleased with how his plans work out. With the lucky nature of the year, he could also benefit from some good offers.

Overall, whether born in 1936 or 1996, the Fire Rat can enjoy a special and gratifying year. The Year of the Dragon will give him an excellent chance to put his skills to good use and pursue his interests, and many Fire Rats will achieve encouraging results. The Fire Rat will also benefit from the support of those around him and, with a willing attitude, can gain a lot from his various activities.

TIP FOR THE YEAR
Make the most of your opportunities, because a lot can follow on from what you do this year. If you were born in 1996, be disciplined in your studying. What you do now can be valuable preparation for the opportunities that lie ahead.

The Earth Rat

The Dragon year can bring encouraging developments for the Earth Rat, with many ideas and plans proceeding well. Another positive feature of the year will be the opportunities that it brings, and by being adaptable, the Earth Rat can benefit. In so many ways this can be a good and favourable year for him.

One of the Earth Rat's strengths is his keen and curious nature. He has an enquiring mind and takes an informed interest in a great many things. Over the year his curiosity could be whetted on several occasions, and by following up whatever catches his attention, he can derive considerable satisfaction from his activities. Some Earth Rats may decide to give time to a cause, project or charity, and for many the Dragon year can open up some interesting and rewarding avenues to explore.

The Dragon year also encourages enterprise and the Earth Rat may be tempted to use his existing skills in new ways, perhaps by furthering an idea, promoting some work he has completed or setting himself a particular challenge. In addition, for Earth Rats who have recently retired or do so this year, this is an excellent time for taking up new activities and looking at other ways in which they could use their skills and strengths. By using their time well and seizing their opportunities, they will often find that interesting results can follow on.

The Earth Rat will also value his social life over the year, and some of his friends who have specialist knowledge could be especially helpful with some of his activities and ideas. Also, by keeping active and becoming involved in new pursuits, there will be good chances for the Earth Rat to widen his social circle over the year. Any Earth Rats who may, because of work or other commitments, have neglected their social life in recent times and would welcome new friends will find the Dragon year can help rectify this by giving them the chance to meet new people. Mid-April to June and November to early January 2013 could see a lot of social activity and, for those alone, even romantic possibilities. This is certainly a year for pleasing personal developments.

The Dragon year will also be a time of opportunity as far as the Earth Rat's work is concerned. Many Earth Rats will have been giving some thought to their current position and to what they would like to do in the future. Some will be planning retirement or hoping to reduce their hours and so give themselves more time for other activities. These Earth Rats should consult those who are in a position to advise them on their plans, particularly on the financial implications, as well as talk their thoughts and ideas over with their loved ones. Although what they decide may be a big personal step, with full consultation and support they will feel satisfied that the right choice is being made.

For those Earth Rats who are still keen to take their career further and have certain goals they want to reach, the Dragon year can bring some interesting opportunities. For many, this can be an important and personally significant year.

The Dragon year is also favourably aspected as far as financial matters are concerned, and some Earth Rats will benefit from a bonus, the fruition of a policy or a gift. However, while this upturn will be welcome, the Earth Rat will need to manage his finances carefully. This includes budgeting ahead for more substantial purchases as well as taking measures to help both his present and future situation. With discipline and care, he will fare much better.

This need for good management also applies to travel and holiday plans. Making early allowance for these will enable the Earth Rat to do – and enjoy – a lot more.

One of the key characteristics of the Earth Rat is the importance he attaches to his family and the Dragon year will bring some special occasions for him to enjoy. Not only will his loved ones be supportive, but over the year they will be keen to help the Earth Rat in his decision-making as well as encourage him in his various activities. A combined approach will be of benefit to everyone concerned. There will also be successes to celebrate, whether the Earth Rat's own or those of someone close to him, and time spent with his loved ones will be very much part of his year.

Overall, the Year of the Dragon holds considerable promise for the Earth Rat. In particular it will offer him the opportunity to become involved in new activities and use his time and skills in different ways. By being willing and receptive, he can derive much personal value from what he does this year. His personal life is also favourably aspected, and both domestically and socially, he will find himself in increasing demand, with some rewarding times and activities to enjoy.

TIP FOR THE YEAR
This is a year for development and personal growth. By following up your ideas and interests you can not only benefit from what you do but also find new possibilities arising. The Dragon year is one of considerable potential. Use it well.

FAMOUS RATS

Ben Affleck, Ursula Andress, Louis Armstrong, Lauren Bacall, Dame Shirley Bassey, Kathy Bates, Irving Berlin, Silvio Berlusconi, Kenneth Branagh, Marlon Brando, Charlotte Brontë, Jackson Browne, George H. W. Bush, Glen Campbell, Jimmy Carter, Jeremy Clarkson, Aaron Copland, Cameron Diaz, David Duchovny, Duffy, Noël Edmonds, T. S. Eliot, Eminem, Colin Firth, Clark Gable, Liam Gallagher, Al Gore, Hugh Grant, Lewis Hamilton, Thomas Hardy, Prince Harry, Haydn, Charlton Heston, Buddy Holly, Mick Hucknall, Henrik Ibsen, Jeremy Irons, Samuel L. Jackson, LeBron James, Jean-Michel Jarre, Scarlett Johansson, Gene Kelly, Avril Lavigne, Jude Law, Melissa Leo, Gary Lineker, Lord Andrew Lloyd Webber, Ian McEwan, Katie Melua, Claude Monet, Richard Nixon, Jo Nesbø, Ozzy Osbourne, Sean Penn, Katy Perry, Sir Terry Pratchett, Ian Rankin, Lou Rawls, Burt Reynolds, Jonathan Ross, Rossini, William Shakespeare, Donna Summer, James Taylor, Leo Tolstoy, Henri Toulouse-Lautrec, Spencer Tracy, the Prince of Wales, George Washington, the Duke of York, Emile Zola.

6 FEBRUARY 1913 ⁓ 25 JANUARY 1914   *Water Ox*

24 JANUARY 1925 ⁓ 12 FEBRUARY 1926   *Wood Ox*

11 FEBRUARY 1937 ⁓ 30 JANUARY 1938   *Fire Ox*

29 JANUARY 1949 ⁓ 16 FEBRUARY 1950   *Earth Ox*

15 FEBRUARY 1961 ⁓ 4 FEBRUARY 1962   *Metal Ox*

3 FEBRUARY 1973 ⁓ 22 JANUARY 1974   *Water Ox*

20 FEBRUARY 1985 ⁓ 8 FEBRUARY 1986   *Wood Ox*

7 FEBRUARY 1997 ⁓ 27 JANUARY 1998   *Fire Ox*

26 JANUARY 2009 ⁓ 13 FEBRUARY 2010   *Earth Ox*

THE
OX

THE PERSONALITY OF THE OX

The more considered the way,
the more considerable the journey.

The Ox is born under the signs of equilibrium and tenacity. He is a hard and conscientious worker and sets about everything he does in a resolute, methodical and determined manner. He has considerable leadership qualities and is often admired for his tough and uncompromising nature. He knows what he wants to achieve in life and, as far as possible, will not be deflected from his ultimate objective.

The Ox takes his responsibilities and duties very seriously. He is decisive and quick to take advantage of any opportunity that comes his way. He is also sincere and places a great deal of trust in his friends and colleagues. He is, nevertheless, something of a loner. He is a quiet and private individual and often keeps his thoughts to himself. He also cherishes his independence and prefers to set about things in his own way rather than be bound by the dictates of others or influenced by outside pressures.

The Ox tends to have a calm and tranquil nature, but if something angers him or he feels that someone has let him down, he can have a fearsome temper. He can also be stubborn and obstinate and this can lead him into conflict with others. Usually he will succeed in getting his own way, but should things go against him he is a poor loser and will take any defeat or setback extremely badly.

The Ox is often a deep thinker and rather studious. He is not particularly renowned for his sense of humour and does not take kindly to new gimmicks or anything too innovative. He is too solid and traditional for that and prefers to stick to the more conventional norm.

His home is very important to him and in some respects he treats it as a private sanctuary. His family tends to be closely knit and the Ox will make sure that each member does their fair share around the house. He tends to be a hoarder, but he is always well organized and neat. He also places great importance on punctuality and there is nothing that infuriates him more than to be kept waiting, particularly if it is due to someone's inefficiency. The Ox can be a hard taskmaster!

Once settled in a job or house, the Ox will quite happily remain there for many years. He does not like change and he is also not particularly keen on travel. He does, however, enjoy gardening and other outdoor pursuits and he will often spend much of his spare time out of doors. He is usually an excellent gardener and whenever possible will make sure he has a large area of ground to maintain. He usually prefers to live in the country rather than the town.

Due to his dedicated and dependable nature the Ox will usually do well in his chosen career providing he is given enough freedom to act on his own initiative. He invariably does well in politics, agriculture and in careers that need specialized training. He is also very gifted artistically and many Oxen have enjoyed considerable success as musicians or composers.

The Ox is not as outgoing as some and it often takes him a long time to establish friendships and feel relaxed in another person's company. His courtships are likely to be long, but once he is settled he will remain devoted and loyal to his partner. He is particularly well suited to those born under the signs of the Rat, Rabbit, Snake and Rooster. He can also establish a good relationship with the Monkey, Dog, Pig and another Ox, but he will find that he has little in common with the whimsical and sensitive Goat. He will also find it difficult to get on with the Horse, Dragon and Tiger – the Ox prefers a quiet and peaceful existence and those born under these three signs tend to be a little too lively and impulsive for his liking.

The female Ox has a kind and caring nature and her home and family are very much her pride and joy. She always tries to do her best for her partner and can be a most conscientious and loving parent. She is an excellent organizer and a very determined person who will often succeed in getting what she wants in life. She usually has a deep interest in the arts and is often a talented artist or musician.

The Ox is a very down-to-earth character. He is sincere, loyal and unpretentious. He can, however, be rather reserved and to some he may appear distant and aloof. He has a quiet nature, but underneath he is very strong-willed and ambitious. He has the courage of his convictions and is often prepared to stand up for what he believes to be right, regardless of the consequences. He inspires confidence and trust and throughout his life he will rarely be short of people who are ready to support him.

THE FIVE DIFFERENT TYPES OF OX

In addition to the 12 signs of the Chinese zodiac there are five elements and these have a strengthening or moderating influence on the signs. The effects of the five elements on the Ox are described below, together with the years in which they were exercising their influence. Therefore Oxen born in 1961 are Metal Oxen, those born in 1913 and 1973 are Water Oxen, and so on.

Metal Ox: 1961

This Ox is confident and very strong-willed. He can be blunt and forthright in his views and is not afraid of speaking his mind. He sets about his objectives with a dogged determination, but he can become so involved in his various activities that he can be oblivious to the thoughts and feelings of those around him, and this can sometimes be to his detriment. He is honest and dependable and will never promise more than he can deliver. He has a good appreciation of the arts and usually has a small circle of very good and loyal friends.

Water Ox: 1913, 1973

This Ox has a sharp and penetrating mind. He is a good organizer and sets about his work in a methodical manner. He is not as narrow-minded as some of the other types of Ox and is more willing to involve others in his plans and aspirations. He usually has very high moral standards and is often attracted to careers in public service. He is a good judge of character and has such a friendly and persuasive manner that he usually experiences little difficulty in securing his objectives. He is popular and has an excellent way with children.

Wood Ox: 1925, 1985

The Wood Ox conducts himself with an air of dignity and authority and will often take a leading role in any enterprise in which he becomes involved. He is very self-confident and is direct in his dealings with others. He does, however, have a quick temper and has no hesitation in speaking his mind. He has tremendous drive and willpower and an extremely good memory. He is particularly loyal and devoted to the members of his family and has a most caring nature.

Fire Ox: 1937, 1997

The Fire Ox has a powerful and assertive personality and is a hard and conscientious worker. He holds strong views and has very little patience when things do not go his way. He can also get carried away in the excitement of the moment and does not always take into account the views of those around him. He nevertheless has many leadership qualities and will often reach positions of power, eminence and wealth. He usually has a small group of loyal and close friends and is very devoted to his family.

Earth Ox: 1949, 2009

This Ox sets about everything he does in a sensible and level-headed manner. He is ambitious but also realistic in his aims and is often prepared to work long hours in order to secure his objectives. He is shrewd in financial and business matters and is a very good judge of character. He has a quiet nature and is greatly admired for his sincerity and integrity. He is also very loyal to his family and friends and his views are often sought.

PROSPECTS FOR THE OX IN 2012

The Year of the Rabbit (3 February 2011–22 January 2012) will have been a reasonable one for the Ox and a lot is set to happen in the closing months.

In his work the Ox could face new pressures and an increasing workload, but with commitment and dedication he will not only impress but also achieve some creditable results. For some Oxen, including those seeking work, October and early November could see openings worth pursuing.

One of the more favourable aspects of the Rabbit year concerns the Ox's relations with others and in the remaining months he should make the most of his opportunities to meet others. In his work, the contacts he makes could be helpful, while on a personal level he will find himself in demand, with friends to see, events to attend and, for unattached Oxen, affairs of the heart adding something special to this part of the year. September could be interesting socially, as could the weeks approaching and just after Christmas.

In his home life the Ox will continue to do a lot for others and will be kept fully occupied, whether giving advice and assistance, making arrangements or carrying out home maintenance projects. Busy though the last few months of the year may be, he will delight in how certain plans proceed as well as in the love and gratitude shown him by others. On a personal level, the Rabbit year can often be a special and rewarding time for the Ox.

With so much domestic and social activity, as well as the purchases the Ox will want to make in the last months of the year, he will, however, need to keep a close watch on spending. He should also avoid risks and take care if lending to another person. Without a proper agreement, problems could follow. Oxen, be warned.

However, the Year of the Rabbit will have given the Ox the chance to use his talents in many ways and will leave him with some satisfying achievements to his credit.

The Year of the Dragon starts on 23 January and will be a variable one for the Ox. The Ox likes to follow carefully laid plans and could feel uncomfortable with the pace and spontaneous nature of the Dragon year. It is one which will test his patience but will nevertheless give him valuable new experience.

In his work the Ox should focus on his responsibilities but also remain aware of what is going on around him. Sometimes new initiatives could change his role and he will need to adapt. Also, while he is likely to have misgivings about some of the new developments, he should be wary of being too obtuse. To appear inflexible or intransigent could be to his detriment. For many Oxen, whatever their views, the best policy in the Dragon year will be to work hard and keep their heads down.

However, while some parts of the year will be demanding, the Ox can still derive much value from it. Changes in his role will often give him the chance to broaden his experience and prove himself in another capacity. By rising to the challenge and using this year to further his skills, he will be both helping his current situation and widening his scope for the future.

Many Oxen will remain with their present employer this year and build on their experience, but for those keen on making a change or looking for work, the Dragon year can bring interesting developments. Although their quest may not be easy, by considering a wide range of positions, many could secure a job in a different capacity that will prove an interesting challenge. March, May, August and November could see encouraging developments, but the Dragon year will be fast-moving throughout, with opportunities arising quickly and sometimes taking the Ox by surprise.

Financially, with his existing commitments, some repairs that may be needed and all the other plans he will want to carry out, the Ox may find his spending easily mounting up. Whenever possible, he should set funds aside for specific requirements and watch his outgoings. Fortunately his disciplined nature will help, but the better control he has over his finances, the better he will fare.

One particular characteristic of the Dragon year is the niggles and petty irritations it can bring. These can range from annoying delays and muddles over transactions to excessive bureaucracy concerning benefits, payments or some other important matter. Some of what occurs this year could exasperate the Ox, and to help minimize these more awkward aspects, he should pay special attention to important correspondence and keep paperwork and receipts carefully. By being thorough, he will find some problems can be averted or at least more easily dealt with when they arise.

Many Oxen will be leading busy and sometimes pressured lifestyles this year and in view of this it is also important that the Ox does not neglect his own well-being. To skimp on exercise or a healthy diet could leave him lacking his usual energy and prone to minor ailments.

In this busy year he should also allow time for his interests and recreational pursuits. No matter what he may enjoy doing in his spare time – something practical, sporting, creative or even educational – some regular 'me time' will do him good as well as bring him pleasure.

In addition he will be grateful for the support of his friends and should never forget that they will be glad to assist if called upon to do so. While the Ox can be a somewhat private individual, he should also take up the social invitations he receives as well as go to any events that appeal to him. By doing so, he may meet some helpful people who in time can become loyal friends. April, May, July and September are likely to see the most social opportunities.

The Ox's home life will keep him busy during the year and there will need to be good co-operation and some flexibility as routines and work schedules change. Here the Ox's methodical nature will help, particularly in thinking adjustments through and giving advice as needed. However, while the year will bring its pressures, there will also be pleasures. These may include success that comes after considerable effort and good news that the Ox will be keen to share. Domestically and personally, the Dragon year will contain some richly rewarding times.

Nevertheless, it can also highlight an Ox weakness: when delays occur or problems arise, he is not slow to vent his feelings. In view of the irritations that are likely this year, he should try to show greater patience as well as watch his temper.

Overall, although the Ox may not always feel comfortable with the year's often heady pace, by concentrating on what he has to do and showing a willingness to adjust to new developments he can enjoy some notable achievements, add to his circle of friends and gain valuable new experience. And what he does this year can be taken further in 2013, the Year of the Snake, which is a particularly good one for him.

The Metal Ox

The Metal Ox has a great many strengths. He is determined, persistent and takes his responsibilities seriously. He is very much a no-nonsense sort and rather than delay or procrastinate, he simply likes to get on with things. However, despite his noble intentions, he could find the Dragon year frustrating. Some of his plans and hopes could be difficult to realize and he could also have a few problems to deal with. This may not be the smoothest of years for him, but despite its vexations, the Metal Ox is made of strong stuff and will not only have the chance to show his strengths but also find that out of difficulty new possibilities can arise.

In his work he is likely to see considerable change. Not only may he be given different objectives but also see his role expanded in new ways. Many Metal Oxen could be faced with adapting to new working practices and could be concerned about some of the developments that take place and the speed with which they are introduced.

However, while the Metal Ox may find parts of the year demanding, some of the tasks and objectives he is given will allow him to gain experience in new areas and prove himself in a different capacity. For the many Metal Oxen who decide to remain with their present employer this year, the experience they gain can be an important stepping-stone to future progress.

For those intent on change or seeking work, the Dragon year can open up some interesting possibilities. Securing a position will not be easy, but by considering different ways in which they could use their skills, obtaining advice and looking at training possibilities, quite a few Metal Oxen will gain a new position that will be a base from which they can later progress. And, with their prospects greatly improved next year, any additional skills they can gain can be to their benefit in the near future. March, May, August to mid-September and November could see particularly encouraging developments.

Another important feature of the year will be personal development, and many Metal Oxen will decide to enrol on courses or start a study programme, perhaps to gain an additional qualification. Finding time for this may sometimes be difficult, but what the Metal Ox is able to achieve can be a valuable legacy of the year.

Throughout the year the Metal Ox should also be open to opportunities. Although he will have plans and hopes for 2012, he should not regard these as set in stone. Sometimes new ideas will arise or situations change, and by being flexible he will stand more chance of benefiting. During the Dragon year the winds of change and chance blow strongly.

One area which could see sudden developments is travel. While the Metal Ox may prefer to plan ahead, this year he may well have the chance to go away at short notice. There could also be some particularly interesting travel possibilities towards the end of 2012 and early in 2013.

The Metal Ox should, however, keep watch over his spending throughout the year. Without care, he could find his outgoings creeping up. This is a time for good financial management. In addition the Metal Ox needs to pay attention to tax and benefit matters as well as any other important documents he may receive. Delay or missed details could be to his disadvantage. Metal Oxen, take note, and do be thorough.

Although, with all his various activities, the Metal Ox will be kept busy over the year, he should also make sure that his social life is not neglected. By keeping in regular contact with his friends he will not only benefit from their support but also enjoy the times spent together. His work and interests can also introduce him to new people, and Metal Oxen who are alone and would welcome more contact with others will find that taking up invitations and going to events in their area can lead to some significant new friendships being made. Mid-March to the end of May, July and September could see the most social activity.

In the Metal Ox's home life, this will be a busy year, with plans and routines subject to change. Adjustments will need to be made, but with co-operation, new patterns can quickly become established. Some Metal Oxen could also see family members leave home, particularly as children start university or take a new job, and here the Metal Ox's attentive nature can help others through what can be a daunting stage in their life.

With his practical nature, the Metal Ox will often have projects he will be keen to carry out over the year, but again this is a time for flexibility. Some plans may have to be put back or altered to fit in with other arrangements, but in some cases the delay could be a blessing in disguise as better alternatives arise.

In general, the Year of the Dragon may not be the smoothest of years for the Metal Ox. However, by adapting to the situations in which he finds himself and doing his best, he can greatly add to his experience, and his persistence, discipline and personal qualities can lead to both present and future achievements. A challenging but significant year.

TIP FOR THE YEAR
Look to develop your skills and knowledge. Also, be adaptable as situations change and opportunities arise. What opens up now can be to your long-term advantage.

The Water Ox
This will be a variable year for the Water Ox. Progress will not be easy and parts of the year frustrating. However, while the Dragon year will bring its challenges, it will also have very definite benefits. The effort the Water Ox can put in and the skills he can show will give him the experience necessary for future success. In many ways this is a

year of preparation for the better times ahead, especially next year.

At work the Water Ox will often find his level of responsibility changing, with increased targets and objectives to meet. Not only can this add to his workload, but delays can occur, bureaucracy take time and people not be as co-operative or efficient as the Water Ox would like. At times he may be exasperated, but he should remain focused and do his best. His application and commitment will be noticed, and when targets are met and certain results achieved, the success will be all the more deserved.

Another important factor of the year is that by rising to the challenge, the Water Ox will be adding to his experience and having the chance to demonstrate a wide range of skills. This will be to his benefit when opportunities arise in the future or he looks to move on.

For those Water Oxen who feel the time is now right for change, March, May, August and November could bring some interesting possibilities, but opportunities do need to be taken quickly.

For Water Oxen seeking work, there can be important developments in store. Obtaining a new position will not be easy, but by considering the different ways in which they could use their experience and making a special effort with their applications, these Water Oxen will find doors opening for them. Results this year will come from hard work and giving that little bit extra, but with his prospects much improved next year, the experience the Water Ox gains now can be instrumental in his future progress.

Financially, with personal commitments, accommodation plans and travel costs, the Water Ox will have many demands on his resources and will need to keep a close watch on spending and budget ahead. If he does not do so already, keeping a set of accounts could be helpful. Also, if he takes on any new commitment or enters into an agreement, he should check the terms and obligations and keep any paperwork and guarantees safely. This is no year for risk or oversight.

In view of the busy nature of the year it is also important that the Water Ox keeps his lifestyle in balance and sets aside some time for relaxation and exercise. With this being an innovative time, should a fitness discipline, activity or recreational pursuit be introduced that appeals to him, he should follow it up. What he starts this year can bring him a great deal of pleasure and possible benefit both now and in the future.

He should also make sure he keeps in regular contact with his friends. If meeting up is not always possible, a phone call or e-mail could be a good way to stay in touch. Contact with others can do the Water Ox a lot of good over the year, especially as it will give him the chance to discuss current activities and benefit from advice. April, May, July, September and early 2013 could see some good social opportunities.

Domestically, the Water Ox will again see a lot of activity this year. He will give considerable help to both younger and more senior relatives and in addition will do much to ensure the smooth running of domestic life. While busy, this will often be very rewarding, and there could be a notable personal or family occasion to enjoy later on in the year.

Overall, the Year of the Dragon will ask a lot of the Water Ox and will not always be easy or straightforward.

However, one of the Water Ox's strengths is his conscientious nature, and by doing his best and rising to the challenge, he can gain valuable experience and demonstrate his redoubtable qualities. The Dragon year may test him, but it will pave the way for some significant developments, particularly in the following Year of the Snake. What is achieved this year should not be underestimated, for its benefits can be considerable.

TIP FOR THE YEAR
Make full use of any chances to further your experience and gain new skills. Also, keep your lifestyle in balance and preserve time for your personal interests, friends and loved ones. These are important and special parts of your life. Be sure to treasure them.

The Wood Ox

The Wood Ox is both conscientious and ambitious. He is not one for fuss and sets about his activities in a quiet and methodical way. And his approach and style serve him well, allowing him to make steady progress. In 2012 he will continue to make headway, but this will not be without considerable effort on his part. The Dragon year can be challenging and the Wood Ox will not always be comfortable with the developments it brings. However, amid the pressures, there will be some special and personally significant times to enjoy.

At work, many Wood Oxen will have established themselves in a company or organization and will not only have built up expertise in their present role but also made good contacts and friends. Over the year many will have the chance to build on this and be offered other responsibilities. However, while this represents progress, there could be a lot to learn and some adjustments to make, and the shift in role may sometimes be more difficult than the Wood Ox anticipated. Parts of the year can be exacting, but the Wood Ox is never one to shrink from a challenge and with time and patience will not only prove himself in a new capacity but will also find the experience helpful for the future. The Dragon year may not be easy but it can be instructive, and often significant in the longer term.

For Wood Oxen who decide the time has come for a change, as well as those seeking work, events can move in curious ways. Obtaining a new position may be difficult, but by keeping alert, making enquiries and talking to contacts and those in a position to advise, the Wood Ox will find some interesting possibilities emerging. Sometimes these could be in an area or industry that is unfamiliar to him, but he will welcome the chance to do something different. Again any new role can be daunting, with a lot to learn, but what is achieved this year can lead to more possibilities opening up in the future.

Another factor in the Wood Ox's favour will be the opportunities he will have to work with new colleagues. Many will respond well to his quiet, conscientious nature and senior staff will be keen to support him, including putting him forward for training. March, May to early June, August and November could see some important developments.

The progress the Wood Ox makes at work can lead to a rise in income, but throughout the year money matters will

THE OX

need care. The Wood Ox should keep a close watch on spending and be vigilant when dealing with important paperwork or making new commitments. Financially, this is a year to be alert and thorough, and if anything concerns him at any time, the Wood Ox should seek clarification and advice.

A particular feature of the Dragon year is its sudden opportunities, and there could be chances for the Wood Ox to travel at short notice, perhaps to take a break or visit others. His interests can keep him active, too, and if he has the chance to attend events, shows and concerts, again perhaps at short notice, he should try to go. Admittedly the Wood Ox does like to plan ahead, but by being open to the more spontaneous nature of the year he can get to do some interesting and fun things.

Once again he will value his close circle of friends over the year, and changes in his work and the various activities he pursues can also bring him into contact with others and result in some important new friendships being made. April, May, July, September and the start of 2013 could see the most social activity and, for the unattached, affairs of the heart are promising. Here again the Dragon year can bring sudden developments, and although the Wood Ox may prefer to take his time, for a few, finding love can be sudden and glorious.

The Wood Ox's home life will also see a lot happen this year. There will be important decisions to be made, some upheaval as plans take shape and also times of personal and family celebration. While a lot will work out favourably, there will be fraught moments when plans are disrupted or delayed (patience is not always a Wood Ox strong point!) and pressures mount. The Wood Ox should accept these as best he can and resolve to work around them. The year will contain its annoyances, but these should not be allowed to get out of proportion or undermine what can be a personally rewarding time.

Overall, the Year of the Dragon can be a demanding one for the Wood Ox, but by rising to its challenges and doing his best, he will learn a lot, develop new strengths and win the respect of many. Headway made now can also have considerable bearing on his future progress. And his relations with others can be strong and meaningful, with many positive developments to enjoy.

TIP FOR THE YEAR
Being ambitious, you realize there are times when you need to push yourself forward and take on new and sometimes uncomfortable challenges. This is such a year. Make the most of your chances to extend your skills, as you can do your prospects a lot of good. Also, consult others and listen closely to their advice. The support you receive can be significant and your good relations with others can help you in many ways.

The Fire Ox
The Fire Ox can accomplish a lot this year, but it will require considerable effort. Progress will not be easy or automatic, but with persistence and hard work, important headway can be made.

For the Fire Ox born in 1997 there is a Chinese proverb that it could be helpful to keep in mind this year: 'Study hard when you are young or you'll regret it when you are old.' In the Dragon year the young Fire Ox should make every effort with his studying. This is his opportunity to prepare himself for what lies ahead. While the world of work and other responsibilities may be several years away, what he can learn now can bear important fruit later. This is no time to waste.

Also, while he will have his preferred subject areas, the Fire Ox should not be discouraged if certain pieces of work do not get the marks he was hoping for. This will give him the chance to recognize what he did wrong and avoid this in future. For some, it can also be a wake-up call that more effort is required. The Dragon year can be demanding, but it is by being stretched and challenged that the young Fire Ox will learn more.

If, however, at any time he is struggling with a certain subject, it is important that he seeks guidance. Doing nothing can only compound his anxiety and there are many around him who will be only too willing to help.

As the Fire Ox sets about his various activities, he will find new strengths emerging and should consider how he can best build on these. Again, those around can be encouraging and if the Fire Ox is open to instruction and advice, some interesting possibilities can emerge. For the more musical Fire Ox (and many Oxen do have good musical skills), there could be the chance to learn an instrument or join a school band or orchestra, while for the sporting, extra tuition could be made available. Whatever his interests, with effort and willingness the young Fire Ox can gain a lot from the year.

He will also value his close circle of friends and the support they offer can be important. Over the year his interests will bring him into contact with others, too, and he will enjoy a good understanding with many.

In his home life the Fire Ox will need to be forthcoming and willing to help as required. The emphasis of the Dragon year is on effort and willingness, and whether in his home life, school work or interests, commitment will enable the Fire Ox to get the most out of it and enhance his prospects for the future.

For Fire Oxen born in 1937, this will be an interesting but sometimes niggling year. The Fire Ox is a redoubtable character and has a firm will and resolve. Much of the year will go well for him, but it will not be without its irritations. Whether dealing with delay, bureaucracy or misunderstandings, there will be occasions which will test the Fire Ox's patience. However, while he may be annoyed, he needs to be careful not to exacerbate difficult situations but focus on their resolution. In particular, he should check facts, get advice and consider the best way forward. With determination and resourcefulness, the more awkward aspects of the year can be defused or averted, but throughout the year the Fire Ox does need to be on his mettle.

Nevertheless, there will be other aspects of the Dragon year that the Fire Ox will particularly value, including spending time with his family and enjoying the often good bond he has with younger relations. In addition he will often be keen to make some purchases to improve his home, and by considering his options carefully and talking his ideas over with those around him, he will be pleased with his choices, even if some undertakings do take longer than envisaged.

The Fire Ox will also find long-held interests bringing him particular pleasure and will enjoy following through certain ideas, contacting other enthusiasts or attending interest-related events. Gardening (including indoor gardening) will delight many Fire Oxen and such interests can do the Fire Ox a lot of good in this sometimes tricky year.

With the variable aspects, he will, though, need to be vigilant when dealing with finance and important paperwork. Problems can arise if certain procedures are not followed. Fire Oxen, take note. Be careful and thorough and do seek advice if necessary.

In general, the Year of the Dragon will not be the easiest for the Fire Ox. He will need to be careful not to exacerbate problems with moments of stubbornness or intransigence. Awareness, patience and some flexibility will be required. But for both the younger and more senior Fire Ox, the year will bring opportunities to enjoy personal interests and develop skills. And family and friends will be supportive and effort well rewarded.

TIP FOR THE YEAR
Be prepared to work hard. Although results may sometimes be slow in coming, your efforts and tenacity will prevail and can benefit you in many ways, both now and in the future.

The Earth Ox

The Earth Ox is a realist. He has good judgement and a talent for gauging situations, and these abilities will serve him well this year. This may not be the easiest of years for him, but he can gain a lot from it as well as enjoy some deserving successes.

For those Earth Oxen in work the Dragon year can be demanding. Many will see changes being introduced which will not only impact on their role but also require considerable adjustment. The Earth Ox may have misgivings about what is happening, but he will find it best to concentrate on his duties and keep a relatively low profile. This is not a time to rock the boat or be inflexible.

However, while parts of the year will be challenging, the Earth Ox will still have the chance to put his experience to good use. His judgement can be a tremendous asset this year and colleagues will often recognize and value his contribution.

The majority of Earth Oxen will remain in their current position over the year and adapt as required. However, for those seeking a new role, the Dragon year can bring some interesting developments. Securing a new position will not be easy, but the Earth Ox is persistent and by keeping alert and considering a range of possibilities may well secure a position that gives him the chance to do something very different. This may be temporary, however, and this is a year when the Earth Ox will need to be adaptable. March, May, August and November could see some interesting work developments, but events move quickly in the Dragon year and whenever the Earth Ox sees a vacancy that appeals to him, he should be swift in following it up.

There will also be some Earth Oxen who choose to retire or reduce their working commitments over the year and again this will be a time of change and personal adjustment.

Whatever his situation, the Earth Ox will need to be careful when dealing with paperwork and financial matters this year. He does need to give these his full attention and seek advice on anything that concerns him. Also when considering large purchases or entering into agreements, he should check the terms and conditions and that his requirements are being met. Again, without sufficient attention, problems can ensue. This is very much a year for being vigilant and aware.

If possible, however, the Earth Ox should try to make provision for a holiday. With all that he does and the pressures he is likely to have to cope with in the Dragon year, a change of scene can do him a lot of good. There may be the chance to go away at short notice and if a travel offer or invitation appeals to him, the Earth Ox should follow it up.

Another rewarding aspect of the year concerns the Earth Ox's personal interests. Over the year many Earth Oxen will be keen to take certain interests further, possibly by going on courses or setting themselves a particular project. By allowing themselves the time to do this, they can find their efforts particularly rewarding. Any Earth Oxen who feel unfulfilled over the year would do well to consider activities they could enjoy and new interests they could start. By doing something purposeful, they could transform their situation.

As with most Oxen, the Earth Ox can have a quiet and reserved nature, but over the year he should make the most of his social opportunities as well as keep in contact with his friends. This is no year to distance himself from what is going on or to keep himself to himself. Friends can be particularly supportive and encouraging and can offer valuable advice on important decisions.

In addition some Earth Oxen will give thought to their well-being over the year and those who join an exercise class or decide to keep fit in other ways will find that a great deal of fun and mutual support can be had. In the Dragon year the Earth Ox's social life can bring him a great deal of pleasure.

His home life will also see much activity, and with the changes and pressures he may be experiencing in his work situation, along with the important decisions others may be facing, there will need to be good liaison and co-operation in his household. The more discussion and awareness there is, the better for all. However, while home life will often be busy, it will also mean a great deal to the Earth Ox, particularly as plans are realized (even if they take longer than anticipated) and some notable family occasions enjoyed. This is very much a year favouring communication, joint effort and shared decision-making.

Overall, the Year of the Dragon can be a demanding one for the Earth Ox and throughout he will need to remain aware, thorough, careful and adaptable. However, while there will be pressures, personal interests can be especially satisfying and the Earth Ox will value the support of others.

TIP FOR THE YEAR
Although some of the developments of the year may concern you or bring increased pressure, you can learn a lot from them. Be your resourceful self and rise to the challenge. Considerable benefits can follow on from what you are able to accomplish this year.

FAMOUS OXEN

Lily Allen, Hans Christian Andersen, Peter Andre, Gemma Arterton, Johann Sebastian Bach, Warren Beatty, Kate Beckinsale, David Blaine, Napoleon Bonaparte, Albert Camus, Jim Carrey, Charlie Chaplin, George Clooney, Natalie Cole, Bill Cosby, Diana, Princess of Wales, Marlene Dietrich, Walt Disney, Patrick Duffy, Jane Fonda, Edward Fox, Michael J. Fox, Peter Gabriel, Elizabeth George, Richard Gere, Ricky Gervais, Julia Gillard, William Hague, Handel, King Harald V of Norway, Adolf Hitler, Dustin Hoffman, Hal Holbrook, Anthony Hopkins, Billy Joel, King Juan Carlos of Spain, John Key, B. B. King, Keira Knightley, Mark Knopfler, Burt Lancaster, Kate Moss, Alison Moyet, Eddie Murphy, Jack Nicholson, Leslie Nielsen, Barack Obama, Gwyneth Paltrow, Oscar Peterson, Paula Radcliffe, Robert Redford, Lionel Richie, Wayne Rooney, Tim Roth, Rubens, Meg Ryan, Amanda Seyfried, Jean Sibelius, Bruce Springsteen, Meryl Streep, Lady Thatcher, Alan Titchmarsh, Scott F. Turow, Vincent van Gogh, Zoë Wanamaker, Sigourney Weaver, the Duke of Wellington, Arsène Wenger, W. B. Yeats.

26 JANUARY 1914 ～ 13 FEBRUARY 1915   *Wood Tiger*

13 FEBRUARY 1926 ～ 1 FEBRUARY 1927   *Fire Tiger*

31 JANUARY 1938 ～ 18 FEBRUARY 1939   *Earth Tiger*

17 FEBRUARY 1950 ～ 5 FEBRUARY 1951   *Metal Tiger*

5 FEBRUARY 1962 ～ 24 JANUARY 1963   *Water Tiger*

23 JANUARY 1974 ～ 10 FEBRUARY 1975   *Wood Tiger*

9 FEBRUARY 1986 ～ 28 JANUARY 1987   *Fire Tiger*

28 JANUARY 1998 ～ 15 FEBRUARY 1999   *Earth Tiger*

14 FEBRUARY 2010 ～ 2 FEBRUARY 2011   *Metal Tiger*

THE
TIGER

THE PERSONALITY OF THE TIGER

It's
the zest,
the enthusiasm,
the giving the little bit more,
that makes the difference.
And opens up so much.

The Tiger is born under the sign of courage. He is a charismatic figure and usually holds very firm views. He is strong-willed and determined and sets about most of his activities with tremendous energy and enthusiasm. He is very alert and quick-witted and his mind is forever active. He is a highly original thinker and is nearly always brimming with new ideas or full of enthusiasm for some new project or scheme.

The Tiger adores challenges and loves to get involved in anything that he thinks has an exciting future or that catches his imagination. He is prepared to take risks and does not like to be bound either by convention or the dictates of others. He likes to be free to act as he chooses and at least once during his life he will throw caution to the wind and go off and do the things he wants to do.

The Tiger does, however, have a somewhat restless nature. Even though he is often prepared to throw himself wholeheartedly into a project, his initial enthusiasm can soon wane if he sees something more appealing. He can also be rather impulsive and there will be occasions in his life when he acts in a manner he later regrets. If he were to think things through or be prepared to persevere in his various activities, he would almost certainly enjoy a greater degree of success.

Fortunately the Tiger is lucky in most of his enterprises, but should things not work out as he hoped, he is liable to suffer from severe bouts of depression and it will often take him a long time to recover. His life often consists of a series of ups and downs.

He is, however, very adaptable. He has an adventurous spirit and rarely stays in the same place for long. In the early stages of his life he is likely to try his hand at several different jobs and he will also change his residence fairly frequently.

The Tiger is very honest and open in his dealings with others. He hates any sort of hypocrisy or falsehood. He is also well known for being blunt and forthright and has no hesitation in speaking his mind. He can be rebellious at times, particularly against any form of petty authority, and while this can lead him into conflict with others, he is never one to shrink from an argument or avoid standing up for what he believes is right.

The Tiger is a natural leader and can rise to the top of his chosen profession. He does not, however, care for anything too bureaucratic or detailed, and he does not like to obey orders. He can be stubborn and obstinate and throughout his life he likes to retain a certain amount of independence in his actions and be responsible to no one but himself. He likes to consider that all his achievements are due to his own efforts and he will not ask for support from others if he can avoid it.

Ironically, despite his self-confidence and leadership qualities, he can be indecisive and will often delay making a major decision until the very last moment. He can also be sensitive to criticism.

Although the Tiger is capable of earning large sums of money, he is rather a spendthrift and does not always put his money to its best use. He can also be most generous and will often shower lavish gifts on friends and relations.

The Tiger cares very much for his reputation and the image that he tries to project. He carries himself with an air of dignity and authority and enjoys being the centre of attention. He is very adept at attracting publicity, both for himself and the causes he supports.

The Tiger often marries young and he will find himself best suited to those born under the signs of the Pig, Dog, Horse and Goat. He can also get on well with the Rat, Rabbit and Rooster, but will find the Ox and Snake a bit too quiet and serious for his liking, and he will be highly irritated by the Monkey's rather mischievous and inquisitive ways. He will also find it difficult to get on with another Tiger or a Dragon – both partners will want to dominate the relationship and could find it difficult to compromise on even the smallest of matters.

The Tigress is lively, witty and a marvellous hostess at parties. She takes great care over her appearance and is usually most attractive. She can be a very doting mother and while she believes in letting her children have their freedom, she makes an excellent teacher and will ensure that her children are well brought up and want for nothing. Like her male counterpart, she has numerous interests and likes to have sufficient independence and freedom to go off and do the things she wants to do. She has a most caring and generous nature.

The Tiger has many commendable qualities. He is honest, courageous and often a source of inspiration to others. Providing he can curb the wilder excesses of his restless nature, he is almost certain to lead a fulfilling and satisfying life.

THE FIVE DIFFERENT TYPES OF TIGER

In addition to the 12 signs of the Chinese zodiac there are five elements and these have a strengthening or moderating influence on the signs. The effects of the five elements on the Tiger are described below, together with the years in which they were exercising their influence. Therefore Tigers born in 1950 and 2010 are Metal Tigers, those born in 1962 are Water Tigers, and so on.

Metal Tiger: 1950, 2010
The Metal Tiger has an assertive and outgoing personality. He is very ambitious and while his aims may change from time to time, he will work relentlessly until he has obtained what he wants. He can, however, be impatient for results and become highly strung if things do not work out as he would like. He is distinctive in his appearance and is admired and respected by many.

Water Tiger: 1962

This Tiger has a wide variety of interests and is always eager to experiment with new ideas or satisfy his adventurous nature by going off to explore distant lands. He is versatile, shrewd and has a kindly nature. He tends to remain calm in a crisis, although he can be annoyingly indecisive at times. He communicates well with others and through his many capabilities and persuasive nature usually achieves what he wants in life. He is also highly imaginative and is often a gifted orator or writer.

Wood Tiger: 1914, 1974

The Wood Tiger has a friendly and pleasant personality. He is less independent than some of the other types of Tiger and more prepared to work with others to secure a desired objective. However, he does have a tendency to jump from one thing to another and can easily become distracted. He is usually very popular, has a large circle of friends and invariably leads a busy and enjoyable social life. He also has a good sense of humour.

Fire Tiger: 1926, 1986

The Fire Tiger sets about everything he does with great verve and enthusiasm. He loves action and is always ready to throw himself wholeheartedly into anything that catches his imagination. He has many leadership qualities and is capable of communicating his ideas and enthusiasm to others. He is very much an optimist and can be most generous. He has a likeable nature and can be a witty and persuasive speaker.

Earth Tiger: 1938, 1998

This Tiger is responsible and level-headed. He studies everything objectively and tries to be scrupulously fair in all his dealings. Unlike other Tigers, he is prepared to specialize in certain areas rather than get distracted by other matters, but he can become so involved in what he is doing that he does not always take into account the opinions of those around him. He has good business sense and is usually very successful in later life. He has a large circle of friends and pays great attention to both his appearance and his reputation.

PROSPECTS FOR THE TIGER IN 2012

The Year of the Rabbit (3 February 2011–22 January 2012) is an encouraging one for the Tiger and in what remains of it he can fare well.

One of the most favourably aspected areas is his own personal development, and in the remaining months of the Rabbit year he should continue to build on his knowledge and skills, including taking up any training that may be available in his work and undertaking any study and practice he can do by himself. This can not only help his present situation but also be personally satisfying.

For Tigers who are seeking work or looking to change what they do, the closing months of the Rabbit year can see some interesting possibilities, and it would be worth these Tigers keeping alert for opportunities. Many will now find their persistence paying off.

The Tiger will also benefit from the support and good-will of those around him. He can look forward to an increasing number of social occasions, and affairs of the heart can make this a special time. August and November could be particularly busy months.

Domestically, there will be a lot the Tiger wants to do, but ideas do need to be talked through and planned care-fully. The earlier some arrangements are made, the better, otherwise the Tiger may find it is not always possible to fit in all he wants. This particularly applies to meeting up with relations and friends and to travel. The last few Rabbit months will require good organizing.

Overall, the Rabbit year can be a satisfying one for the Tiger, particularly in terms of personal growth.

The Year of the Dragon starts on 23 January and can be a potentially rewarding one for the Tiger. However, it can bring volatile situations and the Tiger will need to watch his impulsive nature. Acting too hastily or without suffi-cient care can bring problems. This is a generally good year, but the Tiger does need to be vigilant.

At work, the aspects are promising. The Tiger is blessed with a fertile imagination and is capable of coming up with many fine ideas. Over the year his creativity and enterprise can bring some excellent results and lead to him making good headway. If he sees ways of improving efficiency or output, or a solution to a problem, he should put his ideas forward. With his general resourcefulness and ability to think out of the box, he can do his reputation and prospects a lot of good. In 2012 it is worth Tigers making that extra effort.

While the aspects are generally promising, a cautionary note does, however, need sounding. If, after a success, the Tiger becomes overconfident or rash, or rushes something through, he risks undermining some of the good he has done. The Dragon year can place traps for the unwary and the Tiger does need to remain on his mettle.

Often as a result of his current activities, he may well have the chance to put in for greater responsibilities. However, if he considers prospects are limited where he is, he should explore new possibilities. Dragon years favour initiative and the Tiger will often be well placed to benefit from any openings that arise. April, May, September and November could see some important work opportunities.

The aspects are also encouraging for Tigers seeking work. Although the job-seeking process can be difficult, the Tiger should have self-belief and make the most of his strengths and style. If he takes particular care with his applications, his qualities will be noticed and ultimately often rewarded.

Progress at work can help financially and the Tiger may also be able to supplement his earnings by putting an idea, hobby or interest to profitable use. However, while the aspects are promising, he will need to remain disciplined. In any enterprise or major transaction, he should check the facts and, if necessary, obtain appropriate advice. In addition he would do well to watch his spending. With his many plans and an often busy lifestyle, he does need to keep track of outgoings and budget accordingly.

This can be an inspiring year, though, and one in which the Tiger should make the most of his talents and originality. Tigers who enjoy creative or expressive pursuits could find some ideas developing in an encouraging way.

In view of the fast-moving nature of the year and the effort the Tiger puts into so many of his activities, however, there is a risk that he could become preoccupied with what he is doing and some areas of his life could suffer as a result. It is essential the Tiger remains aware of this and keeps his lifestyle in balance, including giving time to those around him.

This warning apart, Dragon years are exciting and can be personally rewarding for the Tiger. For the unattached, romance can figure prominently, with some Tigers finding love in an unexpected way. However, if it is to endure, time should be allowed for each partner to get to know the other better and so put the relationship on a firmer foundation.

The Tiger's interests and various activities can lead to some good social opportunities over the year, and he should listen closely to others and take careful note of any advice and suggestions close friends may give. Some of what they say could be both significant and prophetic. April, June and the last quarter of the Dragon year could be a busy time socially.

The Tiger's home life will also see much activity over the year and it is important there is good communication and co-operation between all parties. Without this, home life could be conducted in a whirl of activity and there is the risk that tensions (sometimes caused by over-tiredness) could result. To prevent this, it is important that the Tiger preserves some quality time to spend with his loved ones and that there are interests and activities all can appreciate. Again, that extra bit of time and attention can make a difference this year.

Overall, the Dragon year is one in which the Tiger can use his skills and creativity to good effect. It is a time for pushing forward, with fortune favouring the active and enterprising. The year can bring some interesting new opportunities and the Tiger would do well to follow these up. With mindfulness of others and good use of his abilities, he can make this a good and satisfying year.

The Metal Tiger

The metal element has an important influence on the Tiger, reinforcing his determination and strong will. When the Metal Tiger has decided on a course of action, he will not change his mind easily. However, in 2012 he would do well to be more accommodating. This can be a year of opportunity, but to benefit fully the Metal Tiger will require a flexible approach, especially as chances may suddenly open up for him.

For Metal Tigers in work this can be a significant year. Although they will often be content in their role, change is on the way. New tasks and objectives could be given and they could find their working practices being substantially altered. This will require some adjustment, but by being flexible and accepting the new, the Metal Tiger will often find developments working out well and giving him new incentive. Some Metal Tigers will have the chance to focus on more specific responsibilities and use their skills in a more fulfilling way. Work-wise, the Dragon year will certainly see a lot happening for many Metal Tigers, but despite the disruption, there is the chance to make good headway this year.

For Metal Tigers seeking work or keen to move on from where they are, the Dragon year can have surprising developments in store. Although the Metal Tiger will by now be skilled in particular areas, by being prepared to consider a wide range of possibilities and, in some cases, taking advantage of retraining or other courses, he could secure a position that is completely different from what he has done before. Again, this could involve readjustment, but it will give the Metal Tiger the new challenge he has been seeking. This is a year to be open to chance. April, May, September and November could see particularly interesting possibilities, but whenever the Metal Tiger sees an opening, he should act quickly.

Another important feature of the year will be the support the Metal Tiger receives. Long-term colleagues and contacts could be especially helpful and if ever the Metal Tiger finds himself in a dilemma and would welcome advice, he should ask for it. Similarly, when exploring possibilities, he should talk to those who have the expertise to advise. Not only can he benefit from information given but sometimes also be alerted to opportunities worth considering. In the Dragon year the Metal Tiger needs to be forthcoming.

This importance of contact with others also applies to his social life. During the year he could get deeply involved in various activities, and without care, there is a risk that some friendships could lapse and the Metal Tiger miss out on aspects of life that could bring him pleasure. No matter how busy he may be, he should aim to remain in contact with his friends as well as go to any social events that appeal to him. Not only can the social contact do him good but it will also allow him to benefit from the encouragement and advice certain friends can give. April, June and the closing months of the Dragon year could see the most social opportunity.

THE TIGER

Another important aspect of the Dragon year is that it brings new opportunities. As the Metal Tiger has such wide-ranging interests, during the year he could discover a new subject or activity that particularly intrigues him. If so, he should follow this up. In this fast-moving year it is important the Metal Tiger makes time for himself, for recreation and for pursuing his own interests and ideas.

For the unattached or lonely Metal Tiger, a further benefit of this will be the way existing or new interests bring him into contact with others and, for some, lead to significant new friendship or romance. Here again the Dragon year will have its surprises.

There will also be good travel opportunities. Many Metal Tigers will have the chance to visit areas new to them, although they will need to keep a watch on spending and make allowance for more expensive outlay. With good financial discipline, the Metal Tiger will find he is able to go ahead with his plans, but without this, they could be delayed. The Dragon year requires careful financial management.

In his home life, however, the Metal Tiger can look forward to some special times. There could be family news, an anniversary or other occasion to mark, and some exciting times in the Metal Tiger household. This can be a pleasing year domestically, but throughout, the Metal Tiger will need to be mindful and involved and spend quality time with those close to him. To make assumptions or become too preoccupied (always a risk this year) could result in problems. Metal Tigers, take note, and do remain attentive and aware.

Generally, the Dragon year is full of possibility for the Metal Tiger and by making the most of what arises and being willing to adapt and adjust, he can take great pleasure from what he is able to achieve.

TIP FOR THE YEAR
Spend time with those who are important to you. This is a year of considerable promise, but you do need to keep your lifestyle in balance and preserve time for others as well as for enjoying your achievements.

The Water Tiger

This is a year of considerable opportunity for the Water Tiger. Not only does it mark the start of a new decade in his life, but some of his actions will have important implications for the longer term. And with his enthusiasm and ability to put himself across, the Water Tiger will have much working in his favour.

In his work the aspects are particularly encouraging. Although many Water Tigers will have made good headway in recent years, quite a few will still not feel properly fulfilled. Over the year these Water Tigers should give serious thought to the direction they would like their career to take. Some may decide to look for a greater role in their current organization, while others, feeling they have achieved all they can where they are, will be ready to take on different challenges. The Dragon year is a time for action and as these Water Tigers contemplate their future, interesting developments can start to occur.

For some, internal reorganization in their current place of work will give them the chance to take on a more senior role, while for those keen to move elsewhere, events can take a curious course and they could find themselves being offered a position quite quickly on the strength of their experience. This may be an extension of what they have been doing or allow them to use their experience in new ways.

The aspects are also encouraging for Water Tigers seeking work. While there will be disappointments along the way, openings can occur suddenly, sometimes in an almost fortuitous manner. Friends, former colleagues and employment officials the Water Tiger may have contact with could all alert him to new possibilities. With advice, encouragement and his own very determined nature, he can find important doors opening for him. April, May, September and late October to early December could see interesting developments, but with the aspects so encouraging, possibilities could arise at almost any time.

Another positive feature of the year will be the way the Water Tiger is able to enjoy and develop his personal interests. With his keen and creative nature, he will often have projects or challenges to tackle and ideas he wants to follow up. Although his free time may be limited this year, by preserving time for interests and recreational pursuits, he can get a lot of pleasure and personal benefit from his activities. Here again his fiftieth year is one for following up ideas and making the most of his opportunities. For any Water Tiger who has neglected his personal interests of late, this would be an excellent time to start something new.

Travel will be on the agenda for many Water Tigers, particularly towards the end of 2012 and in early 2013, and some will decide to mark their fiftieth birthday with a special holiday. With careful planning, this could be one of the highlights of the year. In addition, the spontaneity that characterizes the Dragon year could lead to the chance to go away at short notice.

The progress the Water Tiger makes at work can also lead to an increase in income, but with travel possibilities and his existing commitments, he will need to keep good control of his spending and make early provision for plans and more substantial purchases. To do all he wants will require good management and discipline.

Important paperwork will also require close attention, as delay or error could cause problems and be to the Water Tiger's disadvantage. Water Tigers, take note and, where important matters are concerned, do be thorough.

With his outgoing nature, the Water Tiger will enjoy the various social opportunities of the year and his close friends can be especially helpful. Any Water Tiger who has experienced recent difficulty can find certain friends giving important help this year and there could also be good chances to meet others and, for the unattached, sometimes find romance. April, May and November to January 2013 could be busy and rewarding months socially.

The Water Tiger can also look forward to some special times in his home life. Not only will loved ones be keen to mark his fiftieth birthday in style, but many Water Tiger households will see change, possibly due to work changes or a family member moving out, possibly to further their education or seek work experience elsewhere. A lot is set to happen in 2012 and while there will be times when the Water Tiger will feel anxious, by offering support and doing what he can, he can make these important transitions easier. Throughout the year, if tired or pressured, he does need to be careful not to take tensions out on others. Fortunately most Water Tigers are mindful of those around them, but irritability can lead to problems. Water Tigers, take note, be open and forthcoming and do make the most of this often rewarding year.

Overall, the Year of the Dragon will be an important one for the Water Tiger, with his determination, enthusiasm and many ideas opening up excellent possibilities. This is a time for taking on new challenges, and socially and domestically it will also see some notable occasions. The Water Tiger's fiftieth year will be an important one and will often help shape the next few years.

TIP FOR THE YEAR
Look to move forward. By developing your ideas and strengths, you can not only gain a lot personally but also find other opportunities following on. Be active, be enterprising and be sure to make the most of yourself and this special year.

The Wood Tiger

This will be a year of interesting opportunity for the Wood Tiger and although certain plans may not go as envisaged, it is a time for making headway and for important personal developments.

The Dragon year is a fast-moving one and during it the Wood Tiger will need to keep alert and informed about what is going on around him. If he becomes too absorbed in his own activities or does not take sufficient account of current developments, he could find himself at a disadvantage. Wood Tigers, take note, especially as a great deal is possible for you this year.

In his work the Wood Tiger could experience considerable change. Colleagues could move on and new procedures be introduced, and parts of the year will be demanding and sometimes uncomfortable, but it is very much a case of keeping informed and adapting as necessary. In time, some very definite benefits will emerge. Not only will the Wood Tiger get to further his experience but also to work with other colleagues, some of whom can become good contacts and friends, and this can enhance his prospects for the future.

A feature of the Dragon year will be the speed with which developments take place. Chances could come the Wood Tiger's way quite suddenly and he could find that an application he makes is quickly followed up. To benefit fully, he will need to be flexible and make the most of opportunities *as they arise*. The first few weeks of the Dragon year could be especially busy, with April, May, September and November also seeing interesting possibilities.

For Wood Tigers seeking work, again chances can arise suddenly. After a period of few suitable opportunities or a spate of rejections, several interesting openings could occur at once and some Wood Tigers could find themselves in a dilemma about which to pursue. However, by following their instincts, many will not only quickly become established in a new line of work but also find their new position has possibilities for later development. Work-wise, this is a year of considerable potential.

Also, if the Wood Tiger's work or interests are in any way expressive, he should make the most of his talents this year, putting forward his ideas, promoting his work and developing his expertise. Interesting developments may well follow on.

With his often busy lifestyle, it is also important the Wood Tiger gives some attention to his own well-being and ensures he has a healthy diet and sufficient exercise and rest. To drive himself relentlessly could leave him prone to colds and other minor ailments. Wood Tigers, take note.

The Wood Tiger should also keep in regular contact with his friends as well as attend any social events that appeal to him. This can help to keep his lifestyle in balance and certain friends could prove especially helpful with some of the decisions and situations he faces over the year. April, June and the last quarter of the Dragon year could see much social activity, but throughout the year the Wood Tiger's work situation and interests will often give him the chance to widen his social circle.

His home life will also be busy this year and he may well find himself assisting both younger and more senior relations as well as dealing with quite a few home mainte-nance and improvement projects. At busy times, he would find it helpful to focus on priorities and postpone other plans. Also, if at any time he feels tired or anxious, he should avoid taking his vexations out on others. With busy lifestyles, tensions can sometimes arise and, without care, risk undermining rapport and understanding. Wood Tigers, take note and be mindful.

However, while parts of the year will be demanding, to compensate there will also be times that can be special.

Some Wood Tigers will see an addition to their family or have a career or personal success to mark, and many will enjoy shared interests and the sometimes unexpected travel opportunities the Dragon year can bring.

The Wood Tiger's progress at work can also lead to an increase in income, but this will be an expensive year. With his many plans, hopes and accommodation expenses (which could involve a move), he will need to keep careful control of his outgoings. Also, if taking on any major obligation, he should check the details and, if necessary, obtain appropriate advice. This is no time for risk or making assumptions.

Generally, the Year of the Dragon is a busy and promising one for the Wood Tiger, but it is a case of being flexible and making the most of his situation. Experience gained now can be a major factor in the future. Creative activities are also favourably aspected and throughout the year the Wood Tiger will value the support of those around him, although he does need to remain attentive, be forthcoming and preserve quality time for family and friends. With care, however, this can be an exciting year with far-reaching developments.

TIP FOR THE YEAR
Be aware and avoid immersing yourself so fully in certain activities that other parts of your life begin to suffer. Keep a good balance in your lifestyle and adapt as chances arise. This is a year of possibility. Use it well.

The Fire Tiger
The Fire Tiger has great enthusiasm and knows that he is capable of a great deal. In the Dragon year, his prospects are

good. However, events may not work out as originally planned. This can be a year of surprise and unanticipated decisions, but also personally rewarding experiences.

To get the most from 2012, the Fire Tiger will need to keep alert and be flexible. This is no year to be tied to one particular course of action but to adjust to situations as they unfold.

This is especially the case at work. In recent times many Fire Tigers will have impressed with their conscientious nature and ability to learn. This year, many will be given a chance to build on their position and to learn more about their role and industry. Sometimes these opportunities may not be what the Fire Tiger envisaged, but what he is able to accomplish this year can prove helpful in the longer term.

Fire Tigers who feel they could better their prospects by moving elsewhere may also be surprised by events. Sometimes they may be turned down for a particular position but offered another as an alternative, or be attracted to something which marks a considerable change from what they have been doing. Again it is a case of being flexible and making the most of chances *as they occur*. This also applies to Fire Tigers seeking work. By considering a wide range of possibilities and seeking advice, many will secure a position which has good chances of future development. The key to progress in 2012 is to adapt, learn and be open to possibility. Late March to May, September and November could see some encouraging developments, but such is the nature of the year that opportunities could arise at almost any time.

With their future in mind, some Fire Tigers will also decide to add to their qualifications or gain additional skills.

This not only represents an investment in themselves but also in their future. Personal and professional development is something all Fire Tigers would do well to consider this year, as the benefits can be far-reaching.

The Dragon year encourages creativity and expression, and those Fire Tigers who enjoy the arts, whether performing, attending events or in some other capacity, should set time aside to enjoy and develop their interests. For many, this can be an inspiring and productive time.

The Dragon year can also see important personal developments. For those Fire Tigers with a partner there could be exciting news and some key hopes can now be realized. However the Fire Tiger should remember that the Dragon year can have surprises in store and sometimes plans may need reconsidering as situations change. The Fire Tiger may need to show flexibility and pay attention to the views of loved ones. Also, pressures, decisions and dilemmas can occasionally lead to anxious or fraught moments. Fire Tigers, take note. This can be a personally exciting year, but inattention and lack of care can bring problems.

Although the Fire Tiger likes to take responsibility for his own affairs, he would also do well to draw on the assistance of others, including senior relatives. If he talks over his hopes or current situation, he could be given useful advice and assistance. This is a year for good communication.

The Fire Tiger will also value his social life and while existing commitments may mean he has to cut back on going out, if he keeps in regular contact with his friends he will not only enjoy sharing news but also appreciate the social occasions he does go to all the more. For some, a new pursuit or activity introduced during the year could be enjoyable. April, June and the last quarter of the year could see the most social activity and, for the unattached, a chance meeting could suddenly become significant.

Travel, too, is favourably aspected, with interesting opportunities arising, especially in the closing months of the Dragon year.

Generally, the Year of the Dragon offers great possibility for the Fire Tiger. In his work he will often be encouraged to make more of his skills and potential, and any qualifications gained can strengthen his prospects. His relations with others will also be important and this can be an exciting time, with many plans and hopes being realized. However, the Dragon year is fast-moving and as situations change, the Fire Tiger will need to adapt and, crucially, stay mindful of others. Overall, though, a good, fortunate and progressive year.

TIP FOR THE YEAR
Be open to opportunity. Remember that there are many ways forward and by making the most of yourself and your current situation, you can gain a great deal. Also, pay close attention to those who are dear to you and value their support and advice. You have much in your favour this year. Use it well.

The Earth Tiger
This will be an interesting year for the Earth Tiger and it holds considerable opportunity. However, to gain the most from it the Earth Tiger will need to make the most of situations as they are rather than as he would like them to be. This is a time to be accommodating and flexible.

For Earth Tigers born in 1998, this can be a particularly rewarding year. As they learn more, many will revel in the opportunities now becoming available to them. Whether furthering their computer skills or developing their interests in sport, music, art or other subject areas, these Earth Tigers will often find themselves being encouraged to explore new concepts and become more proficient in what they do. With the Earth Tiger's thirst for knowledge and liking for practical activity, this can be an inspiring time.

However, while the young Earth Tiger can make progress this year, he will need to put in time and effort. Results will need to be worked for and should the Earth Tiger find certain subjects challenging, he should not become disheartened or give up too easily. With an open mind and willingness to try, he is capable of making great strides this year. With the success he does enjoy, he will gain considerably in confidence, and any Earth Tigers who may be slightly retiring and hold themselves back will be likely to show new capabilities this year.

In addition to the progress made in his education, the young Earth Tiger will be keen to further certain interests, especially those he can share with his close friends. The Dragon year is an often vibrant and colourful time, with a variety of new styles and fashions emerging, and many Earth Tigers will enjoy following the latest new trend.

A lot that the young Earth Tiger does over the year will have a good social element and there will be many chances to meet new people. His relations with others will generally go well, but problems could still arise and there may be a clash of personality or a difference of opinion over some matter. If so, the young Earth Tiger should be careful not to let the matter escalate or get out of proportion. 'Least said, soonest mended' may often be the best approach this year. If, at any time, a particular situation should worry the young Earth Tiger, he should talk to others. Whether at home, school or, if necessary, via a helpline, there are people he can turn to for help. Generally this is a very encouraging year for the young Earth Tiger, but if he finds himself in any difficulty, he owes it to himself to be forthcoming.

In his home life there will be considerable activity, and with those around him leading busy lifestyles, any assistance he is able to give will be valued and will also help rapport and understanding. In addition many Earth Tigers will enjoy a variety of family activities, including, for some, a holiday away. The Dragon year can bring some particularly enjoyable times and again, the more willing and involved the young Earth Tiger is, the more he stands to gain.

For the Earth Tiger born in 1938, this can also be an interesting year. However, during it the Earth Tiger will need to remain aware and be prepared to adapt as situations require. If he is flexible, he will fare much better.

One particular area of interest will be accommodation, and quite a few Earth Tigers will be keen to acquire new items for their home and make other improvements. Their options and requirements need careful consideration and, in some instances, professional advice, but the more time given to major purchases and plans, the better the eventual result will be.

The Earth Tiger also needs to be careful when entering into any large transactions and dealing with financially related paperwork. Delay, a lost document or a mistake could be to his disadvantage. In the Dragon year bureaucratic matters can be troublesome, and care and vigilance are required.

The Earth Tiger can, however, derive great satisfaction from his personal interests over the year. Creative pursuits are especially well aspected and many Earth Tigers will enjoy the way their ideas develop and the variety of things they get to do. With his alert and curious nature, the Earth Tiger will also appreciate some of the social events and other occasions he goes to over the year. In addition, many Earth Tigers will enjoy participating in local activities or a special interest group.

The Earth Tiger will also play an important part in the lives of those dear to him. Grandchildren and great-grand-children could be particularly grateful for his support and some assistance he gives over the year can prove very help-ful. Many Earth Tigers can also look forward to taking part in a special event this year, perhaps involving an anniver-sary or their family increasing in number. Parts of the year will certainly be busy and exciting. However, at all times the Earth Tiger should remember that if he is troubled by any matter, he should seek advice. Those around will be delighted to reciprocate his many kindnesses.

Overall, the Year of the Dragon will be a busy and event-ful one, and for the Earth Tiger, whether born in 1938 or 1998, it is very much a case of being aware of what is happening and making the most of the current situation. Over the year the Earth Tiger does need to be forthcoming and also listen carefully to the views and advice of those around him, but personal interests and creative pursuits are favourably aspected and by using his time well and seizing his opportunities, the Earth Tiger can derive considerable satisfaction from his achievements and enjoy this full and interesting year.

Be open-minded and ready to consider new possibilities. With a willing and flexible approach, plans can be improved and more can be achieved.

FAMOUS TIGERS

Paula Abdul, Amy Adams, Kofi Annan, Sir David Attenborough, Christian Bale, Queen Beatrix of the Netherlands, Victoria Beckham, Beethoven, Tony Bennett, Tom Berenger, Chuck Berry, Usain Bolt, Jon Bon Jovi, Sir Richard Branson, Matthew Broderick, Emily Brontë, Garth Brooks, Mel Brooks, Isambard Kingdom Brunel, Agatha Christie, Charlotte Church, Phil Collins, Robbie Coltrane, Sheryl Crow, Tom Cruise, Penelope Cruz, Charles de Gaulle, Leonardo DiCaprio, Emily Dickinson, David Dimbleby, Dwight Eisenhower, Queen Elizabeth II, Enya, Roberta Flack, Frederick Forsyth, Jodie Foster, Megan Fox, Lady Gaga, Crystal Gayle, Buddy Greco, Germaine Greer, Ed Harris, Hugh Hefner, William Hurt, Ray Kroc, Shia LaBeouf, Stan Laurel, Jay Leno, Matt Lucas, Groucho Marx, Karl Marx, Marilyn Monroe, Demi Moore, Alanis Morissette, Rafael Nadal, Robert Pattinson, Jeremy Paxman, Marco Polo, Beatrix Potter, Renoir, Kenny Rogers, the Princess Royal, Dylan Thomas, Liv Ullman, Jon Voight, Julie Walters, H. G. Wells, Oscar Wilde, Robbie Williams, Dr Rowan Williams, Tennessee Williams, Sir Terry Wogan, Stevie Wonder, William Wordsworth.

14 FEBRUARY 1915 ⁓ 2 FEBRUARY 1916   *Wood Rabbit*

2 FEBRUARY 1927 ⁓ 22 JANUARY 1928   *Fire Rabbit*

19 FEBRUARY 1939 ⁓ 7 FEBRUARY 1940   *Earth Rabbit*

6 FEBRUARY 1951 ⁓ 26 JANUARY 1952   *Metal Rabbit*

25 JANUARY 1963 ⁓ 12 FEBRUARY 1964   *Water Rabbit*

11 FEBRUARY 1975 ⁓ 30 JANUARY 1976   *Wood Rabbit*

29 JANUARY 1987 ⁓ 16 FEBRUARY 1988   *Fire Rabbit*

16 FEBRUARY 1999 ⁓ 4 FEBRUARY 2000   *Earth Rabbit*

3 FEBRUARY 2011 ⁓ 22 JANUARY 2012   *Metal Rabbit*

THE
RABBIT

THE PERSONALITY OF THE RABBIT

Whenever
Wherever
With whoever.
Always I try to understand.
Without this one flounders.
But with understanding,
at least you have a chance.
A good chance.

The Rabbit is born under the signs of virtue and prudence. He is intelligent, well mannered and prefers a quiet and peaceful existence. He dislikes any sort of unpleasantness and will try to steer clear of arguments and disputes. He is very much a pacifist and tends to have a calming influence on those around him. He has wide interests and usually a good appreciation of the arts and the finer things in life. He also knows how to enjoy himself and will often gravitate to the best restaurants and nightspots in town.

The Rabbit is a witty and intelligent speaker and loves being involved in a good discussion. His views and advice are often sought by others and he can be relied upon to be discreet and diplomatic. He will rarely raise his voice in anger and will even turn a blind eye to matters that displease him just to preserve the peace. He likes to remain on good terms with everyone, but he can be rather sensitive and takes any form of criticism very badly. He will also be the first to get out of the way if he sees any form of trouble brewing.

The Rabbit is a quiet and efficient worker and has an extremely good memory. He is very astute in business and financial matters, but his degree of success often depends on the conditions that prevail. He hates being in a situation which is fraught with tension or where he has to make sudden decisions. Wherever possible he will plan his various activities with the utmost care and a good deal of caution. He does not like to take risks and does not take kindly to change. Basically, he seeks a secure, calm and stable environment, and when conditions are right he is more than happy to leave things as they are.

The Rabbit is conscientious and because of his methodical and ever-watchful nature he can often do well in his chosen profession. He makes a good diplomat, lawyer, shopkeeper, administrator or priest, and he excels in any job where he can use his superb skills as a communicator. He tends to be loyal to his employers and is respected for his integrity and honesty, but if he ever finds himself in a position of great power he can become rather intransigent and authoritarian.

The Rabbit attaches great importance to his home and will often spend a lot of time and money maintaining and furnishing it and fitting it with all the latest comforts – the Rabbit is very much a creature of comfort! He is also something of a collector and there are many Rabbits who derive much pleasure from collecting antiques, stamps, coins, *objets d'art* or anything else which catches their eye or particularly interests them.

The female Rabbit has a friendly, caring and considerate nature, and will do all in her power to give her home a happy and loving atmosphere. She is also very sociable and enjoys holding parties and entertaining. She has a great ability to make the maximum use of her time and although she involves herself in numerous activities, she always manages to find time to sit back and enjoy a good read or a chat. She has a great sense of humour, is very artistic and is often a talented gardener.

The Rabbit takes considerable care over his appearance and is usually smart and well turned out. He also attaches great importance to his relations with others and matters of the heart are particularly important to him. He will rarely be short of admirers and will often have several serious romances before he settles down. He is not the most faithful of signs, but he will find that he is especially well suited to those born under the signs of the Goat, Snake, Pig and Ox. Due to his sociable and easy-going manner he can also get on well with the Tiger, Dragon, Horse, Monkey, Dog and another Rabbit, but he will feel ill at ease with the Rat and Rooster, as both these signs tend to speak their mind and be critical in their comments and the Rabbit just loathes any form of criticism or unpleasantness.

The Rabbit is usually lucky in life and often has the happy knack of being in the right place at the right time. He is talented and quick-witted, but he does sometimes put pleasure before work and wherever possible will opt for the easy life. He can at times be a little reserved and suspicious of the motives of others, but generally will lead a long and contented life and one which – as far as possible – will be free of strife and discord.

THE FIVE DIFFERENT TYPES OF RABBIT

In addition to the 12 signs of the Chinese zodiac there are five elements and these have a strengthening or moderating influence on the signs. The effects of the five elements on the Rabbit are described below, together with the years in which they were exercising their influence. Therefore Rabbits born in 1951 and 2011 are Metal Rabbits, those born in 1963 are Water Rabbits, and so on.

Metal Rabbit: 1951, 2011

This Rabbit is capable, ambitious and has very definite views on what he wants to achieve in life. He can occasionally appear reserved and aloof, but this is mainly because he likes to keep his thoughts to himself. He has a quick and alert mind and is particularly shrewd in business matters. He can also be very cunning in his actions. He has a good appreciation of the arts and likes to mix in the best circles. He usually has a small but very loyal group of friends.

Water Rabbit: 1963

The Water Rabbit is popular, intuitive and keenly aware of the feelings of those around him. He can, however, be rather sensitive and tends to take things too much to heart. He is very precise and thorough in everything he does and has an exceedingly good memory. He tends to be quiet and at times rather withdrawn, but he expresses his ideas well and is highly regarded by his family, friends and colleagues.

Wood Rabbit: 1915, 1975

The Wood Rabbit is likeable, easy-going and very adaptable. He prefers to work in a group rather than on his own and likes to have the support and encouragement of others. He can, however, be rather reticent in expressing his views and it would be in his own interests to become a little more open and let others know how he feels on certain matters. He usually has many friends, enjoys an active social life and is noted for his generosity.

Fire Rabbit: 1927, 1987

The Fire Rabbit has a friendly, outgoing personality. He likes socializing and being on good terms with everyone. He is discreet and diplomatic and has a very good understanding of human nature. He is also strong-willed and provided he has the necessary backing he can go far in life. He does, not, however, suffer adversity well and can become moody and depressed when things are not working out as he would like. He has a particularly good manner with children, is very intuitive and there are some Fire Rabbits who are even noted for their psychic ability.

Earth Rabbit: 1939, 1999

The Earth Rabbit is a quiet individual, but nevertheless very astute. He is realistic in his aims and prepared to work long and hard in order to achieve his objectives. He has good business sense and is invariably lucky in financial matters. He also has a most persuasive manner and usually experiences little difficulty in getting others to fall in with his plans. He is held in high esteem by his friends and colleagues and his views are often sought and highly valued.

PROSPECTS FOR THE RABBIT IN 2012

The Year of the Rabbit (3 February 2011–22 January 2012) will have been an encouraging one for the Rabbit and the closing months will see the fulfilment of certain hopes and some fine personal times.

The Rabbit always attaches great importance to his relations with others and at the end of his own year he will find himself in demand. Socially, there will be more chances to go out, with parties, interest-related events and other forms of entertainment to look forward to. September, December and early January could be particularly busy times. For the unattached, romantic opportunities beckon, while those enjoying new-found romance could find this now becoming far more meaningful.

In the Rabbit's home life there will be increased pressure, with a lot to do, think about and plan. Fortunately the Rabbit is an excellent organizer, but this is a time for joint effort and drawing on the help of others. Many Rabbit households will have celebrated some exciting news during the year, or will do so in the closing months. Rabbit years are often domestically memorable for Rabbits.

At work, the Rabbit can also see important developments, and for those seeking a position or looking to progress, October and early December could bring interesting possibilities to pursue.

Overall, the Rabbit can accomplish a great deal in his own year, although to get the full benefit he does need to put himself forward and act with determination.

The Rabbit is very perceptive and is able to gauge situations well. And these abilities will be very useful to him in the Dragon year. This starts on 23 January and is a time for proceeding carefully and warily. It will be a variable year for the Rabbit, but by remaining alert and thorough, he can do much to minimize or escape its more awkward aspects.

One of the Rabbit's strengths is that he likes to plan and be well organized. However, in the Dragon year situations can be volatile. New developments can be rushed or carried through quickly and many a Rabbit will be left feeling uneasy or under pressure. However, while parts of the year may be difficult, it can still be a constructive time.

At work, many Rabbits will decide to remain in their present position, particularly if they are relatively new to it, and to use the year to become more established in their line of work. However, while this may be their intention, Dragon years are eventful and favour innovation. As a result, many Rabbits will find themselves affected by the winds of change and having to cope with new procedures and additional duties. The Dragon year can be a hard taskmaster. However, while the Rabbit may have misgivings over certain developments, by concentrating on what has to be done, he can add considerably to his reputation. The results he achieves and his fine use of his skills could lead to him being offered a greater role or finding himself well placed for promotion. The Dragon year will be challenging but it will also give many Rabbits the chance to use their strengths to good effect.

For Rabbits who are keen to move from where they are (and sometimes the changes that are introduced will be the deciding factor), as well as those seeking work, the Dragon year can be tricky. Not only will there be fierce competition in the job market but there may be few positions available in the type of work they favour. However, the Rabbit is resourceful and realistic. By thinking carefully about his situation and getting appropriate advice, he could identify opportunities which would give him the chance to broaden his skills. These may involve training and readjustment, but may offer the chance for the Rabbit to become established in a new position with the potential for later development.

It will require considerable effort to make headway this year, but the opportunities will be there and need to be taken as they arise. The second half of the year will be generally easier than the first, with April and the period from September to November being key times.

With his careful and methodical nature, the Rabbit usually manages his finances well, but in the Dragon year he needs to be wary. In particular, if he has a problem or doubt over any financial matter he should seek clarification, including, when appropriate, professional advice. Also, if tempted by any speculative ventures or 'too good to be true' offers, he should be careful. All may not be as it appears and if he is to avoid loss or regret, he needs to investigate what is involved and consider the implications carefully. This is no year for risk or oversight. Rabbits, take note.

However, while the aspects call for financial caution, the Rabbit can derive great pleasure from his home and social life. Many Rabbits regard their home as a sanctuary and, once there, thankfully close the door on outside pressures. And with the demands of the year, many Rabbits *will* close the door and devote more time to their loved ones, set about satisfying projects and enjoy shared interests. The year will see much domestic activity, including adding new comforts and altering the décor of certain rooms, and the Rabbit's fine taste and creative ideas will be very much in evidence.

Another strength of the Rabbit is his ability to enjoy good rapport with many people. Over the year he will do much to encourage and advise his loved ones, and they will often be grateful for his attention, kindness and contribution to home life.

With his personable nature, the Rabbit is also a keen socializer and over the year will value going out and relaxing, unwinding and meeting his friends. Often, as a result of those he knows, he will find himself being introduced to new people over the year and his social circle is set to widen. Any Rabbit who is alone or discontented, perhaps as a result of recent events, will find that if he goes out and perhaps takes up new interests, there will be excellent chances to make new friends. Romantic prospects are also encouraging, with new or existing romances both capable of bringing much happiness. March, July, August and December could see the most social activity.

Another satisfying aspect of the year will be the Rabbit's personal interests. Whether gardening, sport, creative, outdoor or other pursuits, these can again provide a useful break from some of the other pressures of the year. Rabbits have a knack for using their time well and rather than regard this as a particularly progressive year at work, many will view it as a time to improve the quality of their personal life and will be able to do this to good effect.

Overall, the Year of the Dragon will not be the easiest of times for the Rabbit. He will often feel uncomfortable with its sudden bursts of activity and change. However, by focusing on his objectives, he will be able to impress others. Interesting opportunities will arise for many Rabbits in their work. But it will be their home and social life which will be particularly special this year. For many, personal interests will also be a source of much pleasure, and for the unattached, affairs of the heart will often delight.

The Metal Rabbit

This will be a reasonable year for the Metal Rabbit and as it gets underway he would do well to give some thought to what he would like to see happen over the next 12 months. Having ideas in mind and talking them over with others will not only help him prioritize what he wants to do but also make him more aware of possibilities. As many Metal Rabbits will find, once ideas take shape, information, opportunities and assistance can quickly follow on. There is a definite element of synchronicity working in the Metal Rabbit's favour this year and sometimes the speed with which things happen will take him by surprise.

His home life will be particularly special this year. As with many Rabbits, the Metal Rabbit tends to regard his home as a buffer from outside pressures and over the year he will delight in certain domestic projects. These could include carrying out refurbishments and altering décor as well as buying new equipment and installing home comforts. However, while he may have clear ideas about what he wants, the Metal Rabbit would do well to take advice on certain purchases, especially where equipment is involved. Sometimes he could learn of something that better meets his requirements and/or is more economical.

In addition to enjoying the benefits his various plans and purchases bring, the Metal Rabbit will also take pleasure in following the activities of family members. Those who are grandparents could particularly enjoy time spent with grandchildren. Also, while the Metal Rabbit may not want to appear interfering, some assistance he gives to a particular family member could be more significant than he may realize. Indeed, among the Metal Rabbit's virtues are his caring nature and ability to empathize, and both will be valued by his loved ones over the year. Another of his talents lies in encouraging joint activities, and his contribution to home life can lead to many treasured moments.

However, while a lot will go well, no year is ever free from problems, and at more difficult times, the Metal Rabbit needs to be open and forthcoming. If he discusses his concerns with those around him, support, solutions and compromise can be more easily found. Generally this will be a very positive year for home life, but when problems and niggles raise their head, they do need to be dealt with quickly *and* with understanding.

One area which *will* require special care this year will be finance. When entering into any new agreement the Metal Rabbit does need to check the details and consider the implications. He also needs to deal with financially related paperwork carefully. Without sufficient attention, problems could arise and the Metal Rabbit could find himself at a disadvantage. Fortunately, his usually astute nature will help, but financially this is a year to avoid risk or rush.

More encouragingly, the Metal Rabbit will derive considerable pleasure from his personal interests this year and will be able to put his knowledge and skills to effective use. By making the most of his opportunities, skills and ideas, he can make this a personally rewarding time.

With his sociable nature and various interests, he will also enjoy meeting up with his friends as well as going to social events that appeal to him. In addition, by keeping informed about what is going on in his locality, he could discover a new activity, course or facility that is of interest to him and has potential benefit. Again, it is important that he remains aware and open to opportunity. March, July to early September and December could see the most social activity, although at most times of the year the Metal Rabbit will have interesting things to do.

In his work he can find this a demanding and sometimes tricky year. With changes often taking place and new objectives being set, his routine could be substantially altered. However, while this may be unsettling, the best policy for the Metal Rabbit is to concentrate on his specific responsibilities and adapt as required, including taking on new duties if need be. What happens now can often create new opportunities for him in the future, but in the meantime it is a case of doing his best in sometimes volatile situations.

For Metal Rabbits who are keen to move on from where they are or are seeking work, again it is a case of being open to chance. Events can work in curious ways in the Dragon year and some Metal Rabbits may be offered a position they thought it was unlikely they would get. Some may also find they are eligible for retraining. By being aware of what is available and putting themselves forward, they may find their enterprise leading to an interesting (and sometimes surprising) new opportunity. April and late August to November could see some significant developments.

Overall, a lot is set to happen in the Dragon year and while there will be pressures and some adjustments to be made, it will be a generally satisfying time. The Metal Rabbit's relations with family and friends will mean a lot to him this year and he will also derive considerable pleasure from developing his interests and perhaps becoming involved in something new. This is very much a year to be open to chance and set ideas in motion. Important benefits can often follow on.

TIP FOR THE YEAR
Make the most of swift-moving developments or sudden opportunities. Be active and use your ideas to advantage.

The Water Rabbit
'The sun and moon move back and forth like a shuttle' runs a Chinese proverb, and this constant ebb and flow will

be very evident for the Water Rabbit this year. Some months will see considerable activity while others will be sluggish, although in the main this will be a pleasant and generally constructive time.

In recent years many Water Rabbits will have experienced change in their work and will be content to remain where they are this year. However, as the year develops, many will be encouraged to become involved in new initiatives or training or take on greater responsibilities. What they do now can considerably broaden their skills and prepare them for future opportunities, particularly in the auspicious Snake year that follows.

For Water Rabbits who are keen to widen their experience by moving elsewhere, as well as those seeking work, the Dragon year can again be important. Obtaining a new position will not be easy, with some months seeing little apparent progress. However, like the sun and moon, situations change, and after lulls and disappointments, interesting opportunities can suddenly appear. The Water Rabbit will need to keep alert and be aware that when events happen in the Dragon year, they happen quickly. April and September to November could see some good opportunities, but whenever the Water Rabbit sees a possibility, he should act without delay.

A valuable legacy of the year can be the skills the Water Rabbit is able to develop during it. If he has particular career aspirations, extra studying or qualifications can do much to strengthen his prospects. Similarly, for any Water Rabbit with thoughts of changing career or becoming self-employed, this would be an excellent year to take advantage of training or refresher opportunities as well as seek professional advice. Positive steps taken now can greatly help the Water Rabbit's future situation.

This emphasis on personal development also applies to other areas of his life. If there are particular interests he is keen to develop, he should aim to set time aside for them.

In addition he should also give consideration to his current lifestyle and, if lacking regular exercise, seek advice on the most appropriate way to remedy this. Any attention he can give to his lifestyle and personal development can reward him well this year.

The Water Rabbit is generally careful in money matters, but over the year he will need to remain thorough and vigilant. When considering large purchases or transactions, he should check the details and implications, and if tempted by any speculative or more risky undertaking, understand what is involved and his potential liabilities. If he has questions or uncertainties, he does need to get these addressed before proceeding.

When possible, he should, however, aim to make provision for a holiday during the year. A change of scene can do him considerable good.

With his sincere and genial nature, the Water Rabbit enjoys company and will particularly appreciate the various social events he attends over the year. There will also be good opportunities to make new friends and contacts. March, July, August, December and early January 2013 could be particularly busy months socially.

However, there could also be some awkward moments, possibly when a friend seeks advice over a tricky problem or the Water Rabbit hears news or a rumour affecting someone he knows. At such times, he should check the facts and be honest in expressing his views. He should also stand firm and not allow himself to be pressured into saying or doing something against his better judgement. The Water Rabbit dislikes awkwardness, but some parts of the year will require him to be firm and stand his ground. Fortunately, such difficult moments will be few and will not affect all Water Rabbits, but is something to remain aware of during the year.

The Water Rabbit's home life will be a source of much contentment during the year. As always, he will follow the fortunes of his loved ones with fond interest and those close to him will particularly value his care and support. In view of pressures the year may bring, certain plans may need to be reconsidered or rearranged and the Water Rabbit and other household members will need to be flexible and patient. However, for the most part home life will go well.

Overall, the Year of the Dragon will be an interesting one for the Water Rabbit, with some months seeing a great deal happening and others being slow and uneventful. He can make some important gains this year, particularly through developing his skills and knowledge. He does need to be vigilant in money matters, but generally he will be content with how events work out and his home life will often be a source of great personal pleasure.

TIP FOR THE YEAR
Keep alert. Opportunities can arise suddenly and need to be seized quickly. Also, build on your skills and interests. They can not only bring you much personal satisfaction, but also open up possibilities for the future.

The Wood Rabbit

One of the strengths of the Wood Rabbit is his ability to adapt and make the most of his situation, and this year his skills can prove of considerable value.

In 2012 the Wood Rabbit will see change and face some important decisions, and his actions can have great significance. However, he should not allow himself to be hurried or forced into action, but should consider the implications carefully and draw on the support of others in deciding the best way forward. His ability to sense what is right for him will be an important factor this year.

One area which will see considerable development will be the Wood Rabbit's work. Dragon years favour enterprise and change, and many Wood Rabbits will be given new objectives or have the chance to widen their role. This will often require learning new procedures and using skills in other ways, but by adapting (a Wood Rabbit strength) and being willing to learn, he can take an important step in his overall career development. The Dragon year may be demanding, but will prepare him for some of the significant opportunities that lie ahead, especially next year.

Another factor in the Wood Rabbit's favour is his ability to work well with others. He is a good team player and can once again help his situation by liaising well with colleagues and seizing his chances to network and get himself better known. Some contacts made this year can become loyal and helpful friends.

Also, if at any time the Wood Rabbit finds himself in a complex situation, whether related to some aspect of his work or a decision he has to make, it is important he seeks the opinion of others. He will often benefit from their advice. The Dragon year favours an open and forthcoming approach and is no time to keep his concerns to himself.

This also applies to those Wood Rabbits who decide to move on from where they are or are seeking work. By contacting agencies and prospective employers as well as exploring various options, many will find their drive and initiative rewarded, possibly with a position that is very different from what they have done before. Work-wise, the Dragon year can ask a lot of the Wood Rabbit and require him to adapt and learn, but its longer-term value can be considerable. April and late August to November could see some important opportunities.

In money matters the Wood Rabbit will need to be careful. Although he may be keen to improve his situation, he should be wary of any risky, speculative or 'get rich quick' scheme he may hear about. All may not be as it at seems and he should check the details and implications. However, while caution is needed, the Wood Rabbit can also benefit from some luck over the year, perhaps being able to make certain home purchases at reduced prices or take advantage of last-minute travel opportunities. When he has specific ideas or require-ments in mind, it would certainly reward him to keep alert.

Although he will have many calls on his time, he should also make sure he keeps his lifestyle in good balance, preserving time for rest, exercise and personal interests. Where certain pursuits are concerned, if he joins other enthusiasts he can not only benefit from a pooling of ideas and support but also from social opportunities. Wood Rabbits who have let their interests lapse in recent years or would welcome something new to do will find it well worth joining a social group or enrolling on a course.

With this year favouring his relations with others, the Wood Rabbit will value his social life, and March, July to early September and December will see the most social activity. For Wood Rabbits who are feeling low or have had some recent personal difficulty to contend with, a new friendship could become significant.

The Wood Rabbit always sets great store by his home life, and domestically this can be a full and satisfying year, with those close to him valuing his ability to attend to so much. However, while the Wood Rabbit may be willing, there are limits. At busy times, he should ask for help, and rather than putting pressure on himself to get various undertakings finished, he should accept that some tasks may take longer than anticipated. When facing decisions or sudden change, it is also important he talks over what is happening with his loved ones. Not only can they offer support and advice, but interesting possibilities may arise from the discussion.

Overall, the Year of the Dragon will be an interesting and personally rewarding one for the Wood Rabbit. In his work situation, by making the most of chances and changes, he can add considerably to his experience and prepare the way for later opportunities, and his home and social life and personal interests will bring him much contentment.

TIP FOR THE YEAR
Further your skills and experience. With a willing approach, you can sow important seeds for the future. Also use your fine personal gifts to advantage. Get to know others and build up contacts. You can impress many this year and some can be helpful both now and in the future.

The Fire Rabbit

This will be a variable year for the Fire Rabbit. Some aspects of his life can bring great happiness, while others can bring disappointment. However, life rarely runs smoothly and not only will the good more than outweigh the bad, but the Fire Rabbit will get to experience a great deal.

One area which does require especial care is finance. The Fire Rabbit will need to manage his outgoings carefully and, as far as possible, budget ahead. When conducting any large transaction he needs to check the implications and, if applicable, seek advice. This is no year for risk, and if tempted by more speculative ventures, he should be wary. Financially, this is a year for vigilance and discipline.

This can also be a demanding year work-wise. New schemes may be introduced and working patterns altered, and few will remain unaffected by what happens. The Fire Rabbit may be concerned about developments, but by doing his best and being willing to adapt, he can not only make encouraging headway but also gain valuable new experience. And what he accomplishes this year can prepare him for future advances.

Many Fire Rabbits will remain with their current employer over the year and not only become more established but also experienced in the workings of their industry. With his ability to work well with others, the Fire Rabbit should make the most of networking opportunities and, if appropriate, consider joining a professional organization. This can greatly help his prospects.

For Fire Rabbits who decide to move on or are seeking work, the Dragon year can open up interesting possibilities. Their quest will not be easy, but by widening the range of what they are prepared to consider and adapting existing skills, many will secure a new position, often one with scope for further development. April and September to November could see some important chances.

However, while many Fire Rabbits can make good headway over the year, there will also be disappointments. Certain applications may not go their way and plans may not materialize. While this can be disheartening, the Fire Rabbit can learn a lot from what happens and strengthen his ideas and approach. An important value of the Dragon year is its instructive nature.

The Fire Rabbit can, however, derive considerable pleasure from his interests and recreational pursuits this year. He could well be attracted by a new activity and whether it allows him more chance to go out, to get additional exercise or to develop his ideas and creativity, it can often benefit him. For any Fire Rabbits who have thoughts of taking a particular interest further, this would be an excellent year to explore ideas.

A particular strength of the Rabbit is his ability to relate to others, and over the year the Fire Rabbit can look forward to some wonderful times in both his social and personal life. For those with a partner, there will be some exciting plans to share, although these may change as the year progresses. The Dragon year has an element of surprise to it and just as some choices are made, something more suitable could suddenly become available. It would certainly be to the Fire Rabbit's advantage to keep aware and be flexible.

Although the Fire Rabbit will be keen to take responsibility for his own affairs, at times of decision or concern, he should also draw on the advice of more senior relations.

They can offer useful advice or mention certain things he may not have fully considered. The Fire Rabbit has a special place in the lives of many and when pressures are great or he faces complex decisions, he should talk to those who have his best interests at heart.

In addition to family support, the Fire Rabbit can look forward to a pleasing social life. Due to other commitments and financial considerations, he may be more selective in his socializing, but this will not stop him from thoroughly enjoying himself when he does go out. For those who are alone, perhaps having moved to a new area or seen a change in their situation, the Dragon year will bring good opportunities to build up a new social circle. For the unattached, existing or new-found romance can make the year all the more special. Where the Fire Rabbit's relations with others are concerned, this can be an often significant year, with March, July, August and December seeing the most social activity.

Overall, the Year of the Dragon will be mixed for the Fire Rabbit. There will be great happiness, including some often wonderful times spent with others, but there will also be pressures, particularly work-wise, as the Fire Rabbit adapts to changing situations. However, he will learn a great deal, discover new personal qualities and prepare himself for future opportunities. The Dragon year, while sometimes demanding, can leave a lasting legacy.

TIP FOR THE YEAR
Use your people skills well and make the most of opportunities to meet others. Also, develop your skills and interests. What you do this year can both reward you now and

prepare you for the important opportunities soon to emerge, especially next year.

The Earth Rabbit

This will be a reasonable year for the Earth Rabbit. While it will contain its pressures, there will also be a lot for the Earth Rabbit to enjoy.

For Earth Rabbits born in 1939 the year can generally progress well. However, certain areas can be problematic. As with all Rabbits, the Earth Rabbit should be especially careful when dealing with important paperwork and matters of finance. This includes keeping all receipts and guarantees safe as well as checking that insurance and other policies are up to date and adequate. This is no year for lapses, risks or making assumptions.

A feature of the Dragon year is the speed with which things happen and there could be occasions when the Earth Rabbit feels hassled or hurried into making a decision. At such times it would be worth him holding firm and addressing any uncertainties before proceeding. He should not act against his better judgement. However, while the aspects require care, the Earth Rabbit is by nature astute and over the year his perceptiveness will guide him well.

Another of the Earth Rabbit's strengths is that he is interested in a great many things and always keen to further his knowledge as well as try out ideas. And over the year his interests and hobbies can develop in an encouraging manner. Not only will he be pleased with what he does, but he can also find the social aspects beneficial. Whether sharing interests or meeting other enthusiasts, many Earth

Rabbits will enjoy sharing their knowledge and the company certain pursuits bring. Any Earth Rabbits who would welcome new friendships would do well to find out about activities in their area. This can reward them well.

Another pleasing element to the year will be the travel opportunities that arise, and if the Earth Rabbit sees a holiday offer or short break that appeals to him he should try to go. Some Earth Rabbits may also be tempted by more local trips or outings and by making the most of such chances can get to do some interesting things.

The Earth Rabbit has a neat and orderly nature and over the year may well decide to carry out projects on his home, perhaps changing the décor of certain rooms and/or tidying out storage areas. Such projects can prove very satisfying and even lead to the Earth Rabbit rediscovering items of special meaning or coming up with new ideas in the process. Projects in the Dragon year can often have hidden benefits or open up new possibilities.

The Earth Rabbit will take a keen interest in the activities of family members over the year and, being so caring, may also worry about them at times. Rather than keep these concerns to himself, he should let others know and, if applicable, seek professional advice. In any difficult matters this year, the Earth Rabbit should remember he is not alone and there are relatives, friends, help centres and professionals willing to support and advise if need be. This reminder only applies to a few Earth Rabbits, but those who do have times of concern should remember this.

In general, however, this will be a good year and the Earth Rabbit will enjoy sharing plans, carrying out home projects and participating in the various activities that take place.

For Earth Rabbits born in 1999, this will be an interesting and encouraging year. The young Earth Rabbit will have a great number of subjects to study and will sometimes feel daunted by the scope of what he has to do, but by being willing and putting in the effort, he can make encouraging progress, including in some areas which up until now he may have found more difficult.

Another important aspect of the year will be the chance the Earth Rabbit will have to try new activities. In the process he may acquire new skills that will be significant in the future.

He will also value the support of his close friends throughout the year, and Earth Rabbits in new schools could make what will become lifelong friendships. Relations with others will generally go well, but should any problems arise, it is important that the Earth Rabbit is forthcoming and lets others know rather than keeps his worries to himself. Also, the young Earth Rabbit should avoid going against his instinct. Sometimes high jinks or moments of foolhardiness can backfire. Earth Rabbits, take note. Needless risks can lead to problems.

For both the younger and more senior Earth Rabbit, the Dragon year can be personally rewarding. By making the most of their situation and opportunities, they can accomplish a great deal. New activities can often give rise to other possibilities too. This is very much a year which rewards a keen and willing attitude. The Earth Rabbit will also value the support of others, though if any problems arise, it is important he seeks advice. Overall, this will be an interesting year, but throughout the Earth Rabbit needs to remain aware and stay true to his own feelings and better judgement.

Embrace your opportunities. With a positive approach, you can gain a great deal. Shared pursuits will also often bring you pleasure.

FAMOUS RABBITS

Margaret Atwood, Drew Barrymore, David Beckham, Harry Belafonte, Pope Benedict XVI, Ingrid Bergman, St Bernadette, Jeff Bezos, Kathryn Bigelow, Gordon Brown, Michael Bublé, Nicolas Cage, Lewis Carroll, Fidel Castro, John Cleese, Confucius, Marie Curie, Johnny Depp, Novak Djokovic, Albert Einstein, George Eliot, W. C. Fields, James Fox, Sir David Frost, Cary Grant, Ashley Greene, Edvard Grieg, Oliver Hardy, Seamus Heaney, Tommy Hilfiger, Bob Hope, Whitney Houston, Helen Hunt, John Hurt, Anjelica Huston, Chrissie Hynde, Enrique Inglesias, Clive James, Henry James, Sir David Jason, Angelina Jolie, Michael Jordan, Michael Keaton, John Keats, Lisa Kudrow, Gina Lollobrigida, George Michael, Sir Roger Moore, Andrew Murray, Mike Myers, Brigitte Nielsen, Graham Norton, Michelle Obama, Jamie Oliver, George Orwell, Sarah Palin, Edith Piaf, Brad Pitt, Sidney Poitier, Romano Prodi, Ken Russell, Elisabeth Schwarzkopf, Neil Sedaka, Jane Seymour, Neil Simon, Frank Sinatra, Sting, Quentin Tarantino, J. R. R. Tolkien, KT Tunstall, Tina Turner, Luther Vandross, Sebastian Vettel, Queen Victoria, Muddy Waters, Orson Welles, Hayley Westenra, Walt Whitman, Robin Williams, Kate Winslet, Tiger Woods.

3 FEBRUARY 1916 ⌒ 22 JANUARY 1917   *Fire Dragon*

23 JANUARY 1928 ⌒ 9 FEBRUARY 1929   *Earth Dragon*

8 FEBRUARY 1940 ⌒ 26 JANUARY 1941   *Metal Dragon*

27 JANUARY 1952 ⌒ 13 FEBRUARY 1953   *Water Dragon*

13 FEBRUARY 1964 ⌒ 1 FEBRUARY 1965   *Wood Dragon*

31 JANUARY 1976 ⌒ 17 FEBRUARY 1977   *Fire Dragon*

17 FEBRUARY 1988 ⌒ 5 FEBRUARY 1989   *Earth Dragon*

5 FEBRUARY 2000 ⌒ 23 JANUARY 2001   *Metal Dragon*

23 JANUARY 2012 ⌒ 9 FEBRUARY 2013   *Water Dragon*

THE
DRAGON

THE PERSONALITY OF
THE DRAGON

I like giving things a go.
Sometimes I succeed,
sometimes I fail.
Sometimes the unexpected happens.
But it is the giving things a go
and the stepping forward
that make life so interesting.

The Dragon is born under the sign of luck. He is a proud and lively character and has a tremendous amount of self-confidence. He is also highly intelligent and very quick to take advantage of any opportunity. He is ambitious and determined and will do well in practically anything he attempts. He is also something of a perfectionist and will always try to maintain the high standards he sets himself.

The Dragon does not suffer fools gladly and will be quick to criticize anyone or anything that displeases him. He can be blunt and forthright in his views and is certainly not renowned for being either tactful or diplomatic. He does, however, often take people at their word and can occasionally be rather gullible. If he ever feels that his trust has been abused or his dignity wounded, he can sometimes become very bitter and it will take him a long time to forgive and forget.

The Dragon is usually very outgoing and is particularly adept at attracting attention and publicity. He enjoys being in the limelight and is often at his best when he is confronted by a difficult problem or tense situation. In some respects he is a showman and he rarely lacks an audience. His views are highly valued and he invariably has something interesting – and sometimes controversial – to say.

He also has considerable energy and is often prepared to work long and unsocial hours in order to achieve what he wants. He can, however, be rather impulsive and does not always consider the consequences of his actions. He also has a tendency to live for the moment and there is nothing that riles him more than to be kept waiting. The Dragon hates delay and can get extremely impatient and irritable over even the smallest of hold-ups.

The Dragon has an enormous faith in his abilities, but he does run the risk of becoming over-confident and unless he is careful he can sometimes make grave errors of judgement. While this may prove disastrous at the time, he does have the tenacity and ability to bounce back and pick up the pieces again.

The Dragon has such an assertive personality, so much willpower and such a desire to succeed that he will often reach the top of his chosen profession. He has considerable leadership qualities and will do well in positions where he can put his own ideas and policies into practice. He is usually successful in politics, show business, as the manager of his own department or business, and in any job that brings him into contact with the media.

The Dragon relies a tremendous amount on his own judgement and can be scornful of other people's advice. He likes to feel self-sufficient and there are many Dragons who cherish their independence to such a degree that they prefer to remain single throughout their lives. However, the Dragon will often have numerous admirers and many will be attracted by his flamboyant personality and striking looks. If he does marry, he will usually marry young, and will find himself particularly well suited to those born under the signs of the Snake, Rat, Monkey and Rooster. He will also find that the Rabbit, Pig, Horse and Goat make ideal companions and will readily join in with many of his escapades. Two Dragons will also get on well together, as they will understand each other, but the Dragon may not find things so easy with the Ox and Dog, as both will be critical of his impulsive and somewhat extrovert manner. He will also find it difficult to form an alliance with the Tiger, for the Tiger, like the Dragon, tends to speak his mind, is very strong-willed and likes to take the lead.

The female Dragon knows what she wants in life and sets about everything she does in a determined and positive manner. No job is too small for her and she is often prepared to work extremely hard to secure her objectives. She is immensely practical and somewhat liberated. She hates being bound by routine and petty restrictions and likes to have sufficient freedom to go off and do what she wants to do. She will keep her house tidy, but is not one for spending hours on housework – there are far too many other things that she prefers to do. Like her male counterpart, she has a tendency to speak her mind.

The Dragon usually has many interests and enjoys sport and other outdoor activities. He also likes to travel and often prefers to visit places that are off the beaten track rather than head for popular tourist destinations. He has a very adventurous streak in him and providing his financial circumstances permit – and the Dragon is usually sensible with his money – he will travel considerable distances during his lifetime.

The Dragon is a very flamboyant character and while he can be demanding of others and in his early years rather precocious, he will have many friends and will nearly always be the centre of attention. He has charisma and so much confidence that he can often become a source of inspiration to others. In China he is the leader of the carnival and he is also blessed with an inordinate share of luck.

THE FIVE DIFFERENT TYPES OF DRAGON

In addition to the 12 signs of the Chinese zodiac there are five elements and these have a strengthening or moderating influence on the signs. The effects of the five elements on the Dragon are described below, together with the years in which they were exercising their influence. Therefore Dragons born in 1940 and 2000 are Metal Dragons, those born in 1952 and this year are Water Dragons, and so on.

Metal Dragon: 1940, 2000

This Dragon is very strong-willed and has a particularly forceful personality. He is energetic, ambitious and tries to be scrupulous in his dealings with others. He can also be blunt and to the point and usually has no hesitation in speaking his mind. If people disagree with him or are not prepared to co-operate, he is more than happy to go his own way. He usually has very high moral values and is held in great esteem by his friends and colleagues.

Water Dragon: 1952, 2012

This Dragon is friendly, easy-going and intelligent. He is quick-witted and rarely lets an opportunity slip by. However, he is not as impatient as some of the other types of Dragon and is prepared to wait for results rather than expect everything to happen at once. He has an understanding nature and is willing to share his ideas and co-operate with others. His main failing is a tendency to jump from one thing to another rather than concentrate on the job in hand. He has a good sense of humour and is an effective speaker.

Wood Dragon: 1964

The Wood Dragon is practical, imaginative and inquisitive. He loves delving into all manner of subjects and can quite often come up with some highly original ideas. He is a thinker and a doer and has the drive and commitment to put many of his ideas into practice. He is more diplomatic than some of the other types of Dragon and has a good sense of humour. He is very astute in business matters and can also be most generous.

Fire Dragon: 1916, 1976

This Dragon is ambitious, articulate and has a tremendous desire to succeed. He is a hard and conscientious worker and is often admired for his integrity and forthright nature. He is very strong-willed and has considerable leadership qualities. He can, however, rely a bit too much on his own judgement and fail to take into account the views and feelings of others. He can also be rather aloof and it would certainly be in his own interests to let others join in more with his various activities. He usually enjoys music, literature and the arts.

Earth Dragon: 1928, 1988

The Earth Dragon tends to be quieter and more reflective than some of the other types of Dragon. He has a wide variety of interests and is keenly aware of what is going on around him. He also has clear objectives and usually has no problems in obtaining support and backing for any of his ventures. He is very astute in financial matters and often able to accumulate considerable wealth. He is a good organizer, although he can at times be rather bureaucratic and fussy. He mixes well with others and has a large circle of friends.

PROSPECTS FOR THE DRAGON IN 2012

The Year of the Rabbit (3 February 2011–22 January 2012) may lack the activity and pace the Dragon favours, but it can still be a useful one for him. Coming before his own year, it will give him the chance to develop his ideas and skills and prepare himself for the exciting prospects that lie ahead.

In his work the Dragon should pay careful attention to developments going on around him. By keeping himself informed, he may have the chance to extend his experience and work with other colleagues. What he does in the closing Rabbit months can do a lot to enhance his reputation and help his prospects. September and December, in particular, could see interesting developments.

The Dragon will need to keep a careful watch on his spending, however, and, whenever possible, make advance provision for any extra outlay as well as travel opportunities occurring late in the year.

He will also see an increase in activity in both his home and social life at this time and could find it helpful to spread out his commitments. Discussion with others and sorting out arrangements early on will not only be better for all but also lead to less pressure and more enjoyable occasions. August and December could be two full and interesting months socially.

As the Rabbit year draws to a close, the Dragon's own year is about to start, and any thought he can give to what he wants to do over the next 12 months could be useful. His fortune is very much on the turn and an auspicious year lies ahead.

The Dragon is born under the sign of luck and, to some extent, makes his luck, due to his own character. By being active and outgoing, he not only knows a great many people but also gets involved in many things and so places himself in a good position to benefit from opportunities.

This, backed by his own earnest nature, stands him in good stead.

The Year of the Dragon begins on 23 January and many Dragons will not only celebrate the start of their own year in style but also be determined to make this a positive one. And their efforts can reward them well.

Almost as soon as the Dragon year begins, if not shortly before, the Dragon will be keen to get certain plans underway. These can apply to almost any area of his life, but a key feature of the Dragon year will be that once the Dragon sets plans in motion, interesting possibilities can quickly arise.

Work-wise, the aspects are particularly encouraging. For Dragons who are established in their profession, there will be good chances to move ahead, and if they keep alert for promotion opportunities, they may be able to make significant progress this year. Very often the responsibilities these Dragons now take on will involve using their skills in new ways and the year can provide interesting challenges which many will relish.

The aspects are also promising for any Dragons who feel staid or unfulfilled in their present position or are seeking work. This is a year to be open to opportunity, and by keeping alert and considering different possibilities, many Dragons will secure an ideal position, often in a different type of work or industry from before. This is a year for change and innovation. March, May, September and October could see some positive developments, but, as Dragons will find, events can happen quickly in their own year and when they see an opportunity, they need to act without delay.

Another important feature of the year will be the chance the Dragon will have to add to his experience and skills. All Dragons should make the most of any training they may be offered, courses they can take or qualifications they can gain. Not only can this have present value but also help their future prospects, with this current period of growth extending well into the following Snake year. Investment made in the Dragon himself will also be an investment in his future.

The progress the Dragon makes at work can also help financially and many Dragons will enjoy an increase in earnings over the year. Some may also be able to supplement their income by putting an idea or interest to profitable use or may benefit from a bonus or gift. However, to make the most of any upturn the Dragon should manage his money carefully and look to reduce any borrowings and make provision for his future. With care, he can improve his situation this year as well as ease certain pressures.

With his genial and outgoing nature, the Dragon will often be on impressive form this year and his social circle is set to increase. Some of those he meets over the year can become important friends and connections. February, March, July and December could be especially active months socially, although at most times of the year the Dragon will have chances to go out and things to do. For the unattached, their own year can bring wonderful romance. Affairs of the heart are superbly aspected and quite a few Dragons could meet their future partner this year. For any who may have suffered hurt in recent years, their own year can see a considerable improvement in their situation.

The Dragon can also look forward to an active home life, although there is a risk that this could become a whirl of activity, and at busy times there will need to be good co-operation and a willingness to help out and share household tasks. Amid the bustle and busyness, it is important that the Dragon preserves some quality time to spend with his loved ones. In this exciting year, he *does* need time to pause, unwind and value the pleasures of home life. He should also be prepared to talk over his thoughts and ideas with his loved ones. Not only can he gain from their insights but he may also be assisted in unexpected ways. However, while this may be a busy year, it can also be a special one, and many a Dragon household will have a special event to celebrate over the year.

In general, the Year of the Dragon is a highly auspicious one for the Dragon himself. It is a time for pushing ahead with plans, and with his energy, determination and style, the Dragon is set to achieve a great deal. For Dragons who have had recent disappointments, this year can mark a distinct change in fortunes and this upturn will continue well into 2013. However, to benefit fully, the Dragon does need to take action and be the instigator of the changes he desires. As he will so often find, however, once he makes a start, a lot can follow on. Fortune in the Dragon year will very much favour the bold and enterprising.

The Metal Dragon
This is a year of considerable possibility for the Metal Dragon and by making the most of his ideas and opportunities, he can enjoy some pleasing results.

One of the Metal Dragon's strengths is his determined nature and once he has set his mind on something, he pursues it with considerable might. Metal Dragons born in 1940 will certainly have plans they will be keen to get underway and will set about them with much gusto. However, while the Metal Dragon will have some definite aims, it is important that he discusses these with his loved ones and friends. Not only can certain ideas be strengthened by their input, but just the process of discussion can help set many in motion.

Many Metal Dragons will feel in expansionist mood this year and be keen to make improvements to their home, including buying new equipment and modifying certain areas. As the process gets underway, the Metal Dragon will enjoy making choices and improvements and delight in what is achieved. Practical activity will occur in many a Metal Dragon household. However, while he may be enthusiastic and determined, the Metal Dragon should avoid having too many projects happening at one time. It is better to concentrate on a few activities and do them well than rush many. Also, if involved in any potentially hazardous or strenuous activity, he should follow the recommended procedures or seek professional help. This is not a year for compromising safety.

There will be some notable family occasions to mark this year, and whether celebrating anniversaries or academic successes or seeing his family increase in number, the Metal Dragon will follow developments with much pride. Certain relations will be especially grateful for his understanding on some matters and many a Metal Dragon will play a valued part in the lives of those who are special to him.

The Metal Dragon has an enquiring nature and over the year several activities or products could attract his attention. These could include fitness or well-being programmes, locally run courses or technology to help with his interests. The Dragon year opens up some good possibilities and the Metal Dragon may well find it advantageous to find out more. Some of what he chooses to do this year can not only be to his benefit but also have a good social element which will add extra appeal.

There will be some good travel opportunities over the year, with many Metal Dragons visiting places of interest or attending some notable events. Many of the Metal Dragon's plans can work out well and the second half of the year can contain some travel highlights.

With home purchases, travel expenses and his various interests, the Metal Dragon should keep tabs on his spending, but by allowing additional time for certain purchases, he could benefit from some attractive offers. The Dragon year does have an element of good fortune about it.

To make the most of this auspicious time, the more senior Metal Dragon does need to move his plans forward as well as consult those around him, but with action and support he will be pleased with what he is able to achieve and this can be a successful year for him.

For Metal Dragons born in 2000, the Dragon year is also one of great opportunity. As the young Metal Dragon learns more and develops his skills, he will find more possibilities opening up for him. New subjects or interests can develop well, and some Metal Dragons could be introduced to an activity they will be keen to take further in following years. For many, this can be an inspiring time.

The young Metal Dragon will also be helped by being open about any problems or uncertainties he may have. Similarly, if wanting to try out certain activities, he will find that by talking to others, more can become possible. This is a year of considerable scope, but to benefit, the young Metal Dragon does need to put himself forward, believe more fully in himself *and* be active and open.

For all Metal Dragons, whether born in 1940 or 2000, this can be an interesting and rewarding year. By being alert to possibility, willing to consult others and ready to take action, they can achieve a great deal. With support, encouragement and the considerable good fortune that will come their way, they can enjoy a pleasing and successful year.

TIP FOR THE YEAR
Embrace the exciting and innovative spirit of the Dragon year and be willing to try new activities and develop ideas. By being open to possibility, you can gain so much.

The Water Dragon

This is the Water Dragon's own year and promises to be a special one. Not only will he have the chance to realize certain hopes and aspirations but also to put his ideas and experience to good use. With the willingness to put himself forward, together with the encouraging aspects, he will find a lot going in his favour.

In order to make the most of his own year the Water Dragon should decide on what he wants to do. If he gives some thought to ways he can take his ideas forward, important possibilities can emerge. To help give momentum to the process, early on in the year he should discuss his thoughts with his loved ones and explore possibilities, as well as obtain relevant information. Positive action will lead to plans becoming possible and many Water Dragons will also benefit from offers of assistance.

The Water Dragon's thinking may concern various aspects of his life, but his work situation may feature prominently. Although he may have made progress in recent years, he may not feel as fulfilled as he would like and may be hankering to make better use of his experience. And over the year many Water Dragons will be given the chance. In many a workplace, changes will be introduced and as a result, quite a few Water Dragons will have the opportunity to change their duties and take on new responsibilities. For those who have been seeking new challenges, their own year can provide them.

A helpful factor will be the excellent working relations the Water Dragon enjoys with his colleagues. As a result, he could become involved in training as well as find colleagues regularly seeking his advice. Over the year his experience will be valued and will help his further progress. March, May, September and October could see some particularly encouraging work developments.

With this being a much more fulfilling year work-wise, most Water Dragons will remain with their present employer, but for those who are keen to make a change or are seeking work, the Year of the Water Dragon can take an interesting course. Obtaining a new position will not be easy, but the Water Dragon's strengths can be very much to his advantage in his own year. By talking to contacts and actively making enquiries, many Water Dragons will uncover new possibilities to consider. For quite a few this can be a year of significant developments and any Water Dragons who have been feeling staid or discouraged can find that a new position they are offered can provide the change and incentive they have been wanting for a long time.

In addition some Water Dragons could be keen to use their skills in other ways, perhaps on a freelance basis or in an enterprising venture. If they obtain good advice and proceed carefully, they will find interesting developments can follow on. There will also be some Water Dragons who will choose to retire this year. For those who do, the Dragon year can again represent the start of a new chapter in their lives. Whatever he chooses to do, the Water Dragon will find his own year full of possibility.

He can also derive much satisfaction from developing his own interests. Here his knowledge and skills can serve him well and if he sets himself some rewarding projects, he will delight in what he is able to do. Joining others, perhaps through taking part in an interest group or enrolling on a course, can also bring support and social opportunities and give added meaning to the Water Dragon's activities. And with the year favouring innovation, if he sees a new activity that appeals to him, especially one related to well-being or personal development, it would be worth him finding out more.

Another favourably aspected area is travel, and if there are any particular destinations the Water Dragon is keen to visit, he should make enquiries and see what is possible. Quite a few Water Dragons could also decide to mark their sixtieth year with a special holiday.

The Water Dragon will also derive much pleasure from his social life. For unattached Water Dragons, particularly those who have experienced personal difficulty of late, the Dragon year can see a considerable improvement in their situation, with new activities, interests and, for some, friendships and romance adding a sparkle to their lives. February, March, July and December could see the most social activity.

This will also be a full and special year in many a Water Dragon household. Loved ones will often be keen to mark the Water Dragon's sixtieth birthday in style and not only could there be celebrations and surprises in store but the year could also be marked by several other pieces of family news. The Water Dragon will be at the forefront of the activities and his organizational skills, attentiveness and many ideas will be appreciated. However, with all the activity, it is important that there is good co-operation and plenty of time is allowed for ambitious home projects.

Financially, many Water Dragons can look forward to an upturn this year, with some benefiting from a gift or the fruition of a policy. However, the Water Dragon will need to keep close control over his spending and make provision for larger outlays. Also, in view of the general activity of the year, he should not put off attending to important paperwork. A delay or oversight could be to his disadvantage. Water Dragons, do take note.

In most respects, however, this can be a fine and encouraging year for the Water Dragon. It is a time to take action and realize plans, and with his strengths and skills and the support of others, he can achieve a great deal. As he will find, once plans are initiated, interesting and sometimes fortuitous developments can quickly follow on. This is the Water Dragon's own year and one offering great possibility.

TIP FOR THE YEAR
Go after what you want. A lot can now become possible for you. Also, value your relations with others. Those close to you can give you valuable support and will be keen to make your own year special. This is your year. Enjoy it. Good luck and good fortune.

The Wood Dragon

This is a year of considerable potential for the Wood Dragon and by setting about his aims and activities in determined fashion, he can make important progress. Not only are the prevailing aspects encouraging, but with his Wood Dragon initiative and the support of others, he will have a great deal in his favour. For any Wood Dragon who may start the year in low spirits or be disappointed with recent progress, this is a year to draw a line under what has gone before and focus on the present and near future. With a positive approach, many a dissatisfied Wood Dragon can enjoy a marked improvement in fortune.

The Wood Dragon's work situation is especially encouraging. For those who have been with the same employer for some time, the in-house knowledge they have built up can make them particularly strong candidates when promotion opportunities arise or staff are required for specific projects. Over the year many will have a chance to make important advances in their career, with some achieving the position they have been working towards for some time.

For Wood Dragons who feel there are limited openings where they are and would like to move on, as well as those seeking work, again the Dragon year can open up significant possibilities. By considering the type of work they would now like to do and making enquiries, many will be alerted to an opening they will be keen to pursue or advised of ways into certain industries or jobs. Sometimes this may require additional training or adapting existing skills, but with willingness and effort, many Wood Dragons can set their career on a new course. For those who do move to a different type of job, the Dragon year can open a new chapter in their working lives. Late February to the end of March, May, September and October could see good opportunities, and even if some applications do not go the Wood Dragon's way, he should not lose heart. With self-belief and persistence, he will find doors *will* open for him.

A further feature of the Dragon year is that it favours enterprise, and some Wood Dragons will see a certain interest or idea progressing in exciting fashion. Again initiative and action can reward the Wood Dragon well this year. Also, if a new activity appeals to him, he should follow it up. By being prepared to try things out, he can often benefit both now and in the future.

Where his own recreation is concerned, if he is sedentary for much of the day or does not tend to get much regular exercise, he should seek advice on the best way to correct this. In this busy and favourable year, he does need to give some consideration to his lifestyle, diet and level of exercise.

When possible, he should also try to take a holiday over the year. Even if he is not able to travel very far, the break from routine can do him a lot of good. There could be additional travel opportunities towards the end of 2012.

The Wood Dragon's financial position is encouragingly aspected and he may well enjoy an increase in income over the year. As a result, he will often decide to go ahead with certain plans and purchases. If looking for something specific, he could find it by chance and often on advantageous terms. His alert nature can reward him well in this lucky year. However, while this is an auspicious time, the Wood Dragon should not be dilatory with filing and paperwork and should attend to financial correspondence promptly. An oversight or delay could incur unnecessary expense. Wood Dragons, take note.

The Wood Dragon will very much value his social life this year and will often have interesting things to do and enjoy. Changes in his work or new pursuits can also lead to some good friends and contacts being made. Any Wood Dragon who may start the Dragon year in low spirits should look ahead rather than back and aim to go out more. Positive action can make an appreciable difference, with new friends and, for some, romance bringing extra meaning to their year.

The Wood Dragon's domestic life can also see exciting developments, possibly including a wedding, a significant anniversary, a graduation or the birth of a grandchild. The Dragon year can certainly be both special and memorable for the Wood Dragon. He will be central to a lot of what goes on and whether helping and advising loved ones or attending to arrangements, his thoughtfulness will be valued by many. However, with this being an already busy year, he does need to avoid placing himself under strain by having too much happening at any one time, especially where practical activities are concerned. Spreading out different undertakings (if possible) will lead to more satisfying results.

Overall, the Year of the Dragon can be a personally rewarding one for the Wood Dragon and by seizing his opportunities and developing his ideas, he can benefit from it as well as enjoy it. As far as both work and personal interests are concerned, this can be a successful and inspiring time. The Wood Dragon's relations with others are also favourably aspected, with pleasing times in both his domestic and social life. This is a year to enjoy and to make his strengths and qualities count.

TIP FOR THE YEAR
Be bold. A lot can happen for you this year, but you do need to put yourself forward. Look for opportunities, develop ideas and consider ways in which you can build on your position. You have a lot to offer and your enthusiasm and drive can bring you some pleasing results.

The Fire Dragon

The Fire Dragon's life can take an interesting course. Some years are disappointing, some see steady growth and there are some that can be dynamic. This year is one of these. It can be a time of important progress and personal success.

One of the Fire Dragon's main strengths is his drive. When inspired, there is no stopping him. As the Dragon year starts, if not shortly before, many Fire Dragons will decide that the next 12 months are a time when they must go after the things they want and *make things happen.*

Those who have felt their progress has been modest in recent years will feel particularly ready for new challenges.

Work prospects are especially encouraging. For Fire Dragons who are well established in a particular company or profession, there will now be an excellent chance to take their career to a new level. As colleagues leave, there could be promotion opportunities, and some Fire Dragons may also consider moving to a new department or role and so furthering their experience. For many there will be interesting options to consider, with the emphasis this year on growth and development.

For Fire Dragons who feel dissatisfied where they are and are yearning for change, again this is a year for action. By looking for alternative positions and even considering retraining or obtaining another qualification, they can find important opportunities opening up. These Fire Dragons should not be too restrictive in the types of work they are considering. By being open to possibility, they could be alerted to a position that is very different from what they have done before but perfect for their skills and temperament.

This also applies to Fire Dragons seeking work. By remaining alert and adaptable, many will be successful in securing a new position and with it the chance to prove themselves in a new capacity. Many can also benefit from some moments of good fortune this year, perhaps learning of an ideal vacancy by chance. By remaining aware and determined to move on, they can make good progress. March, May and mid-August to October could see some encouraging developments and even if some applications do not go the Fire Dragon's way, he can often gain from the feedback given and use this to strengthen future applications.

A feature of the Dragon year is that it rewards initiative, and if the Fire Dragon has an idea he is keen to advance or an interest he is hoping to make more of, he should take action. His enterprise and enthusiasm can serve him well.

With all his plans, hopes and activities, the Fire Dragon will be kept busy over the year, and he does drive himself hard. However, it is important that he keeps his lifestyle in balance and spares a thought for his well-being. To make the most of this auspicious year, he does need to have a nutritious diet as well as allow time for exercise and recreation. Fire Dragons, do take note.

With his outgoing nature, the Fire Dragon will make the most of his social opportunities and impress many of those he meets this year. Some of these, especially connected with his work or interests, could be especially helpful. For Fire Dragons who would welcome a more fulfilling social life, the aspects are encouraging, and by going out more, they could enjoy a transformation in their situation. For some this year can also be marked by exciting and significant romance. February, March, July and mid-November to early January 2013 could be the busiest months socially.

The Fire Dragon can also look forward to a rewarding home life and will do much to support his loved ones. If close relations have decisions to take, his suggestions can do a lot to help. In turn, he will appreciate the many plans and activities he shares, and his home life can bring him much pleasure.

His finances can enjoy an improvement this year and as a result he may well be tempted to go ahead with certain plans and purchases as well as some personal treats, including travel. However, while this is an encouraging time, he should be vigilant with paperwork and avoid rushing important transactions.

The Year of the Dragon can be a significant one for the Fire Dragon. However, to get the most from it, he will need to take action and remain flexible. His relations with others will be important, with some often happy times to enjoy. Overall, this can be a successful and personally rewarding year.

TIP FOR THE YEAR
Go after what you want. With a keen and determined approach, you will find a lot opening up for you. Also, keep your lifestyle in balance, preserving time for your loved ones and own interests. This is a year of opportunity. Use it well.

The Earth Dragon

This will be an important year for the Earth Dragon, bringing both opportunity and personal success. He will be able to build on his experience and qualifications and have the chance to move ahead. A lot is set to happen for him in 2012.

The Earth Dragon's relations with others are especially well aspected and for those with a partner, there will be exciting plans to share. This is a year when long-held plans can at last be realized, and some Earth Dragons may start a family or move to new accommodation. Events can happen in fortuitous ways and, if looking for a new home, the Earth Dragon could stumble upon the ideal opportunity or receive some unexpected assistance.

For Earth Dragons currently enjoying romance, their relationship can lead to marriage or settling down together over the year, while the unattached could meet their soul mate, sometimes in curious circumstances which seemed destined to happen. For many Earth Dragons, this can be a special and personally memorable year.

The Earth Dragon's social life is also favourably aspected and while, in view of his other commitments, he may cut back on going out, he will value the contact he has with his friends. For Earth Dragons who move to a new area, possibly due to work, there will be good opportunities to build up a new social circle and make what will become important friendships. February, March, July and December could be particularly pleasing months socially.

A quality that will serve the Earth Dragon well this year is his enthusiasm. He has great drive and energy and over the year will be keen to develop his ideas and interests. Whether promoting something he can do or furthering a skill, he will find his commitment can lead to encouraging results and in some cases interesting new opportunities. This is a year favouring progress and development. If, however, at any time the Earth Dragon has concerns or is about to enter into a major new commitment, he should consider obtaining professional advice. Similarly, if he is ever in a quandary about a decision, he should talk to others. More senior relatives in particular will often be keen to assist.

There will also be some good travel opportunities for the Earth Dragon, with some arising at short notice. The spontaneity can often add to the fun.

The Dragon year can also see encouraging developments in the Earth Dragon's work. Those relatively new in their position will have good opportunities to develop new skills and become more established. With commitment, they can do their prospects a lot of good and be offered further encouragement, either through additional training or the chance to take on greater responsibility.

For Earth Dragons who are already established in a certain line of work, again there will be opportunities to build on what they have learned. These could come through internal promotion or greater responsibility being offered elsewhere. The Earth Dragon's style and skills can reward him well this year. If appropriate, he should also consider joining a professional organization. Raising his profile can again help his prospects.

For Earth Dragons seeking work this will be a year of interesting developments. Although the job-seeking process can be frustrating, by remaining determined, exploring ideas and putting themselves forward, many will be offered a position which can be a useful entry into a profession. March, May, September and October could see some good chances, and for those who take on a new position early in 2012, there could be further possibilities to pursue later on in the year.

Progress at work will also help the Earth Dragon financially, although, with many personal expenses and commitments, he will need to budget carefully. However, many Earth Dragons could enjoy some financial good fortune, either receiving a gift or being lucky in making a major purchase on advantageous terms.

In general, the Year of the Dragon is an encouraging one for the Earth Dragon. During it he will have the opportunity to make more of his skills and to progress in his work and gain valuable new experience. His personal life can also bring much happiness and make the year all the more special. In 2012 he will have a lot in his favour.

TIP FOR THE YEAR
Build on your strengths and move forward. With energy, commitment and what you have to offer, you can find a lot opening up for you. Also, enjoy your relations with those who are special to you. These can be personally significant times.

FAMOUS DRAGONS

Maya Angelou, Jeffrey Archer, Joan Armatrading, Joan Baez, Count Basie, Maeve Binchy, Sandra Bullock, Alexandra Burke, Michael Cera, Courteney Cox, Bing Crosby, Russell Crowe, Roald Dahl, Salvador Dali, Charles Darwin, Neil Diamond, Bo Diddley, Matt Dillon, Christian Dior, Placido Domingo, Fats Domino, Kirk Douglas, Faye Dunaway, Dan Fogler, Bruce Forsyth, Sigmund Freud, Graham Greene, Rupert Grint, Che Guevara, James Herriot, Paul Hogan, Joan of Arc, Boris Johnson, Sir Tom Jones, Immanuel Kant, Martin Luther King, John Lennon, Abraham Lincoln, Elle MacPherson, Queen Margrethe II of Denmark, Florence Nightingale, Nick Nolte, Sharon Osbourne, Al Pacino, Gregory Peck, Pelé, Edgar Allan Poe, Vladimir Putin, Nikki Reed, Keanu Reeves, Ryan Reynolds, Sir Cliff Richard, George Bernard Shaw, Martin Sheen, Alicia Silverstone, Ringo Starr, Princess Stephanie of Monaco, Dave Stewart, Karlheinz Stockhausen, Shirley Temple, Maria von Trapp, Louis Walsh, Andy Warhol, Mark Webber, Raquel Welch, the Earl of Wessex, Mae West.

23 JANUARY 1917 ～ 10 FEBRUARY 1918   *Fire Snake*

10 FEBRUARY 1929 ～ 29 JANUARY 1930   *Earth Snake*

27 JANUARY 1941 ～ 14 FEBRUARY 1942   *Metal Snake*

14 FEBRUARY 1953 ～ 2 FEBRUARY 1954   *Water Snake*

2 FEBRUARY 1965 ～ 20 JANUARY 1966   *Wood Snake*

18 FEBRUARY 1977 ～ 6 FEBRUARY 1978   *Fire Snake*

6 FEBRUARY 1989 ～ 26 JANUARY 1990   *Earth Snake*

24 JANUARY 2001 ～ 11 FEBRUARY 2002   *Metal Snake*

THE

SNAKE

THE PERSONALITY OF THE SNAKE

I think
And think some more.
About what is,
About what can be,
About what may be.
And when I am ready,
Then I act.

The Snake is born under the sign of wisdom. He is highly intelligent and his mind is forever active. He is always planning and always looking for ways in which he can use his considerable skills. He is a deep thinker and likes to meditate and reflect.

Many times during his life he will shed one of his famous Snake skins and take up new interests or start a completely different job. The Snake enjoys a challenge and he rarely makes mistakes. He is a skilful organizer, has considerable business acumen and is usually lucky in money matters. Most Snakes are financially secure in their later years, provided they do not gamble – the Snake has the distinction of being the worst gambler in the whole of the Chinese zodiac!

The Snake generally has a calm and placid nature and prefers the quieter things in life. He does not like to be in a frenzied atmosphere and hates being hurried into making a quick decision. He also does not like interference in his affairs and tends to rely on his own judgement rather than listen to advice.

At times the Snake can appear solitary. He is quiet, reserved and sometimes has difficulty in communicating with others. He has little time for idle gossip and will certainly not suffer fools gladly. He does, however, have a good sense of humour and this is particularly appreciated in times of crisis.

The Snake is certainly not afraid of hard work and is thorough in all that he does. He is very determined and can occasionally be ruthless in order to achieve his aims. His confidence, willpower and quick thinking usually ensure his success, but should he fail it will often take a long time for him to recover. He cannot bear failure and is a very bad loser.

The Snake can also be evasive and does not willingly let people into his confidence. This secrecy and distrust can sometimes work against him and it is a trait that all Snakes should try to overcome.

Another characteristic of the Snake is his tendency to rest after any sudden or prolonged bout of activity. He burns up so much nervous energy that he can, if he is not careful, be susceptible to high blood pressure and nervous disorders.

It has sometimes been said that the Snake is a late starter in life and this is mainly because it often takes him a while to find a job in which he is genuinely happy. However, he will usually do well in any position that involves research and writing and where he is given sufficient freedom to develop his own ideas and plans. He makes a good teacher, politician, personnel manager and social adviser.

The Snake chooses his friends carefully and while he keeps a tight control over his finances, he can be particularly generous to those he likes. He will think nothing of buying expensive gifts or treating his friends or loved ones to the best theatre seats in town. In return he demands loyalty. The Snake is very possessive and can become extremely jealous and hurt if he finds his trust has been abused.

The Snake is also renowned for his good looks and is never short of admirers. The female Snake in particular is most alluring. She has style, grace and excellent (and usually expensive) taste in clothes. A keen socializer, she is likely to have a wide range of friends and the happy knack of impressing those who matter. She has numerous interests and her opinions are often highly valued. She is generally a calm person and while she involves herself in many activities, she likes to retain a certain amount of privacy in her undertakings.

Affairs of the heart are very important to the Snake and he will often have many romances before he finally settles down. He will find that he is particularly well suited to those born under the signs of the Ox, Dragon, Rabbit and Rooster. Provided he is allowed sufficient freedom to pursue his own interests, he can also build up a very satisfactory relationship with the Rat, Horse, Goat, Monkey and Dog, but he should try to steer clear of another Snake as they could very easily become jealous of each other. The Snake will also have difficulty in getting on with the honest and down-to-earth Pig, and will find the Tiger far too much of a disruptive influence on his quiet and peace-loving ways.

The Snake certainly appreciates the finer things in life. He enjoys good food and often takes a keen interest in the arts. He also enjoys reading and is invariably drawn to subjects such as philosophy, political thought, religion or the occult. He is fascinated by the unknown and his enquiring mind is always looking for answers. Some of the world's most original thinkers have been Snakes, and although he may not readily admit it, the Snake is often psychic and relies a lot on intuition.

The Snake is certainly not the most energetic member of the Chinese zodiac. He prefers to proceed at his own pace and to do what he wants. He is very much his own master and throughout his life he will try his hand at many things. He is something of a dabbler, but at some time – usually when he least expects it – his hard work and efforts will be recognized and he will invariably meet with the success and the financial security he so desires.

THE FIVE DIFFERENT TYPES OF SNAKE

In addition to the 12 signs of the Chinese zodiac there are five elements and these have a strengthening or moderating influence on the signs. The effects of the five elements on the Snake are described below, together with the years in which they were exercising their influence. Therefore Snakes born in 1941 and 2001 are Metal Snakes, those born in 1953 are Water Snakes, and so on.

Metal Snake: 1941, 2001
This Snake is quiet, confident and fiercely independent. He often prefers to work on his own and will only let a privileged few into his confidence. He is quick to spot opportu-

nities and will set about achieving his objectives with an awesome determination. He is astute in financial matters and will often invest his money well. He also has a liking for the finer things in life and a good appreciation of the arts, literature, music and food. He usually has a small group of extremely good friends and can be generous to his loved ones.

Water Snake: 1953

This Snake has a wide variety of interests. He enjoys studying all manner of subjects and is capable of undertaking quite detailed research and becoming a specialist in his chosen area. He is highly intelligent, has a good memory and is particularly astute when dealing with business and financial matters. He tends to be quietly spoken and a little reserved, but he does have sufficient strength of character to make his views known and attain his ambitions. He is very loyal to his family and friends.

Wood Snake: 1965

The Wood Snake has a friendly temperament and a good understanding of human nature. He is able to communicate well and often has many friends and admirers. He is witty, intelligent and ambitious. He has numerous interests and prefers to live in a quiet, stable environment where he can work without too much interference. He enjoys the arts and usually derives much pleasure from collecting paintings and antiques. His advice is often highly valued, particularly on social and domestic matters.

Fire Snake: 1917, 1977

The Fire Snake tends to be more forceful, outgoing and energetic than some of the other types of Snake. He is ambitious, confident and never slow in voicing his opinions, and he can be very abrasive to those he does not like. He does, however, have many leadership qualities and can win the respect and support of many with his firm and resolute manner. He usually has a good sense of humour, a wide circle of friends and a very active social life. He is also a keen traveller.

Earth Snake 1929, 1989

The Earth Snake is charming, amusing and has a very amiable manner. He is conscientious and reliable in his work and approaches everything he does in a level-headed and sensible way. He can, however, tend to err on the cautious side and never likes to be hassled into making a decision. He is adept in dealing with financial matters and is a shrewd investor. He has many friends and is very supportive towards the members of his family.

PROSPECTS FOR THE SNAKE IN 2012

The Year of the Rabbit (3 February 2011–22 January 2012) will have been a generally satisfying one for the Snake, particularly as it will have allowed him to develop his ideas and move ahead in some of his activities. In the remaining months he can continue to make progress, but it may not be straightforward and there will be additional demands on his time.

Many Snakes will find their workload increasing at this time and will have some challenging situations to deal with. However, what is required will make good use of the Snake's knowledge and skills and many Snakes can do their reputation considerable good. For those looking to advance or seeking work, September and the closing weeks of the year could see some interesting possibilities to pursue.

There will also be chances for many Snakes to travel, although, with this and other expenses, the Snake should watch his spending and make provision for extra outlay.

He will also find his personal life becoming busier as the Rabbit year draws to a close. There will be chances to meet up with friends and other social opportunities, while domestically there will be many arrangements to fit in. December and early January could see a great deal of activity. When in company, the Snake should be forthcoming and seek the views of others. He may like to keep his thoughts to himself, but more openness can lead to some useful offers of assistance as well as ease certain pressures.

In general, the Year of the Rabbit can be an encouraging one for the Snake and provided he manages to keep his lifestyle in balance (not always easy in view of all the activity of the year), he can take satisfaction in the many things he has been able to achieve.

The Year of the Dragon begins on 23 January and will be an important one for the Snake. He can fare well, but it is a time for focus, discipline and a certain care. The Snake is not always comfortable with the razzmatazz that so often characterizes Dragon years, but by concentrating on his activities and prioritizing where necessary, he can enjoy some pleasing developments.

At work many Snakes will decide to remain where they are and will continue to use their knowledge and skills to good effect. As the year progresses, many will have the opportunity to expand their role, and if they are offered training, a temporary attachment or the chance to deputize for someone, they should take this up. By building on their experience and showing themselves to be adaptable, they will be improving their prospects for when they do choose to move on or seek promotion.

All Snakes should also work closely with colleagues this year and show that they can be a good team member. Although the Snake can be a private individual, by liaising well with others, taking an informed interest in what goes on and using any chances to network, he can again help his prospects. Any Snake who feels an additional qualification could be helpful or that he is lacking experience in a certain area should consider ways in which he can obtain this. With the exciting opportunities that await in 2013, the Snake's own year, what he can learn now can be of considerable value.

For Snakes who decide to change their job this year, as well as those seeking work, the Dragon year can bring some good possibilities. Although their quest will not be easy, by considering different ways in which they can use their experience, these Snakes can come up with some interesting ideas. By following these up, many will be able to gain a foothold they can move on from in the future.

Again, what is achieved this year can be an important factor in subsequent progress. April, May and August to early October could see some key developments.

In addition to what the Snake can learn at work, this is an excellent year for personal development and if there are particular skills he would like to learn or interests he wants to develop, he should set time aside for this. Some Snakes may also give more attention to their well-being, including taking more exercise and improving their overall diet. With medical advice on the best way to proceed, the Snake can really benefit from this.

The Snake is usually astute in money matters, and while he may well enjoy an increase in earnings this year, he should remain cautious. This includes keeping a close watch on spending and being careful not to succumb to too many impulse buys. Also, when entering into agreements, he should check the terms and implications as well as make provision for any increased outlay. This is not a year to relax his usual guard. In addition, where personal posses- sions are concerned, he needs to be vigilant. A loss or theft could be distressing. Snakes, take note and take extra care with security.

The Snake is usually selective in his socializing and this year his social life may not be as active as in some years, but he will particularly enjoy the times he does meet up with friends and attends events. Many Snakes will also find certain interests have a pleasing social element to them. However, while a lot can go well, the Snake needs to remain aware. Rumours and gossip may trouble him during the year. If they do, he should check the facts and correct any untruths. Fortunately, this will only concern a small minority of Snakes, but it is something to watch. April, July and from mid-November onwards will see the most social activity.

The Snake always attaches much importance to his home life and over the year he will be especially active in helping and encouraging those close to him. When decisions need making or pressures arise, his advice will often be more valued and pertinent than he may realize. Some of the ideas he puts forward will also be appreciated. Whether suggesting ways to make certain aspects of home life easier or trips and events for everyone to enjoy, his input and thoughtfulness can lead to a lot going ahead. In turn, where his own ideas and activities are concerned, he needs to be forthcoming. Loved ones will be supportive and can sometimes help in ways he may not have anticipated. Domestically, this can be a pleasing year and in late November or December there could be some important family news to enjoy.

Overall, the Year of the Dragon will be an interesting one for the Snake and by setting about his activities with care and seizing any chances to add to his experience and knowledge, he can make it of significant value, particularly in terms of preparation for 2013, his own year. It will also contain some very happy moments, especially in his domestic life, although it is a time to guard against carelessness and throughout the year the Snake needs to remain alert and adaptable. Overall, however, a valuable and potentially significant year.

The Metal Snake

This will be a satisfying year for the Metal Snake, with many of his plans and activities developing well. He can also look forward to personal and family success and the Dragon year will contain some memorable high points.

Being the deep thinker he is, the Metal Snake may well already have thought through what he would like to do over the next 12 months and will be keen to set his ideas in motion. These can concern home or garden projects or personal interests, but whatever he chooses to do, the Metal Snake will often enjoy getting his plans underway.

Where home projects are concerned, he should readily involve others. Although he will have very definite preferences, by talking to his loved ones he will find that additional possibilities can arise and combined effort can make certain tasks easier to accomplish. Some of the projects he may be considering could involve redecorating certain rooms, replacing equipment and adding new comforts to his home. A few Metal Snakes may even decide to move to accommodation that is more suitable. The Dragon year will certainly see many decisions being taken and the Metal Snake is likely to be pleased with the benefits that follow, despite the initial disruption. The Dragon year has a strongly practical element to it and is very much one for forging ahead with plans.

However, while a lot can work out well, if tackling anything potentially hazardous, the Metal Snake does need to take care and follow the recommended procedures or obtain professional help. Similarly, if gardening, he should take care if doing anything strenuous. A strain could linger and cause pain and inconvenience. Metal Snakes, take note, and with so much practical activity indicated this year, do be careful.

Most of the major activities are likely to take place in the first half of the year and the second half will be more a time for appreciating what has been achieved and enjoying less arduous activities and some travel.

Throughout the year the Metal Snake will take a keen interest in family activities, including helping those with young children and, in his usual discreet and thoughtful way, passing on advice and suggestions. Many Metal Snakes will have an important family occasion to mark and will be thrilled by what takes place. For those who move, there could be a house-warming party to hold as well.

Another satisfying element of the year will concern the Metal Snake's personal interests. This is very much a time favouring progress in this area. A key message of the year for the Metal Snake is to set himself goals *and* act purposefully.

Although the Metal Snake tends to keep his social life relatively low-key, he will take pleasure in some of the social opportunities that arise over the year, including interest-related events and activities in his area. April, July and closing months of the year could see some especially interesting occasions, with the Metal Snake particularly enjoying some of the conversations he has and the opportunity to share ideas.

In view of some of his plans and activities, he will be involved in some expensive transactions this year and, where possible, should make early provision for these. Also, when entering into an agreement, he should check the terms and obligations carefully. Although he is usually thorough, this is no year for making assumptions or taking risks.

For Metal Snakes born in 2001 this will be an active and interesting year. Both in their schoolwork and their personal interests there will be opportunities to develop their knowledge and skills and put them to satisfying use. However, to benefit from these encouraging times, the young Metal Snake does need to be open to instruction and listen carefully to advice. This is no time to close his mind or be awkward when others want to help.

There could also be some interesting travel opportunities this year and, where possible, the Metal Snake should make the most of these. Whether visiting places of interest or just enjoying the chance to see new areas, he can get a lot of value from his travels.

Whether born in 1941 or 2001, the Metal Snake can find the Dragon year a personally satisfying one. By developing his ideas and making the most of his opportunities, he will be pleased with the way many of his activities develop. This is a year for action, and effort will be well rewarded. The Metal Snake will also be encouraged by the support of others and their input can give his plans added impetus. Overall, a pleasing year.

TIP FOR THE YEAR

Set your ideas in motion. Further opportunities can often follow on. Also, draw on the assistance of those around you. With your initiative and their support, you can achieve a lot more.

The Water Snake

The Water Snake sets about life without fuss. He simply likes to get on with things. However, he could find the Dragon year disruptive. Sometimes circumstances may change or plans take a different course, and the Water Snake will need to keep his wits firmly about him and adapt as required.

This is especially the case in his work. Although the Water Snake may prefer to concentrate on his role and use his skills to their best advantage, changes can occur which can take him away from what he is currently doing. Staff movements may require him to take on other duties, new objectives may be set or he may be given a wider role. He may not seek or desire change this year, but he may well be affected by it. However, what happens can give him the chance to extend his experience and can be instrumental in his later success, often in his own year that follows.

In setting about his duties, it is important that the Water Snake liaises well with his colleagues. Although he is some-times a private individual, this is no year to appear inde-pendent or too removed from what is going on.

For Water Snakes who decide to move on from where they are, possibly for personal or family reasons, as well as for those seeking work, the Dragon year can work in curi-ous ways. Obtaining a position will not be easy, but the Water Snake is resourceful and quietly determined. By keeping alert, exploring possibilities and following up ideas, he may well be successful in his quest. The position he gains may not be what he envisaged – and in the Dragon year he will need to be flexible – but it may allow him to use his abilities in a different capacity. April, May and

August to early October could see some interesting work developments, but generally what the Water Snake can accomplish this year can often have future significance.

The Water Snake is generally careful in financial matters but during the year he will need to keep a close watch on his spending. With large expenses likely, including possible transport and home maintenance costs, as well as all the other purchases he may have in mind, he should budget carefully. He should also take care with his possessions. A loss or theft could cause problems. Water Snakes, be warned and be vigilant.

More positively, the Dragon year can bring some interesting opportunities as far as the Water Snake's personal interests are concerned and by developing his ideas and expressing his creativity, he can make this a personally rewarding time. Sometimes there could be an opportunity for him to make more of his knowledge or promote a skill. Some Water Snakes could be attracted to a new pursuit and the Dragon year's progressive energy will inspire many.

The Water Snake's activities can also bring him into contact with others and he should make the most of this. Not only can he benefit from the advice and encouragement others can give, but he may enjoy meeting people he may not ordinarily see. In the Dragon year it is important that he does not immerse himself so much in his own activities that he isolates himself or misses out on the social possibilities his interests can bring. For some Water Snakes who are unattached, even though they may not be seeking romance, there could be interesting romantic developments in store. The Dragon year can bring surprises which can work out well for many a Water Snake. The second half of the year will have more social opportunities than the first, with April, July and then most notably from mid-November onwards being full and interesting times.

The Water Snake's home life will also keep him occupied and his generally unruffled nature will be much appreciated. Not only will loved ones value the time and attention he gives but also the way he is able to assist with various activities. Over the year his empathy and talent for knowing what to do or how to approach certain matters can prove especially helpful. The Dragon year will also contain some memorable domestic highlights and the closing months will bring additional travel opportunities for the Water Snake to look forward to.

In general, the Year of the Dragon holds interesting possibilities for the Water Snake and although some of it may not work out as envisaged, by being flexible and open to chance, he can learn a considerable amount from it. With next year being his own year, what occurs now can pave the way for the special developments that await. Overall, a busy, different and potentially important year.

TIP FOR THE YEAR
Keep alert and be prepared to make the most of opportunities *as they arise*, even though they may require you to modify your existing plans. Also, do not be too independent in approach. With willingness and the assistance of others, you can enjoy achievements that can prove significant.

The Wood Snake

The Wood Snake is ambitious and adept at using his skills and identifying the right moment to act. And while this will be a generally favourable year for him, he will often feel that more can be gained by working behind the scenes and concentrating on specific activities than embarking on major change.

Many Wood Snakes will now be well established in their line of work and often be content to remain where they are and carry out the duties they know and perform so well. For many this can be a satisfying time which will give them the chance to make more of their knowledge and enhance their standing and prospects. The Wood Snake will also find that getting himself more widely known will help both his present and future situation. In addition, all Wood Snakes should take advantage of any training that may be offered to them. Even though they may know a lot about their area of work already, by keeping their skills up to date and learning about new developments they will be widening their scope for later. One of the key benefits of the Dragon year is that experience gained during it can prove very helpful in the future, especially in the following year, the Snake's own year.

Although many Wood Snakes will remain with their present employer over the year, for those who feel unfulfilled and are keen to move on, as well as those who are seeking work, the Dragon year can be important. By giving careful thought to the type of work they would now like to do and seeking advice, these Wood Snakes can see some interesting possibilities emerging. For some, these could involve retraining, and for a few, relocation, but their efforts will often lead to the chance being offered to prove themselves in a new way. This can be an important platform to build on in the future.

Whatever his situation, throughout the year the Wood Snake's keen and enquiring nature will be very much to his advantage, with more senior colleagues often recognizing and encouraging his talents. April, May and August to early October could see some particularly interesting developments, but throughout the Dragon year there will be possibilities to explore.

The Wood Snake's personal interests can bring him a great deal of satisfaction this year and if he would welcome new challenges, this would be an ideal year to take up something new. The Dragon year is a personally rewarding one for the Wood Snake.

However, although the Wood Snake will be able to go ahead with many of his plans this year, he will need to keep a careful watch on spending. With existing commitments, transport and accommodation costs and the purchases he is keen to make, he will need to control his outgoings and avoid too many impulse buys. This is a year which rewards financial planning and discipline. As with all Snakes this year, the Wood Snake will also need to be vigilant regarding personal possessions and careful when attending to important paperwork. Lack of attention could be to his disadvantage.

Socially, the Dragon year will contain quite few special times, and throughout the year the Wood Snake will again value his close circle of friends. May and November to early January will see the most social activity, but whenever the Wood Snake receives an invitation or hears of an event that appeals to him, he should try to go. However, he does need to be wary of rumour and anything that could lead to potential embarrassment. This is no year for lapses or risk.

A lot will happen in his home life over the year, and with some of those who are close to him facing key decisions, whether in their education, work or personal life, his advice can be pertinent and helpful. The Wood Snake has a talent for gauging situations and recognizing the right course of action, and this will again be appreciated this year.

The Wood Snake himself will take considerable pleasure in some of the home (and possibly garden) projects he decides to tackle. The Dragon year can be a quietly satisfying one for him. However, he does need to take care if involved in anything strenuous as well as avoid unnecessary rush. This is a time for setting about things at a steady pace.

In the second half of the year there could be travel opportunities, and any breaks the Wood Snake can take with his loved ones can do everyone good.

Overall, by setting about his activities with care and concentrating on his objectives, the Wood Snake can make this a personally satisfying year. He has great perception and by making the most of his opportunities this year he can lay an important foundation that he can build on in the exciting and progressive year to follow.

TIP FOR THE YEAR
Spend time with others. Domestically and socially, this can be an interesting and frequently rewarding year, with others valuing your judgement and you benefiting from

their support. In both your work and your recreational activities, aim to meet new people. The contacts you make can be helpful both now and in the near future.

The Fire Snake

The element of fire gives the Snake considerable drive. The Fire Snake is determined and resourceful as well as the source of many fine ideas. In the Dragon year he will have the chance to develop these, even though some of his activities may not work out as anticipated. The Dragon year can have change and surprise in store.

In the Fire Snake's work this can be an interesting and eventful year. Although he will have often thought about the direction he would like his career to take, in the Dragon year he will need to be flexible. Chances can suddenly open up or propositions be put to him which will give him experience in a different area. For those in large organizations, this may mean moving to another department or taking on different objectives. Certainly the Dragon year will give many Fire Snakes the chance to move on from their existing role and learn about different aspects of their industry. This may not be what the Fire Snake was anticipating, but by making the most of the situation, he will not only be extending his experience but also gaining skills that can considerably help his future prospects. This is a year to be willing and adaptable.

For Fire Snakes who feel their prospects could be better served by changing employer or who are seeking work, again the Dragon year can have interesting developments in store. With openings often limited, these Fire Snakes will need to widen the scope of what they are prepared to consider. What they are offered may be different from what they were seeking, but a key value of the year is that it can bring new experience and the discovery of new talents. Also, next year is highly auspicious and skills acquired now can often be significant factors in later progress.

April to mid-June and August to early October could see some particularly interesting work developments, but throughout the year the Fire Snake's resourcefulness will serve him well and when he is given an opportunity or sees a suitable vacancy, he should be quick to respond.

It could also be to his advantage to consider his own personal development. If there are skills or qualifications he feels could be useful, he should see whether it is possible to acquire them. Whether through personal study, enrolling on a course or allowing time for practice, he can enhance his future prospects. Also, he should listen closely to the advice of experts, including more senior colleagues. This can prove important.

The progress the Fire Snake makes at work can lead to an increase in income, but this is a year to be careful in money matters. This includes avoiding unnecessary risk as well as guarding against too many impulse purchases. The Fire Snake should also take care with paperwork, making sure insurance policies offer sufficient cover, important documents are kept safely and correspondence is dealt with within time limits. As with all Snakes, he should take extra care of his possessions too. A loss could prove upsetting.

Although the Fire Snake will have many demands on his time this year, he should still aim to keep in regular contact with his friends. Some he has known for many years could offer especially helpful advice over a personal matter or work decision. In addition, his work and interests can be good ways to meet others and some important contacts can be made. He should, however, be wary of rumour and, if necessary, check out anything that may concern him. April, July and from mid-November onwards could see the most social activity.

In his home life it is important that he is forthcoming. If he is open, rather than keeps his thoughts to himself (a tendency of some Fire Snakes), those around him will have more chance of assisting. This is a year favouring communication and co-operation and the Fire Snake himself will do much to help both younger and more senior relations. However, amid all the activity, if he can set aside time for more pleasurable pursuits, or just enjoying quiet moments with his loved ones, his home life can be made all the more rewarding.

Throughout 2012 it is important the Fire Snake remains open to possibility. There will be some good opportunities over the year but these may not always arise as anticipated. By adapting to the situation, however, the Fire Snake can gain valuable experience and discover new strengths which can help with subsequent progress, especially in 2013. Overall, a pleasant, interesting and potentially beneficial year.

TIP FOR THE YEAR
Value your relations with others and take note of their views and advice. At busy times, keep your lifestyle in balance. Spend some time on your interests, as they can develop in encouraging fashion.

The Earth Snake

This will be an important year for the Earth Snake with considerable bearing on his future. He will have some personal decisions to make which can be of long-term significance.

As with all Snakes, the Earth Snake is thoughtful and gives much consideration to his hopes and plans for the future. However, in the Dragon year it is important that he calls on the advice of others as well. That way he will not only fare better, but could be alerted to possibilities he may not yet be aware of. In addition, throughout the year he will need to be fairly flexible in outlook. Situations can change quickly, and by being adaptable, he can often benefit. Throughout 2012 he should avoid being too independent or narrow in approach.

In his work the Dragon year can bring interesting possibilities. Earth Snakes who are relatively new to their position will often be encouraged to learn more about the organization and industry they are in and given the opportunity to extend their skills. By taking advantage of this, these Earth Snakes can not only become more established but also help their reputation and prospects. Throughout the year they should also work closely with colleagues and use any chances to network. The actual progress these Earth Snakes make in the Dragon year may be modest rather than substantial, but could have considerable bearing on the success that awaits in 2013.

This also applies to Earth Snakes who are already established in a line of work. This is a year to consolidate their position and to develop their knowledge and skills.

For Earth Snakes who are unfulfilled where they are and keen to move on, as well as those seeking work, the Dragon year can have interesting developments in store. Rather than risk drifting into a job, these Earth Snakes should seek advice from employment experts. By considering their skills and, if relevant, taking advantage of training courses, they could be alerted to suitable vacancies. This is a year to be open to possibility. Late March to May and August to early October could see some interesting career developments, but the real value of the Dragon year will be the experience many Earth Snakes now gain.

For Earth Snakes currently studying for qualifications, this can be a highly significant year. By remaining focused on what they have to do, many will be delighted with what they achieve and what this opens up for them. Commitment and effort made now can bear sizeable and significant fruit.

The Dragon year also favours personal development and during it many Earth Snakes will become interested in a new recreational pursuit. Not only can this be an interesting contrast to their other activities, but the Earth Snake will often enjoy the element of personal challenge involved and the social opportunities it can open up. Also, both new and existing interests can be good ways for the Earth Snake to keep his lifestyle in balance and, in some cases, get out of doors and benefit from additional exercise.

The Earth Snake is generally careful in money matters, but he does need to keep a close watch on his spending this year. Impulse buys in particular can mount up and in some cases lead to higher interest payments or the Earth Snake having to cut back on other activities. This is a year for financial discipline.

However, while outgoings need to be controlled, the Earth Snake will be keen to travel this year and should try to make advance provision for this as well as keep alert for any special travel offers. There could be several chances to go away, including in the closing weeks of 2012 or early 2013.

This will also be an active and pleasing year in the Earth Snake's personal life. For those in a serious relationship, the Dragon year will contain some special times. Many Earth Snakes will make some important decisions and commitments, and here the Earth Snake's instincts will guide him well. Talking his hopes and aspirations over with his loved ones will be of benefit, as they have his interests at heart, and more senior relations may be supportive too.

The Earth Snake can also look forward to an interesting and varied social life. Not only will his work and interests introduce him to others, but he will often have opportunities to go out. The Dragon year's vibrant nature will encourage the Earth Snake to make more of himself and this can be an exciting time, particularly for those who move to a new area or would welcome new friends. April, July and from mid-November onwards will be the busiest parts of the year although at most times the Earth Snake will have something to look forward to. And with the Dragon year having important implications, a new friendship or romance could be significant.

Overall, the Year of the Dragon can be a busy one for the Earth Snake. In his work, by showing commitment, listening carefully to advice and being prepared to adapt, he can do his prospects a lot of good. His relations with others are favourably aspected and some Earth Snakes will make major personal decisions or meet someone who will become very special. The effects of the Dragon year can be considerable *and* far-reaching.

Listen closely to loved ones and those who have the experience to help you. With advice, encouragement and support, you can achieve so much more. Also, be open to the new, whether taking on different duties at work or expanding your personal interests. By embracing change and chance, you can set yourself up for the future.

FAMOUS SNAKES

Muhammad Ali, Ann-Margret, Kim Basinger, Ben Bernanke, Björk, Tony Blair, Michael Bloomberg, Michael Bolton, Brahms, Pierce Brosnan, Casanova, Chubby Checker, Jackie Collins, Tom Conti, Cecil B. de Mille, Robert Downey Jr, Bob Dylan, Sir Edward Elgar, Sir Alex Ferguson, Sir Alexander Fleming, Mahatma Gandhi, Greta Garbo, Art Garfunkel, J. Paul Getty, Dizzy Gillespie, W. E. Gladstone, Johann Wolfgang von Goethe, Princess Grace of Monaco, Stephen Hawking, Audrey Hepburn, Jack Higgins, Liz Hurley, James Joyce, Stacy Keach, Ronan Keating, J. F. Kennedy, Carole King, Courtney Love, Mao Tse-tung, Chris Martin, Henri Matisse, David Miliband, Robert Mitchum, Piers Morgan, Alfred Nobel, Mike Oldfield, Jacqueline Onassis, Sarah Jessica Parker, Pablo Picasso, Mary Pickford, Daniel Radcliffe, Franklin D. Roosevelt, Mickey Rourke, J. K. Rowling, Jean-Paul Sartre, Franz Schubert, Shakira, Charlie Sheen, Brooke Shields, Paul Simon, Delia Smith, Ben Stiller, Taylor Swift, Madame Tussaud, Shania Twain, Dionne Warwick, Charlie Watts, Ruby Wax, Kanye West, Oprah Winfrey, Victoria Wood, Virginia Woolf.

11 FEBRUARY 1918 ～ 31 JANUARY 1919   *Earth Horse*

30 JANUARY 1930 ～ 16 FEBRUARY 1931   *Metal Horse*

15 FEBRUARY 1942 ～ 4 FEBRUARY 1943   *Water Horse*

3 FEBRUARY 1954 ～ 23 JANUARY 1955   *Wood Horse*

21 JANUARY 1966 ～ 8 FEBRUARY 1967   *Fire Horse*

7 FEBRUARY 1978 ～ 27 JANUARY 1979   *Earth Horse*

27 JANUARY 1990 ～ 14 FEBRUARY 1991   *Metal Horse*

12 FEBRUARY 2002 ～ 31 JANUARY 2003   *Water Horse*

THE
HORSE

THE PERSONALITY OF THE HORSE

There are many worn paths,
but the most rewarding
is the one you decide on and forge yourself.

The Horse is born under the signs of elegance and ardour. He has a most engaging and charming manner and is usually very popular. He loves meeting people and likes attending parties and other large social gatherings.

The Horse is a lively character and enjoys being the centre of attention. He has many leadership qualities and is much admired for his honest and straightforward manner. He is an eloquent and persuasive speaker and has a great love of discussion and debate. He also has a particularly agile mind and can assimilate facts remarkably quickly.

He does, however, have a fiery temper and although his outbursts are usually short-lived, he can often say things that he will later regret. He is also not particularly good at keeping secrets.

The Horse has many interests and involves himself in a wide variety of activities. He can, however, get involved in so much that he can often waste his energies on projects that he never has time to complete. He also has a tendency to change his interests rather frequently and will often get caught up in the latest craze or 'in thing' until something more exciting turns up.

The Horse also likes to have a certain amount of freedom and independence. He hates being bound by petty rules and regulations and as far as possible likes to feel that he is answerable to no one but himself. But despite this spirit of freedom, he still likes to have the support and encouragement of others in his various enterprises.

Due to his many talents and likeable nature, the Horse will often go far in life. He enjoys challenges and is a methodical and tireless worker. However, should things go against him and he fail in any of his enterprises, it will take a long time for him to recover and pick up the pieces again. Success to the Horse means everything. To fail is a disaster and a humiliation.

The Horse likes to have variety in life and will try his hand at many different things before he settles down to one particular job. Even then, he will probably remain alert to see whether there are any better opportunities for him to take up. He has a restless nature and can easily get bored. He does, however, excel in any position that allows him sufficient freedom to act on his own initiative or brings him into contact with a lot of people.

Although the Horse is not particularly bothered about accumulating great wealth, he handles his finances with care and will rarely experience any serious financial problems.

The Horse also enjoys travel and loves visiting new and faraway places. At some stage during his life he will be tempted to live abroad for a short period of time and due to his adaptable nature will find that he will fit in well wherever he goes.

The Horse pays a great deal of attention to his appearance and usually likes to wear smart, colourful and rather distinctive clothes. He is very attractive to others and will often have many romances before he settles down. He is loyal and protective to his partner, but despite his family commitments he still likes to retain a certain measure of independence and have the freedom to carry on with his own interests and hobbies. He will find that he is especially well suited to those born under the signs of the Tiger, Goat, Rooster and Dog. He can also get on well with the Rabbit, Dragon, Snake, Pig and another Horse, but he will find the Ox too serious and intolerant for his liking. He will also have difficulty in getting on with the Monkey and the Rat – the Monkey is very inquisitive and the Rat seeks security, and both will resent the Horse's rather independent ways.

The female Horse is usually most attractive and has a friendly, outgoing personality. She is highly intelligent, has many interests and is alert to everything that is going on around her. She particularly enjoys outdoor pursuits and often likes to take part in sport and keep-fit activities. She also enjoys travel, literature and the arts, and is a very good conversationalist.

Although the Horse can be stubborn and rather self-centred, he does have a considerate nature and is often willing to help others. He has a good sense of humour and will usually make a favourable impression wherever he goes. Provided he can curb his slightly restless nature and keep tight control over his temper, he will go through life making friends, taking part in a multitude of different activities and generally achieving many of his objectives. His life will rarely be dull.

THE FIVE DIFFERENT TYPES OF HORSE

In addition to the 12 signs of the Chinese zodiac there are five elements and these have a strengthening or moderating influence on the signs. The effects of the five elements on the Horse are described below, together with the years in which they were exercising their influence. Therefore Horses born in 1930 and 1990 are Metal Horses, those born in 1942 and 2002 are Water Horses, and so on.

Metal Horse: 1930, 1990
This Horse is bold, confident and forthright. He is ambitious and a great innovator. He loves challenges and takes great delight in sorting out complicated problems. He likes to have a certain amount of independence and resents any outside interference in his affairs. He has charm and a certain charisma, but he can also be very stubborn and rather impulsive. He usually has many friends and enjoys an active social life.

Water Horse: 1942, 2002
The Water Horse has a friendly nature and a good sense of humour and is able to talk intelligently on a wide range of topics. He is astute in business matters and quick to take advantage of any opportunities that arise. He does, however, have a tendency to get easily distracted and can

change his interests – and indeed his mind – rather frequently, and this can often work to his detriment. He is nevertheless very talented and can often go far in life. He pays a great deal of attention to his appearance and is usually smart and well turned out. He loves to travel and also enjoys sport and other outdoor activities.

Wood Horse: 1954

The Wood Horse has a most agreeable and amiable nature. He communicates well with others and is able to talk intelligently on many different subjects. He is a hard and conscientious worker and is held in high esteem by his friends and colleagues. His opinions are often sought and, given his imaginative nature, he can often come up with some very original and practical ideas. He is usually widely read and likes to lead a busy social life. He can also be most generous and often holds high moral views.

Fire Horse: 1966

The element of fire combined with the temperament of the Horse creates one of the most powerful forces in the Chinese zodiac. The Fire Horse is destined to lead an exciting and eventful life and to make his mark in his chosen profession. He has a forceful personality and his intelligence and resolute manner bring him the support and admiration of many. He loves action and excitement and his life will rarely be quiet. He can, however, be rather blunt and forthright in his views and does not take kindly to interference in his own affairs or to obeying orders. He is a flamboyant character, has a good sense of humour and will lead a very active social life.

Earth Horse: 1918, 1978

This Horse is considerate and caring. He is more cautious than some of the other types of Horse, but is wise, perceptive and extremely capable. Although he can be rather indecisive at times, he has considerable business acumen and is very astute in financial matters. He has a quiet, friendly nature and is well thought of by his family and friends.

PROSPECTS FOR THE HORSE IN 2012

The Year of the Rabbit (3 February 2011–22 January 2012) is a generally encouraging one for the Horse, although in what remains of it he will need to keep his wits firmly about him and be flexible. To be intransigent or too independent could undermine his situation and some of the good he has done.

This need for mindfulness applies to all areas of his life. In his work, he should keep alert and informed and adapt as situations require. However, while pressures may increase, the Horse will often have the chance to develop certain skills, with September and October likely to see some interesting work opportunities.

With the end of the year traditionally being more expensive, the Horse should be careful with his spending at this time and, where possible, spread out seasonal purchases and make advance provision for larger outgoings.

Another expense many Horses will have will be the increased social activity towards the end of the year. Some weeks will be a whirl of activity and some advanced planning could be helpful. The Horse will often enjoy himself at this time, but again he will need to be mindful when in company. A lapse or indiscretion could cause problems. Those in the early stages of a romance should remain particularly attentive and aware.

In his home life, too, it is important the Horse is mindful of those around him and remains open and communicative. In many a Horse household there could be a lot to do in the remaining Rabbit months and the more co-operation there is – including flexibility when making plans – the better.

In general, the Year of the Rabbit can be a satisfying one for the Horse and by remaining aware and adapting as required, he can often benefit from the opportunities that arise and the experience he can gain.

The Dragon year, which begins on 23 January, is characterized by activity and enterprise. And while the Horse likes to be involved in a great many things, this is a year that will require care. This is no time for the Horse to throw caution to the wind or take unnecessary risks. Rather, success will come by proceeding steadily and taking the time to develop activities and plans. This may not be to the Horse's taste, but he will appreciate the Dragon year's liveliness and have some great personal times to look forward to.

One interesting feature of the Dragon year is the opportunities that can suddenly open up. This could be the chance for the Horse to travel at comparatively short notice, to try a new activity or to put in for a surprise vacancy at work. When such chances arise, if the Horse feels they are right for him, he should act swiftly. As many will discover, in Dragon years it is those who seize the moment who benefit most.

At work there will often be excellent chances for the Horse to build on his present situation. Whether through staff movements, new objectives or other opportunities, the Dragon year will give him the chance to move ahead and to develop his skills. However, while this is a year for progress, it can also bring pressures and situations which will test the Horse's patience. Some parts of the year will be demanding but at the same time demonstrate the Horse's strengths and resourcefulness. The Dragon year does not always make life easy for the Horse, but it is by rising to its challenges that he will learn and progress.

For Horses who are keen to move on from where they are, either because of concern over recent developments or the desire for a new challenge, as well as Horses seeking work, the Dragon year calls for effort and initiative. With competition likely to be fierce, the Horse will need to take care when making applications and, where possible, find out more about the position he is putting in for. The extra attention he gives can often be an important factor in his success. March, June, September and November could see some good work possibilities, but events can happen quickly throughout the Dragon year and the Horse needs to remain alert and ready.

The progress many Horses make at work will lead to an increase in income, but here again the year requires caution. This is no time for risk and should the Horse be inclined to speculate, he should check the implications and any liabilities he may have. Without care, misjudgements can be made. Also, when dealing with important paperwork the Horse needs to be thorough and allow adequate time. If he has any uncertainties, it is important that he seeks clarification. Financially, this is a year for vigilance.

Another area which requires care is the Horse's well-being. As he is so active and may have a demanding lifestyle, it is important he allows himself time to rest. To balance this, however, if sedentary for long periods of time he should try to rectify this by making sure he has regular exercise. To cope with the demands of this active year, he does need to give some consideration to his own well-being and, when appropriate, seek medical advice on how best to proceed.

With his outgoing nature, the Horse knows many people and his circle of acquaintances is set to widen still further over the year. He will gel with some people he meets almost immediately and can form important new friendships. As a result, his social life will often be active. This can also be an exciting year for affairs of the heart. Even if some relationships flounder, new ones can often quickly follow on. Cupid's arrow will be aimed at many a Horse this year! March, April, June and August could see the most social activity.

The Horse's domestic life will also be full and interesting. Parts of the year could see some particularly frenetic times. At such times it is very much a case of everyone working together, concentrating on what needs to be done and, if necessary, being prepared to put back or rearrange certain activities or projects. There will certainly need to be flexibility in the Horse household over the year. There could also be several personal successes to celebrate, however, and the Horse will take pleasure in various domestic undertakings.

Another favourably aspected area is travel and if possible the Horse should aim to take a holiday or break during the year. The change of routine can do him a lot of good and some Horses will particularly enjoy trips arranged at short notice.

Overall, the Horse can enjoy positive developments in the Year of the Dragon, but to get results he will need to put in the effort and sometimes overcome challenging situations. Parts of the year will ask a lot of him, but they can demonstrate some of his finer qualities, including his resolve and tenacity. He will need to proceed with caution, but throughout the year he will be encouraged by the positive relations he has with many people, and his home and social life will be active and pleasurable. This can be a satisfying year for him, but it is important he keeps his lifestyle in balance and takes the time to enjoy the rewards his efforts bring. What is achieved will be well deserved.

The Metal Horse

This will be a busy, eventful and also surprising year for the Metal Horse. A lot is set to happen, although throughout the Metal Horse will need to be flexible in approach. With metal as his element, he has a strong will, but to remain too fixed in his thinking could deny him some of the opportunities the Dragon year can present. This is a year to remain alert and make the most of chances *as they occur*.

One of the most positive areas of the year will be the way the Metal Horse is able to develop his skills and experience. For those in education, qualifications they gain now can open up some important opportunities, and by putting in the effort, many can look forward to some impressive results. Similarly, the Dragon year will give newly qualified Metal Horses the chance to build on what they have achieved. This is very much a year favouring personal growth.

This also applies to Metal Horses who left education some time ago but feel it could be useful to gain another skill or qualification. By taking positive action and perhaps enrolling on a course or setting time aside for personal study, they can help open up new possibilities. Commitment and initiative will be recognized and rewarded in 2012.

The Metal Horse's work situation can also see encouraging developments. Metal Horses who are already established in a position will often be encouraged to add to their experience. However, while many will make important headway, parts of the year will be challenging, with an increased workload or problems making some duties difficult. At such times the Metal Horse would do well to remember Henry Ford's observation, 'Problems are often opportunities in disguise.' By doing his best and showing initiative, he can not only gain important new experience but also do his reputation much good.

Metal Horses seeking work should widen the scope of what they are prepared to consider. By showing initiative, many will find important doors opening. The Dragon year could have some surprises in store, with some Metal Horses obtaining a position they did not expect to be offered or finding an ideal one by chance. March, June, September and November could see some good work possibilities.

Progress at work will also help financially, with many Metal Horses increasing their income over the year. However, with many expenses and sometimes deposits or other plans to save for, he still needs to keep a watch on his outgoings. Too many impulse buys could result in him having to forego other activities. This is a year for prudence and the avoidance of unnecessary risk.

However, the Metal Horse should try to make provision for travel over the year. Time away can do him a lot of good as well as allow him to visit some often interesting destinations.

He can also look forward to a full and exciting social life. Once again he will be much in demand with friends and will value their support and loyalty. In addition the Dragon year can give rise to some celebrations and there will be several important and joyful occasions to share.

The Dragon year also very much favours romance. For Metal Horses in a relationship, this can bring great happiness and become more significant over the year. For others, there will be many opportunities to meet new people, and even if some romances flounder in the early stages, new ones can quickly take their place. This can be an active and special year for affairs of the heart, although one word of warning: lapses and indiscretions can hurt and the Metal Horse should not act in ways that could embarrass himself or others, or rebound on him. Metal Horses, take note. March, April, June and August could see the most social activity, although the Metal Horse will rarely be at a loss for things to do.

In view of all the activity of the year, it is important that his interests and recreational pursuits do not get sidelined. These can often allow him to use his skills in other ways and give him the chance to relax. In the Dragon year the Metal Horse does need to keep his lifestyle in balance, and if he feels uninspired by existing interests and ready for a new challenge, he should make it a priority to take up something new.

He should also take care with his well-being over the year. If experiencing a series of long days and late nights, he should allow himself time to relax and catch up. He would also do well to consider his level of exercise and quality of diet, as both can make a difference to his energy and vitality.

He will be grateful for the assistance he receives from family members this year and at times of decision-making or pressure or when he has interesting news to tell, he should be forthcoming. With some relations the Metal Horse can be slightly reticent, but his loved ones *will* appreciate him being open and allowing them the chance to help.

In general, the Year of the Dragon can be an encouraging one for the Metal Horse. While it will bring pressures and some challenging situations, these will often allow him to show his strength of character. With his ambitions and hopes for the future, what he learns now can be an important platform to build on. Personally, this can also be a full and exciting year, with his relations with others often being special. A year for effort, but also one to enjoy.

TIP FOR THE YEAR

Seize any chances to add to your experience. What opens up this year can be potentially significant. Also, value your relations with others. Many people believe in you and are willing to help you. Listen to them.

The Water Horse

This will be a satisfying year for the Water Horse, with much to do and appreciate.

For many of the Water Horses born in 1942, one of the highlights of the year will be their seventieth birthday, which friends and loved ones will be keen to celebrate in style. There could also be surprises in store, with unexpected gifts. Many of these Water Horses will particularly appreciate the opportunity to spend time with people they do not often see, including perhaps re-establishing contact with distant relatives or friends from some time ago. This may be a personally exciting time, with the Water Horse often taken aback by the love, generosity and affection shown him.

The celebrations need not be restricted to the Water Horse himself this year, as family members and close friends could also have milestones and personal successes to mark. One feature of the Dragon year is that it is often a time of festivity and achievement, and this will certainly be the case in many a Water Horse household.

In addition to some of the celebrations that take place, the Water Horse will often join loved ones in various projects around the home. This could include smartening up certain areas (and, for some, having a purge on clutter) as well as adding new equipment and comforts. There is a strongly practical edge to the Dragon year and the Water Horse will be the driving force behind many home improvements. However, while he will be pleased with what is achieved, he should avoid unnecessary rush. It is better that the right choices are made rather than the wrong ones completed in haste. The Water Horse also needs to be aware of the cost implications of his plans and take the time to compare prices and make sure that his requirements are met. The more deliberation there is, the better.

There will be some excellent travel opportunities over the year, with the chance for many Water Horses to take a special holiday. Often this will be something they will enjoy planning, and by reading up about their destination and going well prepared, they will thoroughly enjoy their time away. Some may be able to combine a holiday with a special interest and go to events or visit cultural attractions while they are away.

The Water Horse has an inquisitive nature and could also be attracted to a new activity during the year. Some Water Horses may be interested in courses in their area. The Dragon year can open up good possibilities for the Water Horse and if he is willing to give things a try, he can derive much satisfaction from his activities.

He will also welcome the social opportunities of the year and if a member of a society or interest group (or decides to join one), he could find himself playing an increased role. Any Water Horses who are lonely, perhaps having moved to a new area or seen a recent change in their personal circumstances, should consider going out more and perhaps getting involved in their community. Their actions can make their personal life far more fulfilling. Late February to April, June and August could see the most social activity.

Although this is generally a good year, one thing the Water Horse does need to guard against is rush. This applies to dealing with financial matters and paperwork as well as making purchases. Without care, mistakes could be made, and if the Water Horse has any uncertainties, he should seek advice. Water Horses, take note.

For Water Horses born in 2002 this will be a promising year. During it, they will be able to take their skills and interests further, as well as learn new ones, and will enjoy the opportunity to do more. The young Water Horse will often delight in some of the prospects that now open up for him. Much that he learns this year, whether academically or involving recreational pursuits, can give him worthwhile skills to build on.

Throughout the year the young Water Horse will also value the support of those around him and his humour, zest and enquiring mind will delight (and occasionally exasperate) many. The year promises to be full and interesting.

As he enters a new decade of his life, both the younger and more senior Water Horse will enjoy some important and special moments. In addition to appreciating the support and affection of his loved ones and any special celebrations to mark his tenth or seventieth birthday, he will often delight in the opportunities the year brings. By making the most of his ideas and using his time well, he can make this a satisfying and pleasing time.

TIP FOR THE YEAR

Avoid haste. Be prepared to give your plans time and attention. With effort and commitment, plus the support you will enjoy, you can see a lot happen this year.

The Wood Horse

There is a Chinese proverb which notes, 'As a long road tests a horse's strength, so time will reveal a man's character.' Both aspects of this proverb hold very true for the Wood Horse this year.

The Wood Horse is persistent and practical, and over the year these two qualities will serve him well. The Dragon year can be a demanding one, with some parts going well but others bringing times of pressure and challenge.

One of the more demanding areas concerns the Wood Horse's work. Although many Wood Horses will be content to remain in a position they know well, with duties which suit their talents, change is on the way. Sometimes new management may decide to implement new procedures or staff movements mean the Wood Horse's role is substantially altered. Some of what happens may greatly concern the Wood Horse, especially if he feels certain changes could complicate what he has to do, but he should be patient. Life *will* settle down and as he adjusts to new duties or routines, some unexpected benefits can emerge. There could be the opportunity to use his skills in new ways as well as gain a different insight into the industry or organization in which he works. Also, for Wood Horses who need a new challenge, the Dragon year will provide it. Few will remain untouched by the developments it will bring.

As a result of what happens, the Wood Horse should take full advantage of any training offered. By keeping up to date with developments and widening his skills, he will find his new knowledge helping his present situation and, importantly, widening his scope for later.

For Wood Horses who decide to move on from where they are or are seeking work, the Dragon year can be challenging. With competition fierce, the Wood Horse will need to remain persistent as well as show initiative. When making applications, he should find out more about the position he is putting in for so he can stress his experience and suitability. Dragon years can work in curious ways and some Wood Horses may find they are rejected for one position but offered something different instead. Mid-February to the end of March, June, September and November could see some key developments, but whenever the Wood Horse sees a chance that interests him, he should act without delay. Speed and initiative will be important factors this year.

In financial matters, the Wood Horse will need to exercise care. When entering into new agreements, he should check the terms and implications, and when dealing with financially related correspondence, he should be thorough and prompt. He should also be wary if tempted to speculate. Financially, this is a year for caution and vigilance.

The Wood Horse will also have some large expenses this year, perhaps connected with family, travel or new equipment, and whenever possible he should try to budget for these in advance. With care, he will be able to realize many plans this year, but to do so will require good management.

With travel well aspected, all Wood Horses should try to take a holiday over the year. Not only can this provide a rest from their usual routine but they will often delight in visiting places of interest. For those who enjoy sport, music or culture, it may be possible to combine their travels with a special event or specific site.

The Wood Horse's personal interests can also bring him much satisfaction and by setting time aside for them, he will often be pleased with the different ways in which he can use his knowledge and skills.

Although he will often be kept busy with various commitments, his social life can help keep his lifestyle in balance and he should aim to go out when he can. Certain friends could be especially helpful this year, particularly in view of the pressures the Wood Horse may have to deal with. Mid-February to April, June, August and the last weeks of the year could see the most social activity, but all Wood Horses should keep in regular contact with their friends over the Dragon year and enjoy the social opportunities it can bring. For the unattached, there could also be exciting romantic possibilities in store, with a chance meeting quickly becoming important.

In his home life the Wood Horse can also look forward to some important occasions, with many a Wood Horse celebrating the achievements or news of someone who is special to him. At such times, the Wood Horse's organizational abilities, thoughtfulness and advice will be valued by many. With this a generally busy year, it is also important that household tasks are shared and any problems talked through. This way, not only can some of the year's more trying situations be better managed, but a lot more can happen.

Overall, the Year of the Dragon will be a full and varied one for the Wood Horse. There will be highs, especially involving family achievements and personal interests, as well as lows, when pressures and uncertainties arise. But the Wood Horse is a realist and by doing his best he can emerge from the year with much to his credit.

TIP FOR THE YEAR
Consult your loved ones and those who speak with experience. Also, be forthcoming. With this a busy and pressured year, you must not keep your concerns to yourself. Allow time for your interests, too, as these can develop well and do you good.

The Fire Horse

The element of fire and the Horse character are a powerful combination, making the Fire Horse enterprising and courageous. He has passion and ambition and is set to fare well in the Dragon year. However, while the aspects are encouraging, the Fire Horse will sometimes need to temper his exuberant nature. Headway can be made this year, but should he take risks or push his good fortune too far, problems and disappointments can follow. Fire Horses, take note.

One of the interesting features of the Dragon year is the many new ideas that can emerge. The Fire Horse will be keen to try out some of these and will enjoy some of the developments of the year. For any Fire Horses who are feeling bored or unfulfilled, this is an excellent time to take up a new activity. Many will be attracted to something new and can not only benefit from what they do but also find it can open up possibilities for the future.

The Fire Horse will have some good travel opportunities over the year, including some at short notice. Where possible, he should take advantage of these. He will not only

enjoy the rest they can give but also some of the interesting places he visits. The Dragon year can often satisfy the
Fire Horse's adventurous nature.

With travel and his personal interests, the Fire Horse
will have many expenses this year and to do all he wants,
he will need to keep careful control of his outgoings. If he
enters into new agreements he should also check the terms
and implications, and if tempted to speculate, he should be
particularly careful. Financially, this is a year for caution.

In his home life the Fire Horse can look forward to an
eventful year. In view of all the activity, however, there will
need to be good co-operation and flexibility. Also, with the
Fire Horse and others in his household likely to be considering their options for the future, it is important that
everyone is forthcoming and discusses what is on their
mind. Amid all the activity there will, though, be some
memorable occasions, perhaps including a special birthday,
anniversary or personal success, with the Fire Horse fully
enjoying and participating in what occurs.

With his active and outgoing nature, he will also be in
contact with many people this year and is likely to make
some new acquaintances who can be of considerable help to
him. Any Fire Horses who are lonely should make every
effort to go out more and consider joining an interest
group in their area. Doing something positive will not only
give them some occasions to look forward to but also help
them to meet others. Mid-February to April, June and
August could see the most social activity.

Affairs of the heart are well aspected, but while the
Dragon year can bring the Fire Horse considerable pleasure, he should avoid placing himself in any situation which

could lead to difficulty or embarrassment. Dragon years can punish lapses and those who take risks.

At work there can be encouraging developments. For Fire Horses who are established in a company or profession, there will be opportunities to take on greater responsibilities. Sometimes what happens may take the Fire Horse by surprise, but by showing willing he will not only be able to advance his career but also have the chance to prove himself in a different capacity. The Dragon year will require some flexibility, but is one for steady career growth.

For Fire Horses seeking work or hoping to move on from where they are, it is a case of being open to possibility. They will need to remain alert, but with initiative and determination many will be successful in their quest. March, June, September and November could see positive developments, but the key to career progress this year is readiness to take on new challenges.

Overall, the Dragon year can be a full and interesting one for the Fire Horse. In his work he could benefit from encouraging developments, while his home, social life and interests will all see much activity. The Dragon year will bring opportunities to move forward, but throughout the Fire Horse does need to remain alert and consider the implications of his actions. With care, however, this can be a positive and relatively successful year for him.

TIP FOR THE YEAR
Value your relations with others. Also, make the most of your chances to meet new people. Some could be especially helpful both now and in the near future. Your personable nature can reward you well this year.

The Earth Horse

The element of earth gives the Earth Horse a pragmatic quality, allowing him to read situations well and have good judgement. And these talents will prove very useful in this fast-moving year. By keeping alert and adapting to situations as they arise, the Earth Horse can make important progress as well as enjoy some personal success. This will be a full and busy year with a lot of potential.

The Earth Horse's work situation will see some important developments. As a result of duties they have been performing recently, quite a few Earth Horses will be encouraged to take their career to a new level and be offered a transfer or the chance to take on new responsibilities. Although what is offered is an important recognition of recent good work, the changes could take some adjusting to. Not only will these Earth Horses often have to deal with some complex matters early on, but also new colleagues and a new routine. Work-wise, some parts of the Dragon year will be challenging, but by remaining focused and coming to terms with the adjustments needed, the Earth Horse will find that difficulties and pressures can quickly subside and he can establish himself in his new role. The experience he gains can mark an important stage in his career development. March, June, September and November could see some good opportunities.

For Earth Horses who feel they could help their career by looking elsewhere or who are seeking work, the job-seeking process can often be disheartening, but by showing resolve and self-belief, many could benefit from some interesting openings. These may not always be in the type of work they were originally seeking, but they can often give these Earth Horses the chance to use their skills in a new way. Sometimes developments in the Dragon year may take the Earth Horse by surprise, but despite initial difficulties, they can often bring long-term benefit.

The Earth Horse's progress at work this year will often allow him to increase his income and he may be able to supplement this through an interest or skill he can put to good use. However, he will need to be careful in money matters and should be wary if tempted to speculate or attracted by schemes of dubious merit. If he has doubts over any undertaking, he should seek professional advice. He could also have considerable outgoings this year and will need to remain disciplined in his spending. Too many impulse buys could mean economies later on. Financially, this is a year for discipline.

One treat many Earth Horses will allow themselves, however, will be travel. A holiday and, for some, a chance to visit relations will be appreciated. There could be additional travel opportunities towards the end of the year.

The Earth Horse has a close circle of trusted friends and over the year will be grateful for their support and advice. At times of work pressure, their understanding and input can be helpful and reassuring. In addition, the Earth Horse will also have the opportunity to meet new people this year and will quickly establish a good rapport with some of these. Late February to the end of April, June and August will see the most social activity.

For the unattached, the Dragon year has wonderful romantic possibilities. Some Earth Horses who start the year alone will settle down or marry over the year and affairs of the heart can be exciting and special.

This will be a busy year for the Earth Horse's home life, with many calls on his time. Those who are parents will not only be attending to the needs of their children but also dealing with many other commitments. Some of the year will be demanding and tiring, but here again the Earth Horse's pragmatic approach will be helpful. By organizing his time, concentrating on his priorities and liaising well with others, he can enjoy some very special times amid the activity. In this busy year, he should also draw on the support offered by others as well as be willing to share certain domestic tasks. And while he may be keen for certain home projects to go ahead, he should be patient and tackle these when time allows. The Dragon year may see some hectic moments, but in many an Earth Horse household it can also turn out to be a special time.

With his demanding lifestyle it is also important that the Earth Horse allows himself the time to rest and unwind and pursue his personal interests. In 2012 he must ensure he has some 'me time'.

In general, this will be a busy year for the Earth Horse, but it will also contain some fine opportunities. By making the most of these and adapting as required, he can make progress as well as gain important new experience. His relations with others are favourably aspected and his home life, while busy, could contain some particularly special moments. For the unattached, Cupid's arrow could well strike. Overall, a satisfying year that will offer the chance for the Earth Horse to benefit from his many fine qualities.

TIP FOR THE YEAR

In Dragon years, situations are sometimes fluid. So be aware of developments and make the most of opportunities. What you achieve now can have considerable long-term value. Also, enjoy your relations with others. Their support, love and advice can help you in this busy year.

FAMOUS HORSES

Roman Abramovich, Neil Armstrong, Rowan Atkinson, Samuel Beckett, Ingmar Bergman, Leonard Bernstein, Joe Biden, James Blunt, Helena Bonham Carter, David Cameron, James Cameron, Jackie Chan, Ray Charles, Chopin, Nick Clegg, Sir Sean Connery, Billy Connolly, Catherine Cookson, Elvis Costello, Kevin Costner, Cindy Crawford, James Dean, Clint Eastwood, Thomas Alva Edison, Harrison Ford, Aretha Franklin, Bob Geldof, Samuel Goldwyn, Billy Graham, Gene Hackman, Rolf Harris, Rita Hayworth, Jimi Hendrix, Janet Jackson, Calvin Klein, Lenin, Annie Lennox, Pixie Lott, Sir Paul McCartney, Nelson Mandela, Angela Merkel, Michael Moore, Ben Murphy, Sir Isaac Newton, Louis Pasteur, Katie Price (Jordan), Dennis Quaid, Gordon Ramsay, Lou Reed, Rembrandt, Ruth Rendell, Jean Renoir, Theodore Roosevelt, Helena Rubenstein, Adam Sandler, David Schwimmer, Martin Scorsese, Kristen Stewart, Barbra Streisand, Kiefer Sutherland, Patrick Swayze, John Travolta, Kathleen Turner, Usher, Vivaldi, Robert Wagner, Denzel Washington, Emma Watson, Billy Wilder, Andy Williams, Brian Wilson, the Duke of Windsor, Jacob Zuma.

1 FEBRUARY 1919 ～ 19 FEBRUARY 1920   *Earth Goat*

17 FEBRUARY 1931 ～ 5 FEBRUARY 1932   *Metal Goat*

5 FEBRUARY 1943 ～ 24 JANUARY 1944   *Water Goat*

24 JANUARY 1955 ～ 11 FEBRUARY 1956   *Wood Goat*

9 FEBRUARY 1967 ～ 29 JANUARY 1968   *Fire Goat*

28 JANUARY 1979 ～ 15 FEBRUARY 1980   *Earth Goat*

15 FEBRUARY 1991 ～ 3 FEBRUARY 1992   *Metal Goat*

1 FEBRUARY 2003 ～ 21 JANUARY 2004   *Water Goat*

THE
GOAT

THE PERSONALITY OF THE GOAT

Amid the complexities of life,
it is the ability to appreciate that is so special.

The Goat is born under the sign of art. He is imaginative, creative and has a good appreciation of the finer things in life. He has an easy-going nature and prefers to live in a relaxed and pressure-free environment. He hates any sort of discord or unpleasantness and does not like to be bound by a strict routine or rigid timetable. He is not one to be hurried against his will, but despite his seemingly relaxed approach to life, he is something of a perfectionist and when he starts work on a project he is certain to give his best.

The Goat usually prefers to work in a team rather than on his own. He likes to have the support and encourage-ment of others and if left to deal with matters on his own he can get very worried and tend to view things rather pessimistically. Wherever possible he will leave major deci-sion-making to others while he concentrates on his own pursuits. If, however, he feels particularly strongly about a certain matter or has to defend his position in any way, he will act with great fortitude and precision.

The Goat has a very persuasive nature and often uses his considerable charm to get his own way. He can, however, be rather hesitant about letting his true feelings be known and if he were prepared to be more forthright he would do much better as a result.

The Goat tends to have a quiet, somewhat reserved nature, but when he is in company he likes he can often become the centre of attention. He can be highly amusing, a marvellous host at parties and a superb entertainer. Whenever the spotlight falls on him, his adrenaline starts to flow and he can be assured of giving a sparkling performance, particularly if he is allowed to use his creative skills in any way.

Of all the signs in the Chinese zodiac, the Goat is probably the most gifted artistically. Whether it is in the theatre, literature, music or art, he is certain to make a lasting impression. He is a born creator and is rarely happier than when occupied in some artistic pursuit. But even in this he does well to work with others rather than on his own. He needs inspiration and a guiding influence, but when he has found his true *métier*, he can often receive widespread acclaim and recognition.

In addition to his liking for the arts, the Goat is usually quite religious and often has a deep interest in nature, animals and the countryside. He is also fairly athletic and there are many Goats who have excelled in some form of sporting activity or who have a great interest in sport.

Although the Goat is not particularly materialistic or concerned about finance, he will find that he will usually be lucky in financial matters and will rarely be short of the necessary funds to tide himself over. He is, however, rather self-indulgent and tends to spend his money as soon as he receives it rather than make provision for the future.

The Goat usually leaves home when he is young but he will always maintain strong links with his parents and the other members of his family. He is also rather nostalgic and is well known for keeping mementoes of his childhood and souvenirs of places that he has visited. His home will not be particularly tidy, but he knows where everything is and it will be scrupulously clean.

Affairs of the heart are particularly important to the Goat and he will often have many romances before he finally settles down. Although he is fairly adaptable, he prefers to live in a secure and stable environment and he will find that he is best suited to those born under the signs of the Tiger, Horse, Monkey, Pig and Rabbit. He can also establish a good relationship with the Dragon, Snake, Rooster and another Goat, but he may find the Ox and Dog a little too serious for his liking. Neither will he care particularly for the Rat's rather thrifty ways.

The female Goat devotes all her time and energy to the needs of her family. She has excellent taste in home furnishings and often uses her considerable artistic skills to make clothes for herself and her children. She takes great care over her appearance and can be most attractive to others. Although she is not the most organized of people, her engaging manner and delightful sense of humour create a favourable impression wherever she goes. She is also a good cook and usually derives much pleasure from gardening and outdoor pursuits.

The Goat can win friends easily and people generally feel relaxed in his company. He has a kind and understanding nature and although he can occasionally be stubborn, he can, with the right support and encouragement, live a very satisfying life. And the more he can use his creative skills, the happier he will be.

THE FIVE DIFFERENT TYPES
OF GOAT

In addition to the 12 signs of the Chinese zodiac there are five elements and these have a strengthening or moderating influence on the signs. The effects of the five elements on the Goat are described below, together with the years in which they were exercising their influence. Therefore Goats born in 1931 and 1991 are Metal Goats, those born in 1943 and 2003 are Water Goats, and so on.

Metal Goat: 1931, 1991
This Goat is thorough and conscientious in all that he does and is capable of doing very well in his chosen profession. Despite his confident manner, he can be a great worrier and he would find it helpful to discuss his concerns with others rather than keep them to himself. He is loyal to his family and employers and will have a small group of particularly close friends. He has good taste and is usually highly skilled in some aspect of the arts. He is often a collector of antiques and his home will be very tastefully furnished.

Water Goat: 1943, 2003
The Water Goat is very popular and makes friends with remarkable ease. He is good at spotting opportunities but does not always have the necessary confidence to follow them through. He likes to have security both in his home

life and work and does not take kindly to change. He is articulate, has a good sense of humour and is usually very good with children.

Wood Goat: 1955

This Goat is generous, kind-hearted and always eager to please. He usually has a large circle of friends and involves himself in a wide variety of activities. He has a very trusting nature but he can sometimes give in to the demands of others a little too easily and it would be in his interests if he were to stand his ground more often. He is usually lucky in financial matters and, like the Water Goat, is very good with children.

Fire Goat: 1967

This Goat usually knows what he wants in life and often uses his considerable charm and persuasive personality to achieve his aims. He can sometimes let his imagination run away with him and has a tendency to ignore matters that are not to his liking. He is rather extravagant in his spending and would do well to exercise a little more care when dealing with financial matters. He has a lively personality, many friends, and loves attending parties and social occasions.

Earth Goat: 1919, 1979

This Goat has a considerate and caring nature. He is particularly loyal to his family and friends and invariably creates a favourable impression wherever he goes. He is reliable and conscientious in his work but sometimes finds it difficult to save and never likes to deprive himself of any little luxury he might fancy. He has numerous interests and is often very well read. He usually derives much pleasure from following the activities of the various members of his family.

PROSPECTS FOR THE GOAT IN 2012

The Year of the Rabbit (3 February 2011–22 January 2012) is a generally encouraging one for the Goat, although to make the most of it he will need to remain determined and seize his opportunities. This is particularly the case in the closing months, which promise to be an active and interesting time.

At work, many Goats will face an increased workload, with new objectives to meet. Although demanding, this can not only demonstrate some of the Goat's strengths, but also create opportunities worth pursuing. Goats seeking work should also remain determined. With initiative, many could secure a position in the closing months of the Rabbit year, even if, for some, this may be temporary.

The Goat could also be fortunate in financial matters at this time and if he keeps alert, he can be particularly pleased with certain purchases he makes. His fine taste and eye for quality will prove an advantage. Also, many Goats can look forward to some travel in the final weeks of the year.

The Goat's home and social life will also see much activity as the Rabbit year draws to a close. To do all he wants, he should start his planning early. Both domestically and socially, many Goats will find themselves in demand and will have good reason to value some of the very special relationships they have.

Being born under the sign of art, the Goat has a curious and enquiring nature and will find the Dragon year one of great possibility. It will be an active year, an inspiring one and often a pleasing one.

The Dragon year starts on 23 January and almost as soon as it begins, the Goat will sense change in the air. Events happen quickly in Dragon years and during this one the Goat will need to keep his wits firmly about him.

One of the more positive aspects of the year concerns the Goat's relations with others. With his *joie de vivre*, conversational skills and fondness for being at the heart of things, he will often revel in the social opportunities the Dragon year can bring. Many Goats will find their social life enjoying quite a fillip this year.

For any Goat who may start the year in low spirits, the Dragon year can mark a considerable change in fortune. These Goats should embrace the spirit of the Dragon year and consider taking up new activities or joining social groups. By taking positive action, they can do a lot to bring about the change they desire. Positive new friendships can be made and these can also be exciting times romantically. Quite a few Goats who are unattached at the start of the year will meet someone who can quickly become special. February, April, July and December could see the most social activity, but at most times of the year, the Goat will have interesting things to do.

This will also be an active year in many a Goat household and there will need to be good co-operation and flexibility. The implications of change, whether involving the Goat's work situation or that of another family member, do need to be talked through. This is very much a year for sharing and openness.

Also, although some of the year's events can cause uncertainty, the Goat should not always assume the worst. Some of the pressures or problems will be short-lived and, as Einstein noted, 'In the middle of difficulty lies opportunity.'

Busy though some of the year may be, the Goat will very much enjoy some of the special times he spends with others, and 2012 can bring some very happy occasions.

The Dragon year can also see major developments in the Goat's work situation. With this a year of innovation, he could find himself having to adapt to new procedures and regulations as well as his workload changing. Although this can be daunting, by doing his best and adapting as required, he will gain useful experience. This is no year for him to close his mind to change.

Many Goats will have the chance to make headway in their current place of work, but for those who feel uncomfortable with developments and are looking for a change or seeking work, the Dragon year can again see important developments. To benefit, these Goats will need to be flexible and widen the scope of what they are prepared to consider, but events can take a curious course in the Dragon year and some interesting possibilities arise. Admittedly, any new position may involve a steep learning curve, but by rising to the challenge, many Goats will not only have the chance to establish themselves in an often different type of work but also prepare themselves for future progress, especially in the favourable Snake year that follows. March, May, September and October could see important work developments, but throughout the Dragon year the Goat should be prepared for change and make the most of his opportunities.

The progress he makes in his work can also help financially, but with an often busy lifestyle and many plans in mind, he can find his spending creeping up. Restraint in the early months of the year will give him more chance to go ahead with activities later on in 2012. This is a year for good control of the purse strings.

Overall, the Dragon year will be a busy and demanding one for the Goat, but it can open up many possibilities for him. The events of the year will admittedly bring their pressures, but with support and a certain amount of readjustment, the Goat can enjoy interesting and personally rewarding times. And what he achieves now can often be taken further in the favourable Snake year that follows.

The Metal Goat

With the energy and vibrancy of the Dragon year, the Metal Goat can look forward to an exciting year ahead.

His personal life is especially well aspected and whether partying, socializing or taking part in various activities, he will be very much in demand. His social circle is set to increase over the year and his good humour and straightforward nature will be particularly appreciated. For many Metal Goats, romance can bring added excitement to this already busy year, and even if some relationships do not endure, the year will contain some special times. The beginning of the Dragon year to late February, April, July and December could see the most social activity, but with the aspects as they are, at almost any time of the year the Metal Goat will have a variety of things to do.

For Metal Goats who move over the year, perhaps for education or work, this can be a significant time. Although the early days in a new location can be unsettling, very quickly these Metal Goats will get to meet others and build up a new social circle. This is very much a time of personal growth for the Metal Goat and he will learn a lot from the new situations he experiences.

With some of the pressures and decisions he will have over the year, it is also important that he talks to others and listens to their advice. This is no year to keep concerns or anxieties to himself or deny himself the support others are willing to give. There will also be opportunities for him to reciprocate, possibly doing something for a senior relation.

A positive aspect of the year will be the travel opportunities it will bring, and whether going on holiday or taking some short breaks, the Metal Goat will often enjoy visiting some interesting destinations. Those who decide to travel quite extensively this year will, however, need to go well prepared, and the more they can save and plan in advance, the more they will be able to do while away.

With travel, socializing and other expenses, the Metal Goat will need to keep a close watch on spending this year and be careful if tempted by impulse buys or indulgences. If he enters into any agreement, he should take the time to compare the different terms and options that may be available and be aware of any obligations involved. Financially, this is a year requiring prudence.

Although there will be a lot for the Metal Goat to do this year, with some weeks being especially busy, he should make sure his interests do not suffer as a result. Being born under the sign of art, many Metal Goats have creative talents and should enjoy developing these during the year. With Dragon years favouring innovation, what they do could meet with a pleasing response.

The Metal Goat would also do well to give some consideration to his well-being. Late nights and too much fast food could leave him susceptible to minor ailments. To keep on good form this year it would reward him to pay attention to his diet as well as allow himself the chance to rest and catch up after particularly busy times.

For the many Metal Goats in education, this will be an interesting although demanding year. As their studies progress, a lot will be expected of them and they will sometimes have difficult concepts and skills to master. However, it is through being stretched that the Metal Goat will learn more, and with perseverance and self-belief, he can make valuable headway this year. Focus, discipline and perseverance will be key, but by keeping in mind what certain qualifications can lead to and being prepared to ask in times of difficulty, he will be spurred on. As a result of their studying, some Metal Goats could find new career possibilities to consider and here again the Dragon year can prove important and helpful in the longer term.

For Metal Goats in work, the Dragon year will bring excellent chances to build up their skills and experience. Those already established in a position will often be given more training, and by showing their willingness to learn, they can make pleasing progress and demonstrate their potential for the future. Although the Metal Goat is in the early stages of his working life, he can sow important seeds for the future.

This also applies to Metal Goats seeking work. Obtaining a position will require determination and persistence, and what is offered may be routine and not quite what the Metal Goat may have had in mind, but it can open the way to other possibilities. The long-term benefits of the Dragon year should not be underestimated. March, May and mid-August to October could see some encouraging work developments.

Overall, the Year of the Dragon will be a busy and often personally exciting one for the Metal Goat. Importantly, it will give him the chance to grow and gain life and work experience that he can build on. On a personal level this can be a special and happy year, with the Metal Goat's personal qualities being widely appreciated and bringing him important new friends. A positive and rewarding year.

TIP FOR THE YEAR
Be prepared to put in the effort. Whether studying or in work, a lot will be expected of you and to do well you do need to offer commitment and rise to the challenge. It may not be easy, but the benefits can be far-reaching. Also, draw on the support of others. This can make a big difference this year.

The Water Goat

This will be a pleasing year for the Water Goat and while some parts may be busier and more fraught than he might like, he will generally be satisfied with what he is able to achieve. However, as he will quickly discover, this is a fast-moving year and plans could be disrupted or changed at the last moment. This is very much a time to keep alert and adapt as necessary.

This is particularly the case in his home life. Sometimes the Water Goat and those close to him will have certain ideas they want to follow through, but as these are talked over and decisions are about to be made, something will happen that causes them to be altered. It could be that a stronger idea emerges or the original idea turns out to be impractical or, when considering purchases, something better and more appropriate is discovered. Throughout the year the Water Goat needs to be open-minded and flexible when making arrangements.

Also, there will be a degree of spontaneity to the Dragon year which needs to be taken into account. In some cases the Water Goat may take advantage of a last-minute holiday offer. By making the most of his opportunities, he will very much enjoy some of the things that happen over the year.

As always, he will take a fond interest in the activities of those close to him, although, being so caring, he will sometimes find himself worrying over them as well. However, during the year he will have the chance to talk over any concerns and offer advice, and his ability to empathize and put his thoughts into words will be especially appreciated. Also, while he will do a lot for others this year, in return he will benefit from support in some of his own undertakings, possibly concerning certain tasks, interests he has, problematic equipment or correspondence. There will be a great deal of mutual support and co-operation in the Water Goat's family during the year. In addition, with the Dragon year noted for its celebrations, there could be news or an occasion that gives rise to a party.

The Water Goat will also appreciate meeting up with his friends. Not only will there be news and ideas to share, but for those who have common interests, there could be events to go to and activities to enjoy together. The Water Goat has great social skills, and his warmth, interest and *joie de vivre* will be appreciated by many.

Water Goats who are feeling lonely or a bit dispirited can find the Dragon year bringing the chance of improvement. However, to benefit, they do need to take action and be open to opportunity. It could be there are social groups or activities in their area they could go to or they could offer to assist in their community in some way. By doing something positive they will be giving themselves more chance to meet others, some of whom will be like-minded and possibly in situations similar to their own. The first few weeks of the year, April, July and December could see the most social activity.

With the Dragon year favouring innovation, many a Water Goat will also be tempted to do something different this year. This could be taking up a new recreational pursuit, possibly one connected with well-being, studying an area of interest or learning a new skill. Whatever he decides do, the Water Goat will often delight in starting something new.

With travel, socializing and household purchases and other equipment to buy and maintain, he will have quite a few outgoings this year, with some months seeing more expense than usual. As a result, the Water Goat does need to keep watch on his spending and, where possible, make early allowance for more expensive outgoings. Also, while he may find some paperwork he receives tiresome, to give it scant attention or delay his response could affect some entitlements he may be due. In financial matters, this is a year for control and vigilance.

Although the Water Goat keeps himself fairly active, he could also find it helpful to give some consideration to his general well-being. This includes making sure his diet is nutritious and well balanced and that he takes regular exercise. If he has been neglecting himself of late or feels some improvements could help, by obtaining medical advice on the best way to proceed, he could find his actions not only benefiting him but also, particularly where exercise is concerned, becoming a new interest he will come to enjoy.

Overall, the Year of the Dragon can be a full and exciting one for the Water Goat, but to get the most from it he will need to be adaptable and flexible in his planning. Yet again he will treasure the positive relations he has with others and the Dragon year can open up some interesting opportunities for him. With a willing attitude, he can enjoy and benefit from this busy yet rewarding time.

TIP FOR THE YEAR
Be open to the new. Whether reading up on a new subject, taking up a new exercise discipline, learning a different skill or mastering a new piece of technology or equipment, you can get a lot of satisfaction from starting something different. This is a year of possibility.

The Wood Goat

The Dragon year is a fast-moving one and the Wood Goat will sometimes be concerned by its developments. Changes can suddenly be forced upon him and cause certain plans to be revised. However, while the Dragon year can bring its pressures, there will also be positive developments in store and special times to enjoy.

One of the most important aspects of the year will concern the Wood Goat's work situation. Although many Wood Goats will have been in their career for some time and will be well established, new systems and regulations could be introduced, changes in management could bring in new ways of working and/or new technology could impact on their role. There will be developments this year which will concern many a Wood Goat, but while he may lament the passing of familiar practices, out of change *will* come new opportunity.

To make the most of his situation the Wood Goat will need to be flexible. If he is resistant to change or appears disparaging in any way, he could undermine his present position and lose out on certain opportunities. This is very much a year for adapting as required.

Most Wood Goats will remain with their present employer this year but with greatly changed duties, but for those who decide to move on or are seeking work, the Dragon year can again be significant. Although these Wood Goats may know the type of work they would like, by widening their scope many could secure a position that is very different from what they have done before and gives their career new impetus. March, May and mid-August to the end of October could see important work developments, but throughout the year the Wood Goat will need to remain alert and be willing to adapt.

A major benefit of the year will be the chances he will get to add to his skills. These could come through training in his work and the experience he gets when given a new role as well as through some of what he may read and study privately. By being receptive and embracing the progressive nature of the year, he can gain a lot personally from it as well as find greater fulfilment in what he does.

His development need not be restricted to his work, however. There may also be certain ideas and personal interests that he is keen to take further. Over the year, many Wood Goats will spend time on pursuits that are satisfying and potentially beneficial. For some, new interests started this year could develop in importance in following years.

The progress many Wood Goats make at work can lead to a modest increase in income, and a few may be able to supplement their earnings through an interest, skill or enterprising idea. However, in money matters the Wood Goat will need to be disciplined. As well as planning ahead for major outgoings, he should be wary of risk or buying too much on impulse. This can lead to misjudgement and regret. Financially, this is a year for caution.

Socially, the Wood Goat will particularly value his close circle of friends this year. Some he will have known for a long time, and when changes or problems arise, he will welcome the chance to talk to people he trusts. Talking can often ease certain anxieties as well as put thoughts and situations into better perspective.

In addition to the support of his friends, the Wood Goat will enjoy the social opportunities that arise over the year and there will be quite a few occasions he will particularly appreciate. In addition, interests and activities he pursues can lead to a widening of his social circle, and for any Wood Goats who would welcome new friendships, the Dragon year can help put a sparkle back in their lives. February, April, July and December will see the most social activity.

This will also be a busy year in many a Wood Goat household and some flexibility will be needed. Sometimes changes in work and commitments will mean routines have to be altered or plans adjusted. In addition, opportunities can arise suddenly and to benefit the Wood Goat will have to act quickly. The Dragon year does have a strong element of spontaneity to it which can often lead to some interesting and different occasions for the Wood Goat to enjoy. He will also value the support of his loved ones during the year, particularly when under pressure or facing change. And, while this will be a busy year in many a Wood Goat household, it will also contain its special times as achievements and family news are celebrated.

Overall, the Year of the Dragon will be a demanding one for the Wood Goat, particularly as it will involve change. However, by adjusting to new situations and rising to the challenge, the Wood Goat will have the chance to develop personally as well as benefit from what opens up for him. This is a year to move forward and embrace the new as well as enjoy the opportunities this potentially beneficial year will bring.

TIP FOR THE YEAR

Whether in your work or personal interests, look to develop what you do. The Dragon year will provide good opportunities for you, but these will require you to be open-minded and willing to act. This may be a demanding year, but it is one filled with possibility ...

The Fire Goat

This will be a busy year for the Fire Goat and while it will contain some excellent opportunities, it will also bring pressures and demands. To get the best from it the Fire Goat should decide on his priorities and concentrate on these. If not, there is a risk he could rush from one activity to another without reaping the full rewards of his efforts. Good time management will help a lot this year.

This will be especially the case at work. Over the year many Fire Goats will have to deal with an increased workload as well as take into account changed procedures, new legislation and different colleagues and clients. Parts of the year will be demanding and, being conscientious, the Fire Goat will often worry about all he has to do. Prioritizing will help. By concentrating on his most important activities and using his time and skills effectively, not only will he be able to accomplish a great deal but also have the chance to demonstrate his skills under pressure and widen his experience. It is by being challenged that strengths emerge and reputations are built, and this year the Fire Goat can greatly help his future prospects.

An important aspect of the year will be the training many Fire Goats are given. This could familiarize the Fire

Goat with new duties, equipment or procedures as well as keep him up to date with developments in his company and industry. By making the most of these opportunities, he will not only be demonstrating his desire to progress but will also gain knowledge that can lead on to new possibilities. This is very much a year to be open-minded and willing to learn.

Many Fire Goats will have the chance to take on greater duties in their current place of work, but for those who are keen to move on or are seeking work, the Dragon year can turn out to be an important juncture in their working lives. To benefit, these Fire Goats should be open to possibility. By keeping alert, making enquiries and seeking advice, many could be alerted to a position that is different from what they have done before. Again, what many achieve this year will stand them in excellent stead for the future, especially the opportunities that will arise in 2013. March and May and late August to the end of October could see significant developments, but opportunities can arise quickly throughout the Dragon year.

The Fire Goat's progress at work can lead to an increase in income over the year and many Fire Goats will also benefit from a gift or bonus payment. Quite a few could enjoy some money luck this year, but the Fire Goat should still be careful. With an often active lifestyle and many commitments, he will need to watch his spending and make early provision for more expensive plans. With good control over his budget, he will be able to go ahead with a lot of what he wants to do, but should he proceed on too much of an ad hoc basis, some economizing and revising of plans may be needed. Fire Goats, take note.

With the many demands on his time it is also important the Fire Goat takes care of his own well-being. This includes allowing time to rest and unwind and appreciate the pleasures around him. He would do well to review his diet and level of exercise, and if he feels either needs improving, take advice on the best way to proceed.

He should also make sure his interests do not get side-lined due to the demands of the year. Not only can these give him the chance to do something different but they can also allow him to make more of his creativity and to meet others. With the Dragon year being an enterprising time, some Fire Goats could find interest-related skills or ideas meeting with success and encouragement. This is a year of possibility and the Fire Goat does need to preserve time for himself and the activities he enjoys.

This also applies to his social life. Although frequently busy, the Fire Goat should not deny himself the chance to meet his friends or go to events that appeal to him. Such occasions can do him good as well as bring him pleasure. In addition, many Fire Goats will welcome the advice certain friends can give, particularly as they may have experience that may help. For Fire Goats who are alone, the Dragon year can have some surprises in store, with an existing or new friendship suddenly taking on greater significance. The first few weeks of the year, April, July and December could see some interesting times socially, but throughout the year the Fire Goat will benefit from keeping up his social life.

His home life will see a lot happening over the year and there will need to be good dialogue and liaison between everyone in his household. Certain arrangements may need to be kept fluid as situations change and interruptions occur. However, while the Dragon year will be busy, it will contain some very special moments. There may be a particular birthday, anniversary or achievement to mark and the Fire Goat's home life will mean a great deal to him. His home may also be an important sanctuary in this frequently active year.

In general, the Year of the Dragon holds interesting prospects for the Fire Goat, but to benefit, he does need to channel his energies wisely and focus on priorities. With care, attention and effort, he can learn a great deal and prepare himself for future success. This may be an exacting year but it can be an instructive one, and by meeting its challenges, the Fire Goat will often find it personally fulfilling.

TIP FOR THE YEAR
Keep your lifestyle balanced and preserve time for family, friends and personal interests. Seize any chances to develop your skills. In this busy year, your commitment will reward you well.

The Earth Goat

There is a Chinese proverb which reminds us, 'With aspirations, you can go anywhere; without aspirations, you can go nowhere.' For the Earth Goat, this is very much a year for deciding on his aspirations. The Dragon year has great potential for him and his actions during it will often be of far-reaching significance.

As the Dragon year starts the Earth Goat could find it helpful to take stock of his situation and think carefully about what he would like to accomplish over the next 12 months. He should involve family and close friends in the process, talking over future hopes and aspirations and being honest with his thoughts. Out of this, not only will he become more aware of the action he now needs to take but also benefit from ideas, advice and offers of assistance. The Dragon year is no time to close his mind to possibility, especially in the early months. He may also benefit from some of the sudden opportunities the year will bring and needs to remain both aware and flexible.

The Earth Goat's work situation in particular will see important developments. Although pressures and changes can cause some uncomfortable moments, this is a progressive year which will allow the Earth Goat to take on increased responsibility and further his skills. In view of some of the demands placed upon him, this can be an exacting time, but it will often give the Earth Goat the chance to become better established and add to his reputation. It can also be highly instructive. New procedures may have to be learned and problems overcome, but new initiatives may also offer the opportunity for input and creativity – often a strong point of the Earth Goat. Over the year many Earth Goats will make headway in the organization they work for, with senior colleagues often encouraging them.

For Earth Goats who are seeking work or who decide to move on from where they are, this can be a significant year. These Earth Goats should not only give careful thought to the type of position they would now like but also contact relevant organizations and employment centres for advice. By taking the initiative, many will be successful in getting a foothold in a company or other organization. Once there, by being willing to learn and putting in the effort, they can use this as a platform to build on in the future. March, May, September and October could see important work developments, but this is a fast-moving year and opportunities can arise at almost any time.

To help both his current situation and future aspirations, the Earth Goat, whether in work or seeking it, should also take advantage of any training that may be offered or, if he feels he is lacking skills that are now needed, consider ways in which he can obtain these. If he has to study or enrol on a course in his own time, it will be worth it, for what he does now will be an investment in his future.

The Earth Goat can also derive pleasure from developing certain interests over the year. For those who enjoy creative activities this can be an exciting time, with their work often enjoying a positive response. For Earth Goats who have aspirations to take certain interests further, this is a year to promote what they do.

The Earth Goat's progress at work can lead to an increase in income over the year and some Earth Goats may also find an interest or hobby supplementing their earnings. However, with a busy lifestyle and many expenses, the Earth Goat will need to keep a tight control over spending and make allowance for more expensive plans and commitments. This is the year for good financial housekeeping.

On a personal level, the Earth Goat will find himself in demand. His sincere and attentive nature makes him popular company and over the year he will not only add to his social circle but also make some important new contacts. For some Earth Goats, the Dragon year can also bring the chance of romance and this will add considerable excitement to this full and interesting year. The first few weeks of the year, April, July and December could see the most social opportunities.

The Earth Goat will also see much activity in his home life and will do much to assist his loved ones. Here his ability to empathize will be much appreciated, with both younger and older relations often having good reason to be grateful for his advice and encouragement. In addition, the Earth Goat will enjoy sharing activities and advancing household plans, but in view of the busy nature of the year there will need to be flexibility when making arrangements. With good co-operation, however, the Earth Goat's home life can be both active and frequently rewarding. There could also be some hastily arranged travel opportunities.

Overall, the Year of the Dragon offers the Earth Goat considerable potential, but he does need to focus on his priorities and be flexible when situations change. Though this can be a demanding year, it is a progressive one and the Earth Goat can do himself and his future a lot of good.

TIP FOR THE YEAR
Use your personal skills well. You will be on impressive form this year. This may be a demanding time for you, but your efforts, enterprise and creativity can reward you well and have future value.

FAMOUS GOATS

Pamela Anderson, Jane Austen, Jenson Button, Lord Byron, Vince Cable, Coco Chanel, Mary Higgins Clark, Nat 'King' Cole, Jamie Cullum, Robert de Niro, Catherine Deneuve, Charles Dickens, Ken Dodd, Sir Arthur Conan Doyle, Umberto Eco, Douglas Fairbanks, Will Ferrell, Dame Margot Fonteyn, Jamie Foxx, Noel Gallagher, Bill Gates, Robert Gates, Mel Gibson, Whoopi Goldberg, Mikhail Gorbachev, John Grisham, Oscar Hammerstein, George Harrison, Billy Idol, Julio Iglesias, Sir Mick Jagger, Steve Jobs, Norah Jones, Nicole Kidman, Sir Ben Kingsley, Matt le Blanc, John le Carré, Doris Lessing, Franz Liszt, James McAvoy, Sir John Major, Michelangelo, Joni Mitchell, Rupert Murdoch, Randy Newman, Sinead O'Connor, Michael Palin, Eva Peron, Pink, Marcel Proust, Keith Richards, Julia Roberts, Nicolas Sarkozy, Philip Seymour Hoffman, William Shatner, Gary Sinise, Jerry Springer, Lana Turner, Mark Twain, Rudolph Valentino, Vangelis, Barbara Walters, John Wayne, Fay Weldon, Bruce Willis.

20 FEBRUARY 1920 ⁓ 7 FEBRUARY 1921 *Metal Monkey*

6 FEBRUARY 1932 ⁓ 25 JANUARY 1933 *Water Monkey*

25 JANUARY 1944 ⁓ 12 FEBRUARY 1945 *Wood Monkey*

12 FEBRUARY 1956 ⁓ 30 JANUARY 1957 *Fire Monkey*

30 JANUARY 1968 ⁓ 16 FEBRUARY 1969 *Earth Monkey*

16 FEBRUARY 1980 ⁓ 4 FEBRUARY 1981 *Metal Monkey*

4 FEBRUARY 1992 ⁓ 22 JANUARY 1993 *Water Monkey*

22 JANUARY 2004 ⁓ 8 FEBRUARY 2005 *Wood Monkey*

THE
MONKEY

THE PERSONALITY OF
THE MONKEY

The more open to possibility,
the more possibilities open.

The Monkey is born under the sign of fantasy. He is imaginative, inquisitive and loves to keep an eye on everything that is going on around him. He is never backward in offering advice or trying to sort out the problems of others. He likes to be helpful and his advice is invariably sensible and reliable.

The Monkey is intelligent, well read and always eager to learn. He has an extremely good memory and there are many Monkeys who have made particularly good linguists. The Monkey is also a convincing talker and enjoys taking part in discussions and debates. His friendly, self-assured manner can be very persuasive and he usually has little trouble in winning people round to his way of thinking. It is for this reason that he often excels in politics and public speaking. He is also particularly adept in PR work, teaching and any job that involves selling.

The Monkey can, however, be crafty, cunning and occasionally dishonest, and he will seize any opportunity to make a quick profit or outsmart his opponents. He has so much charm and guile that people often don't realize what he is up to until it is too late. But despite his resourceful nature, he does run the risk of outsmarting even himself. He has so much confidence in his abilities that he rarely listens to advice or is prepared to accept help from anyone.

He likes to help others but prefers to rely on his own judgement when dealing with his own affairs.

Another characteristic of the Monkey is that he is extremely good at solving problems and has a happy knack of extricating himself (and others) from the most hopeless of positions. He is the master of self-preservation.

With so many diverse talents, the Monkey is usually able to make considerable sums of money, but he does like to enjoy life and will think nothing of spending his money on some exotic holiday or luxury he has had his eye on. He can, however, become very envious if someone else has what he wants.

The Monkey is an original thinker and despite his love of company, he cherishes his independence. He has to have the freedom to act as he wants and any Monkey who feels hemmed in or bound by too many restrictions will soon become unhappy. Likewise, if anything becomes too boring or monotonous, the Monkey will soon lose interest and turn his attention to something else. He lacks persistence and this can often hamper his progress. He is also easily distracted, a tendency that he should try to overcome. By concentrating on one thing at a time, he will almost certainly achieve more in the long run.

The Monkey is a good organizer and even though he may behave slightly erratically at times, he will invariably have a plan at the back of his mind. On the odd occasion when his plans do not work out, he is usually quite happy to shrug his shoulders and put it down to experience. He will rarely make the same mistake twice and throughout his life he will try his hand at many different things.

The Monkey likes to impress and is rarely without followers or admirers. Many are attracted by his good looks, his sense of humour, or simply because he instils so much confidence.

Monkeys usually marry young and for it to be a success their partner must allow them time to pursue their many interests and indulge their love of travel. The Monkey has to have variety in his life and is especially well suited to those born under the sociable and outgoing signs of the Rat, Dragon, Pig and Goat. The Ox, Rabbit, Snake and Dog will also be enchanted by his resourceful and outgoing nature, but he is likely to exasperate the Rooster and Horse, and the Tiger will have little patience with his tricks. A relationship between two Monkeys will work well – they will understand each other and be able to assist each other in their various enterprises.

The female Monkey is intelligent, extremely observant and a shrewd judge of character. Her opinions are often highly valued and, having such a persuasive nature, she invariably gets her own way. She has many interests and involves herself in a wide variety of activities. She pays great attention to her appearance, is an elegant dresser and likes to take particular care over her hair. She can be a doting parent and will have many good and loyal friends.

Provided the Monkey can curb his desire to take part in everything that is going on around him and concentrate on one thing at a time, he can usually achieve what he wants in life. Should he suffer any disappointment, he is bound to bounce back. He is a survivor and his life is usually both colourful and eventful.

THE FIVE DIFFERENT TYPES OF MONKEY

In addition to the 12 signs of the Chinese zodiac there are five elements and these have a strengthening or moderating influence on the signs. The effects of the five elements on the Monkey are described below, together with the years in which they were exercising their influence. Therefore Monkeys born in 1920 and 1980 are Metal Monkeys, those born in 1932 and 1992 are Water Monkeys, and so on.

Metal Monkey: 1920, 1980
The Metal Monkey is very strong-willed. He sets about everything he does with dogged determination and often prefers to work independently rather than with others. He is ambitious, wise and confident, and is certainly not afraid of hard work. He is very astute in financial matters and usually chooses his investments well. Despite his somewhat independent nature, he enjoys attending parties and social occasions and is particularly warm and caring towards his loved ones.

Water Monkey: 1932, 1992
The Water Monkey is versatile, determined and perceptive. He also has more discipline than some of the other Monkeys and is prepared to work towards a particular goal

rather than be distracted by something else. He is not always open about his true intentions and when questioned can be particularly evasive. He can be sensitive to criticism but also very persuasive and usually has little trouble in getting others to fall in with his plans. He has a very good understanding of human nature and relates well to others.

Wood Monkey: 1944, 2004

This Monkey is efficient, methodical and extremely conscientious. He is also highly imaginative and is always trying to capitalize on new ideas or learn new skills. Occasionally his enthusiasm can get the better of him and he can get very agitated when things do not quite work out as he had hoped. He does, however, have a very adventurous streak and is not afraid of taking risks. He also loves travel. He is usually held in great esteem by his friends and colleagues.

Fire Monkey: 1956

The Fire Monkey is intelligent, full of vitality and has no trouble in commanding the respect of others. He is imaginative and has wide interests, although sometimes these can distract him from more useful and profitable work. He is very competitive and always likes to be involved in everything that is going on. He can be stubborn if he does not get his own way and he sometimes tries to indoctrinate those who are less strong-willed than himself. He is a lively character, attractive to others and most loyal to his partner.

Earth Monkey: 1968

The Earth Monkey tends to be studious and well read, and can become quite distinguished in his chosen line of work. He is less outgoing than some of the other types of Monkey and prefers quieter and more solid pursuits. He has high principles, a very caring nature and can be most generous to those less fortunate than himself. He is usually successful in handling financial matters and can become very wealthy in old age. He has a calming influence on those around him and is respected and well liked. He is, however, especially careful about whom he lets into his confidence.

PROSPECTS FOR THE MONKEY IN 2012

The Year of the Rabbit (3 February 2011–22 January 2012) can be a satisfying one for the Monkey and while it may lack the activity of some, it will contain good opportunities and the closing months will generally be an encouraging time.

In his work, the Monkey could see important developments and may be asked to take on greater responsibilities as well as help with certain situations. With his resourcefulness and specific strengths, he will not only be appreciated but often in demand. October and November could be busy months with possible opportunities for Monkeys seeking work or hoping to advance their career.

The Monkey's canny sense can also serve him well when shopping. Whether for himself, his loved ones or his home, his purchases will often delight him (and others). If looking for something specific, he could benefit from an advantageous offer, and in certain transactions he can fare particularly well. He will also enjoy the social opportunities that arise, with September and December being particularly active months. However, when in company, he does need to be attentive and take into account the viewpoints of others. A *faux pas* could embarrass.

Similarly, in his home life, the Monkey will need to consult others over plans and try to spread out certain activities rather than having everything concentrated in a short period of time. Advanced planning can lead to some particularly appreciated occasions and for some Monkeys there will be travel opportunities in the final weeks of the Rabbit year too.

The Monkey has an enquiring nature and likes to be active and involved, and the Dragon year will suit him well. It starts on 23 January and is one of great possibility for the Monkey.

With his ability to gauge situations the Monkey will sense, as the Dragon year starts, that this is a progressive time and will feel more inspired to make things happen. If there are aims he has not fulfilled, short-term ambitions he is keen to realize or ideas he wants to take further, now is the time. The Dragon year's vitality and Monkey's resourcefulness are a powerful combination.

At work, many Monkeys will have seen change in recent years and some will no longer feel fulfilled and will be keen to use their skills more fully. This year their situation is particularly encouraging. If already established in a career, their experience and reputation can allow them to make good headway and move their career forward in their current place of work. To help with this, the Monkey needs to keep himself informed of developments. His ability to identify possible openings can stand him in excellent stead.

For Monkeys who are looking elsewhere, as well as those seeking work, the prospects are also encouraging. Although the job-seeking process is never easy, by remaining active, making enquiries and following up vacancies that interest them, they are likely to find their initiative and determination winning through. Again the Monkey's ability to identify and then make the most of opportunity will be an important factor this year. With the active nature of the Dragon year, possibilities could arise at almost any time, but they do need to be followed up. March, April, September and November could see particularly encouraging developments. Also, Monkeys who secure a new position early on in the year could find they have the chance to take on greater responsibilities later on in 2012. Work-wise, this is a year for initiative, effort and progress.

The Monkey's progress at work can also help financially and many Monkeys will enjoy a rise in income over the year. However, any increase could tempt the Monkey to spend and, without care, his outgoings could start to mount. He does need to watch this and, where possible, use any financial improvement to help his overall position. This includes looking to reduce borrowings, saving up for specific requirements and taking advantage of tax incentives to save for the future. With good management, the Monkey can improve his finances this year, but it will require discipline.

The Monkey keeps life interesting by having widespread interests and these can again reward him well this year. He will often enjoy developing some of the things he does as well as sharing interests with others, including going to various events. For the creative Monkey, some ideas or work he produces could bring especial pleasure. The Monkey's enterprising nature is well suited to the vitality and innovation of the year, and for any Monkey who feels ready for a new challenge, this would be an excellent time to consider taking up something different. The Dragon year is a time of interesting possibility, but to benefit, the Monkey does need to act.

Existing and new personal interests will often bring the Monkey into contact with others, and over the year his social life can bring him much pleasure. In addition, he may decide to join an interest or professional group which can introduce him to a new set of people. On a personal level he will be in good form this year and many will respond well to his genial manner. Monkeys who move to a new area will particularly enjoy forming a new social circle and for some who are unattached, romance could strike unexpectedly. April, May, August and December could see the most social activity.

The Monkey's home life can also give him great satisfaction, although there will need to be good co-operation and a willingness to adapt as schedules and situations change. However, the Monkey is particularly adept at working out what is best for everyone – a talent that will be appreciated this year. In addition, he will often be the driving force behind some of the home projects carried out as well as suggesting (and organizing) activities that everyone in his household can enjoy. A lot will revolve around him this year and those close to him will value his special qualities and the time he preserves for family life.

Overall the Year of the Dragon is one of great possibility for the Monkey. It is a time to seize the initiative and turn hopes and plans into reality. By making the effort, seizing his opportunities and using his skills to advantage, he can look forward to some important success. Whether in his work or his personal interests, this is a year for moving forward and making more of himself. As a Monkey he has wide-ranging talents and the Dragon year will give him the chance to shine, but – and it is a *but* – a lot does rest with the Monkey himself. In 2012 he needs to believe in himself and to act with determination. With the prevailing aspects, he can achieve – and, importantly, enjoy – a lot this year, but it will require effort.

The Metal Monkey

The metal element gives the Monkey considerable determination. When the Metal Monkey has set his sights on a certain objective, he works tirelessly to achieve it and over the year his resolve will serve him well. However, the Dragon year will be busy, and without care, the Metal Monkey could find himself spreading his energies too widely or getting distracted from his true aims. In this favourable year, he does need to set his priorities and focus on them.

In his work, this is a year indicating progress and change. Although many Metal Monkeys may feel settled where they are, the Dragon year is not one for standing still. Through changes in personnel or reorganization, more senior positions could become available, offering the Metal Monkey the chance of promotion or the opportunity to switch to other duties. The winds of change will affect many Metal Monkeys this year, but they will often welcome the challenge.

A further feature of the year will be the experience many will be able to gain. Whether through their everyday duties (including dealing with some of the problems and pressures that will arise) or additional training, by furthering their knowledge and skills they can do much to help their present situation as well as widen their scope for later.

For Metal Monkeys who are keen to further their career by moving elsewhere, as well as those seeking work, the Dragon year can again open up important possibilities. By keeping alert and making enquiries, the Metal Monkey may well find his determination leading to a new position. Although this may be a considerable change from what he has been doing, it can not only be an interesting new career challenge but also give him the chance to establish himself with a new employer.

A factor in the Metal Monkey's favour will be his ability to forge good working relations with many people, and he should make every effort to meet new colleagues and establish himself within a team. If applicable, he could also find it helpful to join a professional organization. Raising his profile can do much to help both his present and future situation. What is achieved in 2012 can mark an important stage in the Metal Monkey's personal and career development and be something he can build on in the future. March to mid-May, September and November could see some key developments.

The Dragon year can also open up some interesting possibilities for the Metal Monkey and if a new activity catches his attention, he should follow this up. Similarly, if he has ideas he can develop or put forward, he should do so. This is very much a year for action *and follow-through*. The main stumbling block is the Metal Monkey abandoning projects before seeing them completed or flitting from one activity to another. In the Dragon year he does need to stay focused and use his time effectively.

He should also give some consideration to his lifestyle over the year. Not only should he keep the various strands of his life in good balance, but also make sure he has sufficient exercise and a healthy diet. Sometimes he is so busy that he may neglect these most essential areas, and to be at his best, this is something he needs to watch.

Another area which requires attention this year is finance. Although many Metal Monkeys will enjoy an increase in earnings, the Dragon year will bring many temptations and the Metal Monkey needs to be wary about buying too much on impulse. Also, if tempted by anything risky or speculative, he must be aware of what is involved and the obligations he may be taking on. Without care, money can all too easily be spent and not put to its best use. Metal Monkeys, take note and be careful.

The Metal Monkey enjoys good relations with many people and over the year he may come into contact with many more and make some very good friends. April, May, August and December could see the most social activity. For unattached Metal Monkeys, including those who may have had some personal difficulty in recent years, the Dragon year can see a brightening in their situation, with new interests, new friendships and, for some, important new love adding excitement to their year.

Domestically, there will be a great deal of activity this year and to do all he wants, the Metal Monkey will need to use his time well. Particularly where home improvements are concerned, he should concentrate on one project at a time rather than trying to do too much too quickly. The Dragon year may favour practical activity, but resources – whether energy, time or money – do need to be used wisely. As with so much this year, the Metal Monkey will be helped by listening to the advice of those around him.

Pleasingly, there will also be news to commemorate in many a Metal Monkey household this year, whether an addition to the family, the successful advancement of plans, the Metal Monkey's own success or that of someone close.

Overall, the Year of the Dragon offers great possibility for the Metal Monkey, but he does need to concentrate on his priorities and use his time and energy wisely. To try to do too much too soon or to spread his attention too widely could lead to less satisfying results. Instead, it is a time for discipline, focus and making the most of the chances this year will offer. However, the Metal Monkey will often be encouraged by the love and support of those special to him and can look forward to some exciting developments in his personal life. A busy year and one with far-reaching value.

TIP FOR THE YEAR
You can achieve a great deal this year as well as do much to help your future situation, but you need to use your time well. Concentrate on your priorities and avoid being diverted from your main aims. You have much in your favour this year, but stay focused and disciplined.

The Water Monkey

This year not only marks the start of a new decade in the Water Monkey's life but can be an important year for him. It will give him the chance to move forward as well as enjoy some very special times. He will have a lot in his favour this year.

Although most Water Monkeys will have some idea of their aims for the year, for any who start 2012 dissatisfied, in low spirits or drifting, the Dragon year can be a time of important change and improvement. To help, as the year starts, these Water Monkeys should draw a line under what has gone before and concentrate on the present and near future. With resolve, self-belief and the help and advice available (including from relevant organizations), they can start to bring the improvement they have been wanting. For these Water Monkeys this can be an important time, but it does rest with them to take the initiative and to have faith in themselves.

Many Water Monkeys will already have specific objectives for the year. For those in education, there will be a lot to do. Study-wise, some of the Dragon year will be intensive and personally challenging. It will also give some Water Monkeys chance to get experience in the workplace. However, while these Water Monkeys will be kept busy, they will often be satisfied with the way they feel they are progressing and what their current activities can open up for them.

In addition, many will welcome the scope and flexibility they are given this year through some of their course options. This is a time of considerable possibility and choice for the Water Monkey and he will be pleased with how many of his decisions work out.

Many Water Monkeys will also take considerable pleasure in their personal interests this year. If the Water Monkey is given the chance of extra tuition for an interest-related skill or sees a new activity that appeals to him, he should make the most of it. It is by embracing his opportunities that he can make his twentieth year important and beneficial. Some of what he does can also have a good social element which can add extra meaning and fun to his activities.

For Water Monkeys in work or seeking work, the Dragon year can again see important developments. Those in work, in particular, could see considerable change. If in the early stages of a career, the Water Monkey could find himself being given more specialist training and new objectives to meet. Some of what is asked of him could be challenging and unsettling, but with a willing approach, he can gain experience that can be an essential part of his career development and prepare him for his onward progression.

For Water Monkeys who are not comfortable in their present work position, the Dragon year will bring the chance to re-evaluate what they do. Some may consider more training or an apprenticeship scheme or look for another position elsewhere. The Dragon year encourages choice and progress, and by taking action, many of these Water Monkeys will be able to set their career on a more appropriate path. The initiative, however, does rest with them. This also applies to those seeking work. Although the job-finding process can be wearying, by considering different possibilities and obtaining advice from contacts and agencies, many Water Monkeys will secure that all-important foothold on the career ladder. Late February to mid-May, September and November could see encouraging developments.

With his various interests and a frequently active social life, however, the Water Monkey will need to keep a close watch on his spending. Yielding to too many temptations could lead to later economies or larger interest payments. Also, he should be careful if tempted by dubious or risky undertakings. Without care, losses could be incurred. Water Monkeys, take note and be thorough and disciplined in financial matters.

Despite this need for care, the Water Monkey's social life can bring him a great deal of fun this year. There will be excellent opportunities to meet others, and as the Water Monkey develops certain interests or see changes in his work situation, some valuable new friendships can be made. For some who are unattached, romance can also add excitement to their year. April to early June, August and December could see the most social activity, but at most times of the year the Water Monkey will have something to look forward to.

He will also be given valuable support by family members and those close to him. And although he may be absorbed in his various activities and keen to take his own decisions, he should not let this preclude him from asking for advice or talking through his options when necessary. With greater openness, he can benefit from the advice and assistance others are willing to give. Water Monkeys, do remember this and do be forthcoming.

Overall, the Dragon year has considerable potential for the Water Monkey. In particular, it will allow him to develop certain skills and work towards qualifications and will give him experience he can build on. What he achieves this year can often be instrumental in some of the success he will enjoy in following years. This is also a time to be open to possibility. With a willing 'can do' approach, the Water Monkey will be pleased with what he is able to accomplish, while personally, his twentieth year can see a lot happen and bring some great times to appreciate.

TIP FOR THE YEAR
You may have ideas about what you want to do, but do draw on the advice of others as well as be open to different possibilities. With help, encouragement and a willingness to embrace your opportunities, you can not only make this year special but also significant.

The Wood Monkey
The element of wood helps bring out the progressive qualities of the Monkey. The Wood Monkey is practical, forward-looking and enjoys a wide range of interests, and the Dragon year will keep him pleasantly occupied.

One of the features of the Dragon year is that it encourages the new, and the Wood Monkey may find himself taking up a new recreational interest, advancing an existing interest in a different way or joining an activity group in his area. This is very much a year for moving forward.

The Wood Monkey will also find himself encouraged by others. It could be that by casually mentioning an idea he finds others urging him on and even keen to share in what he is proposing. This is a 'doing' year and, as the Wood Monkey will often find, not only will he enjoy most of what he does but some undertakings will progress in fortuitous ways. This is a year for him to be open to chance and embrace the opportunities that come his way.

Many Wood Monkeys will decide to set time aside for learning skills that could be useful, including computer applications. By furthering his knowledge, the Wood Monkey can take considerable satisfaction from his activities.

Any Wood Monkeys who start the year in low spirits or feeling unfulfilled should seriously consider taking up a new interest or decide on a personal objective for the year. By doing so, they will not only enjoy the chance to absorb themselves in something different but also enjoy the benefits that can follow on. These Wood Monkeys, do take note – and action.

The Wood Monkey often appreciates outdoor activities, and gardening can bring many a great deal of pleasure over the year. The Dragon year can be an active and frequently inspired time and the Water Monkey may also enjoy using local amenities, including parks and recreational facilities, and visiting places of interest.

Joint activities are favourably aspected and the Wood Monkey will be keen to share a lot of what he does this year. His interests in particular can bring him into contact with many people, and new friendships will often be made. For Wood Monkeys who would welcome more contact with others, perhaps having experienced a recent change in circumstances, it would be well worth joining courses or activity groups in their area or meeting up with other enthusiasts. The Dragon year is a highly encouraging one for the Wood Monkey and positive action will reward him well. April to early June, August and December could see the most social activity.

The Wood Monkey can also look forward to an interesting home life this year. Again he will be keen to encourage joint undertakings, and whether considering purchases and improvements for the home or other plans, by talking his ideas over and sharing decisions, he will be pleased with what is accomplished this year. Practical activities will be to the fore, with home projects and some additional equipment or comforts making a noticeable difference to the Wood Monkey's surroundings. However, in setting about his plans he should avoid unnecessary haste and be prepared to look at alternatives rather than make a decision too quickly. Dragon years can give rise to interesting possibilities and to benefit the Wood Monkey does need to be alert and aware.

He will also follow the activities of family members with much interest and the time and assistance he gives younger relations will be greatly appreciated. Here his ability to relate, empathize and help (in often subtle ways) can do a lot of good.

Although the Dragon year is generally favourably aspected for the Wood Monkey, one area which will need care is finance. With home plans, some expensive purchases and other commitments, he does need to watch his outgoings and make early provision for larger expenses. If he has any concerns over a transaction or any financial correspondence he may receive, he should seek advice. This is a year for care and thoroughness.

Overall, however, the Wood Monkey can benefit from a lot that he does in the Dragon year. Whether advancing interests and ideas, taking up new pursuits or tackling home or other projects, he can find his interest and willingness to take action leading to satisfying results. And developments in the Dragon year can sometimes take a curious course, with his actions leading to new possibilities or opening up other opportunities. It can be a different, stimulating and often personally rewarding time for the Wood Monkey, and with his home and social life encouragingly aspected, it can be a good and interesting one too.

TIP FOR THE YEAR
Be flexible and open to possibility. By being willing to explore ideas and try out different activities, you can gain a lot from the year as well as enjoy it.

The Fire Monkey

There is a Chinese proverb which is very apt for the Fire Monkey this year: 'Better to do it than to miss it.' The Dragon year can bring the Fire Monkey some excellent opportunities, but these do need to be grasped. This is a year to act on ideas and realize ambitions, otherwise chances could slip by and eventually be missed.

Almost all areas of the Fire Monkey's life can see important developments. In his work these could be changing times. With many industries undergoing review and adjustment, the Fire Monkey could find his role altering. However, while this may concern him, new opportunities can follow on from what happens and by being willing to adapt and drawing on his considerable experience, he may find himself well placed to take on a greater and often different role.

Also, the Fire Monkey is blessed with an imaginative nature. He is resourceful and can come up with many fine ideas and solutions. These talents can reward him well this year. Ideas he puts forward could meet with a favourable response and for those whose work or interests allow them to create or innovate in some way, this can be a successful and inspired time.

Another factor in the Fire Monkey's favour will be the good working relations he has with many people. Some Fire Monkeys may even be given a mentoring role over the year. With the dynamic energy that tends to characterize Dragon years, change could happen at almost any time, but March to early May, September and November could be significant months.

Many Fire Monkeys will be able to make progress with their current employer this year, but for those who feel the time is right to do something different or are seeking work, this can be a year of important possibility. By considering different ways in which they could use their skills, they could find an opportunity arising which will be a welcome change from what they have previously been doing. Also, while the job-seeking process is never easy, events can proceed in curious ways in the Dragon year and some Fire Monkeys may be offered a position unexpectedly after several rejections. Throughout the year the Fire Monkey will need to be persistent, determined and flexible.

Fire Monkeys who decide on career change this year or feel it could be useful to improve their skills in certain areas should also take advantage of any training or refresher courses that are available to them. Positive action now will not only help the Fire Monkey's current situation but also his future.

The progress the Fire Monkey makes at work can often help financially and he may also benefit from a bonus or gift during the year. However, he will need to budget carefully, especially as domestic and accommodation expenses are likely to be greater than usual this year. If he does not do so already, keeping a set of household accounts could allow him to keep better track of his position. Generally, the more thoroughly he controls his finances, the better. He should also be careful and thorough with paperwork, especially any that is related to finance. In this busy year, he cannot afford to be lax in financial matters.

In his home life, this promises to be an eventful year. There could be a wedding, the birth of a grandchild or another notable family achievement to celebrate. With exciting developments possible and much planning needed, the Fire Monkey will be keen to provide support, and his ability to organize and empathize will be greatly appreciated.

However, while the year will contain its special moments, there will also be pressures and sometimes differences of opinion. These do need to be addressed and a compromise sometimes reached. In addition, though many Fire Monkeys will be keen to carry out home improvements, ample time should be set aside for these and the cost implications carefully considered.

Although the Fire Monkey will be kept busy with his various commitments, he will very much appreciate the opportunities he has go out and meet up with his friends. Not only can such times be convivial, but certain friends could be especially supportive. Fire Monkeys who would welcome a more rewarding social life could find certain interests offering good chances to meet others. April, May, August and December could see the most social activity.

Overall, the Year of the Dragon is a promising one for the Fire Monkey, but to benefit he does need to act with determination. This is a time to make his personal qualities, ideas and experience count. His relations with others will also be important, with some often special times to look forward to in his home life.

TIP FOR THE YEAR
You have much in your favour this year, but you will need to be flexible. Remain positive and determined, and remember it is 'better to do it than to miss it'.

The Earth Monkey

The Dragon year is a time of great possibility and the Earth Monkey will often benefit from the opportunities it will bring.

One of the key features of the Dragon year is the speed with which things happen. This is certainly no year for standing still. The Earth Monkey should keep his wits firmly about him and when an idea occurs to him or an opportunity comes his way, he should act quickly. As the saying reminds us, 'The early bird catches the worm.' This is a year when initiative and fast responses really can pay off.

At work almost all Earth Monkeys will feel the effects of change. Whether through staff movements, the implementation of new procedures or internal reorganization, a lot will be happening. However, while there will be uncertainty and pressure, there will also be opportunities, and as a result of their experience and in-house knowledge, many Earth Monkeys will be well placed to take on a greater role or become involved in specialist projects. Again, the Earth Monkey should keep himself informed and be quick to signify interest. His versatility and willingness to take on new roles will stand him in excellent stead. A further strength is his ability to enjoy good working relations with his colleagues. Being an active team member and using any chances to network can help his reputation and prospects again this year. And the greater his input, the more he will achieve.

Many Earth Monkeys will be able to make progress in their present place of work, but for those keen to move or seeking work the Dragon year can open up some interesting options. Obtaining a new position will not be easy, but by being active in the job-seeking process and emphasizing their experience, many Earth Monkeys will find their determination, energy and commitment leading to an excellent new opportunity. Again, when suitable vacancies arise, the Earth Monkey should act quickly. Speed is of the essence this year.

With this also being a year for innovation, some Earth Monkeys will decide on a complete career change. There could be personal adjustments to be made and much to learn, but these Earth Monkeys will often feel ready for the challenge and this year will mark a new chapter in the working lives of many. March, April, September and November could see some important developments.

Progress at work can also help financially, but with his existing commitments and the plans he is keen to carry forward, the Earth Monkey does need to control his spending and manage his finances with care. Risks, speculation or hasty purchases could lead to regret. Earth Monkeys, take note and do be thorough in all financial matters.

With the pressures of the year it is also important that the Earth Monkey allows time for rest, relaxation and exercise. This may be a successful year, but he will need to balance the various strands of his life. To help, he should make sure his personal interests do not get sidelined. Not only should he preserve regular time for these but also consider setting himself some objectives for the year, perhaps making more of an interest-related skill, developing an idea or going to events. Any Earth Monkey who has let his interests lapse lately or feels his lifestyle has got out of balance should consider taking up something new this year and rewarding himself with some 'me time'.

The Earth Monkey's social life will also help him keep his life in balance. As well as keeping in regular contact with his friends and going to events that appeal to him, if he takes an interest in what is going on in his area, he can often enjoy himself as well as make some new acquaintances. With the Dragon year ushering in important developments, for the unattached, romance could come unexpectedly. April to early June, August and December could see the most social activity.

The Earth Monkey's home life will be busy and several times during 2012 he may despair over all that is being asked of him, but by doing what he can, dealing with pressures as they arise and playing his full part in home life, these busy times can also be made special. Also, if under pressure, it is important the Earth Monkey does not feel he must do everything single-handed but draws on the willingness of others to help when required.

Overall, the Earth Monkey will have much in his favour this year. With his drive, ambition and ability to adapt, he can make the most of the changes the year will bring. This is a time to move forward and take on new challenges, and by doing so, the Earth Monkey will not only feel more fulfilled but also help his long-term situation. The key to success this year is to put himself forward and act quickly. In addition he will benefit from his good relations with others, with his home and social life being active and rewarding.

TIP FOR THE YEAR
Consider taking up a new interest or setting yourself an objective for the year. By doing something positive, you can gain a lot both personally and professionally from the year.

FAMOUS MONKEYS

Christina Aguilera, Gillian Anderson, Jennifer Aniston, Patricia Arquette, Lady Ashton, J. M. Barrie, José Manuel Barroso, Colette, John Constable, David Copperfield, Patricia Cornwell, Daniel Craig, Joan Crawford, Miley Cyrus, Leonardo da Vinci, Timothy Dalton, Bette Davis, Danny De Vito, Celine Dion, Michael Douglas, Mia Farrow, Carrie Fisher, F. Scott Fitzgerald, Ian Fleming, Paul Gauguin, Jake Gyllenhaal, Jerry Hall, Tom Hanks, Harry Houdini, Hugh Jackman, Katherine Jenkins, Julius Caesar, Buster Keaton, Alicia Keys, Don King, Gladys Knight, Taylor Lautner, George Lucas, Bob Marley, Kylie Minogue, V. S. Naipaul, Lisa Marie Presley, Debbie Reynolds, Little Richard, Mickey Rooney, Diana Ross, Tom Selleck, Omar Sharif, Wilbur Smith, Rod Stewart, Jacques Tati, Elizabeth Taylor, Dame Kiri Te Kanawa, Justin Timberlake, Harry Truman, Michelle Williams, Venus Williams.

8 FEBRUARY 1921 ∼ 27 JANUARY 1922   *Metal Rooster*

26 JANUARY 1933 ∼ 13 FEBRUARY 1934   *Water Rooster*

13 FEBRUARY 1945 ∼ 1 FEBRUARY 1946   *Wood Rooster*

31 JANUARY 1957 ∼ 17 FEBRUARY 1958   *Fire Rooster*

17 FEBRUARY 1969 ∼ 5 FEBRUARY 1970   *Earth Rooster*

5 FEBRUARY 1981 ∼ 24 JANUARY 1982   *Metal Rooster*

23 JANUARY 1993 ∼ 9 FEBRUARY 1994   *Water Rooster*

9 FEBRUARY 2005 ∼ 28 JANUARY 2006   *Wood Rooster*

THE
ROOSTER

THE PERSONALITY OF
THE ROOSTER

With a clear destination
and firm will,
I raise my sails
to the winds of fortune.

The Rooster is born under the sign of candour. He has a flamboyant and colourful personality and is meticulous in all that he does. He is an excellent organizer and wherever possible likes to plan his various activities well in advance.

The Rooster is usually highly intelligent and very well read. He has a good sense of humour and is an effective and persuasive speaker. He loves discussion and enjoys taking part in any sort of debate. He has no hesitation in speaking his mind and is forthright in his views. He does, however, lack tact and can easily damage his reputation or cause offence by some thoughtless remark or action. He has a very volatile nature and should always try to avoid acting on the spur of the moment.

He is usually very dignified in his manner and conducts himself with an air of confidence and authority. He is adept at handling financial matters and organizes his financial affairs with considerable skill. He chooses his investments well and is capable of achieving great wealth. Most Roosters use their money wisely, but there are a few who are the reverse and are notorious spendthrifts. Fortunately, the Rooster has great earning capacity and is rarely without sufficient funds to tide himself over.

Another characteristic of the Rooster is that he invariably carries a notebook or scraps of paper around with him. He is constantly writing himself reminders or noting down important facts lest he forgets – the Rooster cannot abide inefficiency and conducts all his activities in an orderly, precise and methodical manner.

The Rooster is usually very ambitious, but can be unrealistic in some of what he hopes to achieve. He occasionally lets his imagination run away with him and while he does not like any interference from others, it would be in his own interests to listen to their views a little more often. He also does not like criticism, and if he feels anybody is doubting his judgement or prying too closely into his affairs, he is certain to let his feelings be known. He can also be rather self-centred and stubborn over relatively trivial matters, but to compensate for this he is reliable, honest and trustworthy, and this is appreciated by all who come into contact with him.

Roosters born between the hours of five and seven, both at dawn and sundown, tend to be the most extrovert of their sign, but all Roosters like to lead an active social life and enjoy attending parties and big functions. The Rooster usually has a wide circle of friends and is able to build up influential contacts with remarkable ease. He often belongs to several clubs and societies and involves himself in a variety of different activities. He is particularly interested in the environment, humanitarian affairs and anything affecting the welfare of others. He has a very caring nature and will do much to help those less fortunate than himself.

He also gets much pleasure from gardening, and while he may not spend as much time in the garden as he would like, his garden is invariably well kept and productive.

The Rooster is generally very distinguished in his appearance and if his job permits he will wear an official uniform with great pride and dignity. He is not averse to publicity and takes great delight in being the centre of attention. He often does well at PR work or any job which brings him into contact with the media. He also makes a very good teacher.

The female Rooster leads a varied and interesting life. She involves herself in many different activities and there are some who wonder how she can achieve so much. She often holds very strong views and, like her male counterpart, has no hesitation in speaking her mind or telling others how she thinks things should be done. She is supremely efficient and well organized and her home is usually very neat and tidy. She has good taste in clothes and usually wears smart but very practical outfits.

The Rooster usually has a large family and takes a particularly active interest in the education of his children. He is very loyal to his partner and will find that he is especially well suited to those born under the signs of the Snake, Horse, Ox and Dragon. Provided they do not interfere too much in his various activities, the Rat, Tiger, Goat and Pig can also establish a good relationship with him, but two Roosters together are likely to squabble and irritate each other. The rather sensitive Rabbit will find the Rooster a bit too blunt for his liking, and the Rooster will quickly become exasperated by the ever-inquisitive and artful Monkey. He will also find it difficult to get on with the anxious Dog.

If the Rooster can overcome his volatile nature and exercise tact, he will go far in life. He is capable and talented and will make a lasting – and usually favourable – impression almost everywhere he goes.

THE FIVE DIFFERENT TYPES OF ROOSTER

In addition to the 12 signs of the Chinese zodiac there are five elements and these have a strengthening or moderating influence on the signs. The effects of the five elements on the Rooster are described below, together with the years in which they were exercising their influence. Therefore Roosters born in 1921 and 1981 are Metal Roosters, those born in 1933 and 1993 are Water Roosters, and so on.

Metal Rooster: 1921, 1981
The Metal Rooster is a hard and conscientious worker. He knows exactly what he wants in life and sets about everything in a positive and determined manner. He can at times appear abrasive and he would almost certainly do better if he were willing to reach a compromise with others rather than hold so rigidly to his beliefs. He is very articulate and most astute when dealing with financial matters. He is loyal to his friends and often devotes much energy to working for the common good.

Water Rooster: 1933, 1993

This Rooster has a very persuasive manner and can easily gain the co-operation of others. He is intelligent, well read and enjoys taking part in discussions and debates. He has a seemingly inexhaustible amount of energy and is prepared to work long hours in order to secure what he wants. He can, however, waste a lot of valuable time worrying over minor and inconsequential details. He is approachable, has a good sense of humour and is highly regarded by others.

Wood Rooster: 1945, 2005

The Wood Rooster is honest, reliable and often sets himself high standards. He is ambitious, but he is also more prepared to work in a team than some of the other types of Rooster. He usually succeeds in life but does have a tendency to get caught up in bureaucratic matters and attempt too many things at the same time. He has wide interests, likes to travel and is very caring and considerate towards his family and friends.

Fire Rooster: 1957

This Rooster is extremely strong-willed. He has many leadership qualities, is an excellent organizer and is most efficient in his work. Through sheer force of character he often secures his objectives, but he does have a tendency to be very forthright and not always consider the feelings of others. If he can learn to be more tactful, he can often succeed beyond his wildest dreams.

Earth Rooster: 1969

This Rooster has a deep and penetrating mind. He is efficient, perceptive and particularly astute in business and financial matters. He is also persistent and once he has set himself an objective, he will rarely allow himself to be deflected from achieving his aim. He works hard and is held in great esteem by his friends and colleagues. He usually enjoys the arts and takes a keen interest in the activities of the various members of his family.

PROSPECTS FOR THE ROOSTER IN 2012

The Rooster sets about life with considerable energy and in the Rabbit year (3 February 2011–22 January 2012) he will have enjoyed some positive times, even though his results may not always have matched his expectations. Rabbit years can be slow-moving and the Rooster will sometimes have been frustrated by the lack of developments. However, as the year draws to a close, many a Rooster will see an increase in activity.

In his work the Rooster could face new pressures, but these will give him the chance to make more of specific strengths and gain additional experience. By making the most of the challenges, he can do his standing and working relations with his colleagues a lot of good. October and November could see interesting work developments, including for Roosters seeking work.

The Rooster's home and social life will also see an increase in activity as the year draws to a close. With the

Rooster's organizational talents and good judgement, many around him will yet again be looking to him to play a key part in what is going on as well as be glad of his views on certain matters. The Rooster will enjoy some of the occasions that are planned for this time, including meeting up with relations or friends he does not often get to see. September and December could be two particularly full and interesting months socially.

The closing months of the year are a more expensive time and as Rabbit years are generally expensive ones for the Rooster, he should try to make early provision for some of the extra outlay he will have and handle his finances with care.

The Year of the Dragon starts on 23 January and will be an excellent one for the Rooster. This is a time when he can forge ahead with plans as well as enjoy pleasing developments in his personal life. For the Rooster, the Dragon year is one of the best.

There is a Chinese proverb which reminds us 'Well begun is half done' and if the Rooster has not already done so, as the year starts he should consider what he would like accomplish in the next 12 months. That way he will not only be able to direct his energy more effectively but also be more alert to the right type of opportunity to pursue. He should also talk his ideas over with those around him. In some cases they could assist in unexpected ways. This may be an auspicious year, but it is not one for the Rooster to adopt too independent a stance.

Work prospects are especially encouraging and any Rooster who has been disappointed with recent progress or is feeling unfulfilled in what he currently does can benefit from some excellent new opportunities. Those who work in relatively large organizations could find their experience and specialist knowledge now coming into their own. If promotion opportunities arise or there is the possibility to move to another section, they will often be well placed to benefit. This is very much a year when the Rooster should look to move his career forward.

If opportunities are limited where he is or he would welcome a more major change, again this is an excellent year to explore possibilities. By making enquiries, getting information and following up vacancies, many Roosters could secure an ideal position and, in the process, give their career new impetus.

The prospects are also encouraging for Roosters seeking work. Although obtaining a position will take considerable effort and the process may at times be disheartening, by making a special effort with their applications and at interview, including finding out more about the organization and what is required, many will secure a position they will be able to build on in the future. A key feature of the Dragon year is that it opens up opportunities that can suit the Rooster well. February to early April, June and November could see encouraging work developments, although with the aspects as they are, possibilities could arise at almost any time and the Rooster will need to remain alert.

Although he will have a lot to do over the year, it is also important that he allows time for recreational pursuits. Not only can these help him to relax and unwind but they can also often be a source of much satisfaction. In particular, if interested in creative pursuits, the Rooster could take great pleasure in pursuing certain ideas. In this active year he does need to allow himself the chance to do things he enjoys rather than remaining continually busy.

He will also value the social opportunities that arise over the year, particularly those that stem from his personal interests, and will often enjoy the chance to talk and socialize as well as go out and attend events. Affairs of the heart are also well aspected. Existing romances will often become more meaningful and quite a few unattached Roosters will meet someone special. Cupid will fire many an arrow in the Rooster's direction this year and this can be an exciting and eventful time. April, July, August and December could see the most social activity, although throughout the year the Rooster will often have interesting things to do.

There will also be a lot of activity in his home life and there will need to be good liaison and a willingness to share household tasks. But while the year will be busy, there will also be personal achievements to mark, including, for some, an addition to the family, as well as joint activities and plans to enjoy. However, practical projects could entail more disruption than anticipated. Also, one practical undertaking can often lead on to another. Improvements will take place in many a Rooster household this year, but the Rooster does need to be prepared for the upheaval.

His progress at work this year can also help him financially, however, and this will often persuade him to go ahead with various plans and purchases he has been considering for a while. If possible, he should make provision for a holiday over the year, as this could be something he particularly enjoys. In addition, if he can use any financial improvement to reduce borrowings or to save towards specific requirements, he may come to be grateful for his prudence. With thoughtful management, he can fare well this year.

In general, the Dragon year is one of considerable possibility for the Rooster and it will give him the opportunity to shine. He has style, presence and energy, and this is a year when he should look to move forward with determination and make the most of his opportunities. He will enjoy good support in many of his undertakings and his relations with others will often be special. This can be a year of considerable and deserving success for him.

The Metal Rooster

The Metal Rooster will have seen a great deal happen over the last few years and the Dragon year will see some of his efforts now paying off. This will be a successful and rewarding year for him and with the following Snake year also favourably aspected, this can be an auspicious stage in his life.

As the Dragon year starts the Metal Rooster would do well to give some thought to his current situation and what he would now like to achieve. By considering possibilities he will not only be reinforcing the progressive nature of the year but also giving himself something to work towards.

In his work the aspects are particularly encouraging. With the considerable experience and knowledge he has behind him, he will often be excellently placed to make progress. By keeping well informed and alert for opportunity, many Metal Roosters will secure promotion during the year or successfully transfer to another employer. As many will find, their reputation will stand them in excellent stead and allow them to move their career forward.

For Metal Roosters who would welcome a change or are seeking work, the Dragon year can again see some interesting developments. By considering what it is they would now like to do and exploring possibilities, these Metal Roosters can benefit from some significant opportunities. Their persistence and self-belief will often triumph and be rewarded with a position the Metal Rooster can build on in the future. February to early April, June and November could see some good opportunities.

The Dragon year can be a time when new activities or crazes can suddenly become popular and if the Metal Rooster should see something that appeals to him or he feels he could benefit from, he should follow this up. It could be related to physical fitness, new products, technology or a subject that interests him, but by remaining aware and being willing to follow up his ideas, the Metal Rooster can derive much value from activities started in the Dragon year.

With the aspects on his side, any Metal Rooster who enjoys creative pursuits should also consider making more of his talents and, if relevant, promoting what he does. His approach and style could bring forth an encouraging response.

Some Metal Roosters may also be able to put an interest or hobby to profitable use. Along with progress at work leading in many cases to an increase in earnings, this can be a financially improved year. In order to make the most of this, the Metal Rooster does, though, need to keep careful control of his outgoings and make provision for any major purchases or deposits he may be required to make. This is a year when good budgeting can make an important difference to how he fares.

With his active and outgoing nature, the Metal Rooster knows many people and can once more look forward to a frequently busy social life. He will get to meet quite a few new people this year and some will become good friends. For the unattached, an unexpected encounter can lead to love and, for some, change everything. April, July to early September and December could see the most social activity.

Domestically, too, a lot is set to happen in 2012 and some long-held hopes can be realized. For Metal Roosters with a partner, this can be a full and exciting year. Many could see an addition to their family and decide to move to better accommodation as well as have a personal or career success to mark. Some may decide to marry, such are the splendid and joyful aspects of the year.

The Metal Rooster will also be encouraged by the support of others. Many will be keen for him to make more of his potential and will advise him well. Over the year he should embrace this help and heed the advice given, and in return he too will encourage and assist many of those around him.

Although so much is in his favour this year, there is one cautionary note to be sounded: with so much happening and his busy lifestyle making his days full and nights sometimes long, the Metal Rooster does need to allow himself time to rest and catch up. To overdo things, skimp on exercise or not eat well could take its toll and lead to minor ailments. To keep himself on good form, he does need to look after himself. Metal Roosters, take note.

Overall, the Dragon year is a time of great personal opportunity for the Metal Rooster and if he uses his strengths and experience to advantage, he can look forward to making considerable progress and enjoying some deserved (and sometimes overdue) success. In 2012 he should act with determination. This is no time to waste. His personal life can also be a source of much happiness and help make this favourable year all the more special.

TIP FOR THE YEAR
Seize the initiative and make your hopes come true. Follow up your ideas and *remain determined*. This can be a successful time, but you do need to make things happen. With your experience and enthusiasm, plus the support of others, you have a great deal in your favour and now is the time to make it count. Good luck.

The Water Rooster

This is a year of considerable opportunity for the Water Rooster and will give him the chance to add to his experience and enjoy an often pleasing social life. Some developments during the year may take a curious course, but the Water Rooster will benefit from many of his activities and they can be of far-reaching value.

For the many Water Roosters in education who will be starting new courses this year, perhaps away from home for the first time, this can be a daunting but exciting time. There will be adjustments to make and new routines to get used to, as well as the challenges new subjects can bring. However, by keeping in mind the benefits of their studying, these Water Roosters will soon become immersed in what they have to do and settled in their new situation.

This is a year of considerable possibility for the Water Rooster and with a willing approach, he can find new opportunities opening up for him. Whether learning new subjects, trying out different pursuits or looking at new career options, he can find this an instructive and inspiring time.

For Water Roosters who are already at work, this is also a time of important developments. These Water Roosters will often be encouraged to take on greater responsibilities and be given further training as well as extra duties. Some might also find staff movements leading to suitable vacancies opening up for them. Almost all Water Roosters will experience change this year and have the chance to move forward.

The aspects are also encouraging for Water Roosters who are seeking work. Here events could take a curious course. By keeping alert for vacancies, many of these Water Roosters could discover a type of work they have not considered before but which will suit their personality and strengths perfectly. Some may find they are eligible for training or decide to take on an apprenticeship. Whatever the Water Rooster decides to do, by being active in the job-seeking process, he will have chances for further development. February to early April, June and November could see interesting possibilities, and for those who experience change early on in the year, further opportunities could occur in the last quarter. Dragon years are fast-moving and eventful.

With his outgoing nature, the Water Rooster enjoys good relations with many and over the year he will get to meet many more. Water Roosters in work can not only quickly become an appreciated member of any team but also make important friends among their colleagues. Similarly, those who find themselves in a new environment this year, perhaps through studying at university or moving for work, will enjoy making a new circle of friends. The Water Rooster's style, empathy and wide-ranging interests make him popular company and the Dragon year will be a busy time socially. For some, it can have the added excitement of romance. April, July to early September and December could see the most social activity.

Although the aspects are encouraging, there will, though, be some Water Roosters who start the year dissatisfied, alone and in a quandary about what to do. For these Water Roosters, the Dragon year can mark a turning point. By resolving to take action, exploring possibilities and, if appropriate, contacting advice centres for help, they can start to bring about the change they seek. It *will* take effort, but it is well worth doing.

With his interests, social life and living expenses, there will be many demands on the Water Rooster's resources this year and he will need to manage his money well. Also, if he takes on any new commitment, he should check the terms and obligations. Financially, this is a time for good control. For Water Roosters in education, there could also be the chance to supplement their means by casual or weekend work and this could not only be financially helpful but also give them useful work experience.

Personal interests are positively aspected, and whether going to events, trying out ideas or furthering skills, the Water Rooster will have both the time and opportunity to achieve a great deal. His activities will often have a good social element too. Some Water Roosters may also become involved in a new interest or recreational activity over the year. This is a time of opportunity and innovation.

With all that will happen for the Water Rooster this year, he will often value the support and assistance that those close to him can give. Relations and long-standing friends will not only follow his progress with interest but also be willing to advise when necessary. With much resting on certain decisions, it is important that the Water Rooster talks over his ideas and options with those around him. Everyone concerned will gain a lot from a spirit of openness. Also, while the Water Rooster will be frequently busy during the year, any help he can give to others, including assisting with household tasks, will be much appreciated.

Overall, a lot is set to happen in the Year of the Dragon, so much so that it can almost be regarded as a new chapter in the Water Rooster's life. Whether educationally or professionally, he will have opportunities to develop his skills and to show his potential. Effort and commitment may be needed, but what the Water Rooster does now can both reward him well this year and often have significant future value. Personally, too, this can also be an active year that brings pleasure and satisfaction.

TIP FOR THE YEAR

Be open to possibility. This is a fast-moving time and by making the most of the opportunities that come your way, you can gain a great deal. What you undertake now can often benefit you in the longer term. This is a fine year for you. Use it well.

The Wood Rooster

The Wood Rooster has a very practical nature. He is forward-looking and likes to plan and keep involved in things. Rarely is he at a loss for something to do and the Dragon year promises to be a full and rewarding one for him.

Over the year there will be several areas that he will be keen to give some attention to. One of these will be his accommodation. Whether redecorating, sorting and tidying out his home or replacing certain items, he will set about what needs to be done with considerable energy. Not only will he enjoy making choices but he will also take pleasure in the results of his actions. However, many Wood Roosters will find that one project can easily lead on to another! Also while the Wood Rooster will be keen to do a lot himself, if any of his projects involves hazardous or strenuous activity, he should take extra care or enlist the help of a professional. This *is* a year of much practical activity but it is no year for risks.

With much attention focused on the home, some Wood Roosters may also feel this a good time to move, perhaps not only to accommodation that better meets their needs but also to an area they have long favoured. The Dragon year is certainly an active one and the Wood Rooster's ideas can lead to a lot happening in his home life.

In addition to all the practical activity, the Wood Rooster will take great pleasure in his contact with family members. There will be developments to follow, news to hear and achievements to enjoy. The Wood Rooster will often be pleased to give time and advice to those close to him and his support may be more appreciated than he may realize.

There will also be good travel opportunities over the year and if the Wood Rooster receives an invitation to stay with others or sees a holiday offer that particularly appeals to him, he should follow it up. Time away with his loved ones can bring him a great deal of pleasure. Again, it is very much a case of making the most of his opportunities this year.

Another area which can bring the Wood Rooster much satisfaction in the Dragon year is his interests. This is a time favouring creativity and enterprise and the Wood Rooster may delight in trying out ideas, taking certain interests further or indeed getting involved in new ones.

His social life can also see some positive developments. Some Wood Roosters will decide to join a local activity or social group over the year and will not only enjoy the chance to meet others but become immersed in the activities going on. This is a time for involvement and sharing.

The Wood Rooster will also value his close circle of friends and enjoy the chance to talk to those he knows well. One friendship could prove especially important and supportive this year, and for the lonely and unattached, the Dragon year has romantic possibilities. April, July, August and December could see the most social activity, although at most times of the year, the Wood Rooster will have interesting things to do and events to look forward to.

His financial prospects are reasonably aspected, but he will need to make adequate provision for expensive plans and purchases and manage his budget well. Also, if authorizing any work to be carried out, particularly on his home, he should check what is covered as well as obtain several quotations. Where finance is concerned, the more thorough he is, the better.

Another area which requires care this year is his well-being. As well as taking care if involved in strenuous activities (including gardening), the Wood Rooster should give some attention to his general level of exercise and the quality of his diet. Some Wood Roosters may choose to take advantage of recreational facilities in their area to improve their lifestyle. Some personal consideration and care can make a noticeable difference this year.

In general, the Year of the Dragon can be a full and interesting one for the Wood Rooster. His many ideas can lead to a lot happening, and with the help of family and friends, he will be pleased with what he is able to accomplish. A personally rewarding and satisfying year.

TIP FOR THE YEAR
Take action. Whether undertaking home projects, pursuing new or existing interests, joining local groups or going out more, you can find your activities bringing you pleasure and benefit.

The Fire Rooster

The Fire Rooster possesses great resolve and when he has objectives he is keen to reach, he will work tirelessly until he has achieved his aims. In the Dragon year his strong will and sense of purpose will lead to a great deal being achieved. This is a positive, progressive and often fortunate time.

With his tendency to plan ahead, as the year starts the Fire Rooster may already have thoughts about what he would like to see happen in the next 12 months. His plans could be work-related, concern ideas or activities he is keen to develop or have to do with special occasions in his home and family life. Whatever he chooses to focus on, by having something definite to work towards, he will not only be able to direct his energies more effectively but also benefit from some particularly good opportunities. This is a year to be active and alert.

At work the aspects are especially encouraging. Dragon years favour enterprise and the Fire Rooster's often extensive experience and resourceful nature can lead to some important success. The Dragon year will give many Fire Roosters the chance to prosper and their contribution (and loyalty) will often be rewarded with promotion or the offer of a more specialist role.

Most Fire Roosters will remain with their present employer over the year, but for those tempted to move elsewhere, the Dragon year can bring some excellent opportunities. Some will find their experience and contacts helpful in their quest. By keeping alert, talking to those they know and making enquiries, they may find their initiative rewarded with an important new position. It may take time, but as the Fire Rooster has so often proved, when he has set his mind to a task he sees it through, and his determination and self-belief will help him prevail this year.

The same is true for Fire Roosters seeking work. By remaining steadfast and resourceful, they may well be successful in securing a new opening. Even if this is in a slightly lesser role than they hoped for, it will often be something they can build on. February to early April, June and November could see some particularly good opportunities, but such are the aspects that at almost any time the Fire Rooster could have ideas worth considering.

Another satisfying aspect of the year will be the way the Fire Rooster will be able to further his experience. Particularly when taking on a new role, he will have an excellent opportunity to learn about other aspects of his work and industry and so extend his skills.

However, the progressive aspects need not be restricted to his work. If there are certain interests he would like to develop or something new catches his attention, he should set time aside to follow this up. By exploring his ideas, he will be able to get much personal value from what he is able to do. For any Fire Roosters who start the Dragon year dissatisfied, it would be well worth considering starting a new pursuit or setting themselves a new challenge.

The progress the Fire Rooster makes at work can also help his financial position. Many Fire Roosters will increase their earnings over the year and some could also receive a gift or bonus or benefit from some financial good fortune. However, to make the most of any improvement, the Fire Rooster would find it helpful to review his current situation and, if he is able, reduce borrowings as well as set money aside for future plans. Careful thought and good financial control will be to his benefit.

With his outgoing nature and wide interests, the Fire Rooster enjoys positive relations with many people and over the year he will again find himself in demand. His circle of acquaintances is set to grow, with April, July, August and December seeing the most social activity. Importantly, any Fire Roosters who, due to personal circumstances, would welcome a more active social life or new friendships (or romance) can find the Dragon year seeing a definite brightening in their situation. By finding out about activities in their area and going out more, they can help bring about the improvement they seek.

The Fire Rooster's home life will also see considerable activity during the year and there will be some personal and family success to look forward to. Some Fire Roosters could become grandparents this year as well as delight in the achievements of a younger relation. There will be moments this year which will bring many a Fire Rooster considerable pride. In addition, he will enjoy planning ideas and tackling projects with his loved ones. This is a year favouring joint effort.

However, although the aspects are favourable, no year is ever free of problems and this one will be no exception. The Fire Rooster takes his responsibilities seriously and there will be occasions when he will feel under pressure. At such times he should focus on priorities rather than spread his energies too widely. Others will be supportive and he should also avail himself of the extra help they can give. Fire Roosters, do remember this.

Also, with this being such a busy year, the Fire Rooster needs to make sure he has regular exercise and a balanced diet. Neglecting his own well-being could leave him prone to minor ailments. If at any time he has any concerns, he should get these checked out.

In many respects, however, this can be a rewarding and personally successful year for the Fire Rooster. By taking the initiative and using his ideas and experience to advantage, he will enjoy advancing his career and the success this brings. His relations with others will also be positive and there will be some meaningful times to enjoy with loved ones. Overall, an auspicious time.

TIP FOR THE YEAR
Decide on your objectives for the year and then take action. Once you start, your activities can develop a momentum of their own and some interesting possibilities can open up. Be bold, be enterprising, believe in yourself and use your personal qualities well. This is a year for progress ... and success.

The Earth Rooster

The Earth Rooster will have seen a lot happen in recent years, some of it good, some disappointing. As the Dragon year starts, he will feel ready in himself to move ahead and will set about his aims with considerable resolve. Pleasingly, his actions will reward him well.

His work prospects are especially encouraging. For Earth Roosters who are well established in a profession, this is a year when they can take their career to a new level. Sometimes openings could occur as more senior colleagues move on or reorganization takes place. With his background and reputation, the Earth Rooster will often be qualified and ready for a greater role. Events can sometimes take a surprising course. When promotion comes or a new position is offered, it may be in a slightly different capacity from what the Earth Rooster was expecting. However, by rising to the challenge, he will quickly immerse himself in his new role.

For Earth Roosters who feel opportunities are limited where they are, as well as those seeking work, the Dragon year can again bring important developments. By carefully thinking through what it is they now want to do and seeking advice from relevant organizations, they can have some interesting possibilities to consider. Again, these Earth Roosters will need to be flexible, but even if what they are looking for is not immediately available, by making applications and remaining determined, many will secure an entry into a new line of work. February to early April, June to mid-July and November could see some encouraging developments.

Progress at work will also help financially and some Earth Roosters will benefit from an additional source of revenue, perhaps from an enterprising idea, extra work or gift. However, while the financial aspects are promising, the Earth Rooster will need to manage his resources well. With his existing commitments and some of the plans and purchases he is keen to undertake, he will need to make advance provision for larger outlays. Also, when considering any major transaction, he should check the terms and obligations and compare the options available to him. This may be a favourable year, but where cost implications are involved, it is no time to rush or be lax. Earth Roosters, take note and, where necessary, take your time and seek appropriate advice.

A satisfying element of the year will be the creative possibilities that open up. Whether putting forward ideas in his work or pursuing a personal interest, this can be an inspiring time for the Earth Rooster and allow him to make more of his often special talents.

With all the activity of the year he does, though, need to balance out his various activities and give himself time to relax and unwind. Also, to keep himself in good form he needs to pay attention to his diet and level of exercise, and if he feels improvements could be made, seek advice. With the Dragon year holding so much potential for him, he should aim to be at his best throughout.

His social life will also see an increase in activity this year and, being a masterful communicator, he will particularly delight in some of the conversations he has, especially when discussing certain developments and ideas. Some talks could particularly inspire him and give him new possibilities to consider. For any Earth Rooster who would welcome new friendships or romance, the Dragon year can also provide some marvellous opportunities. April, late June to August and December could see the most social activity, but on a personal level, many an Earth Rooster will find himself in demand throughout the year.

The Earth Rooster's home life will also see considerable activity, as well as some change. As a result of developments in his own work situation or his partner's, the year could involve some adjustments being made. However, with good co-operation, new patterns can quickly be established and in some cases lead to unexpected benefits. The Earth Rooster will value the often special rapport he has with those close to him and there could be some meaningful family occasions during the year. The Earth Rooster's home life can be another positive aspect of this often significant year.

Overall, the Dragon year holds great possibility for the Earth Rooster and by putting forward ideas and making his experience and personal qualities count, he can make important headway at work and also enjoy some pleasing personal success. In 2012 he will have much in his favour and can make this a fine and satisfying year.

TIP FOR THE YEAR

This is a year of great potential. However, while you have much in your favour, do keep your lifestyle in balance and preserve time for your loved ones and to enjoy the rewards of your efforts.

FAMOUS ROOSTERS

Fernando Alonso, Javier Bardem, Beyoncé, Cate Blanchett, Barbara Taylor Bradford, Gerard Butler, Sir Michael Caine, Enrico Caruso, Eric Clapton, Joan Collins, Rita Coolidge, Daniel Day Lewis, Minnie Driver, the Duke of Edinburgh, Gloria Estefan, Roger Federer, Errol Flynn, Benjamin Franklin, Dawn French, Stephen Fry, Melanie Griffith, Josh Groban, Goldie Hawn, Katharine Hepburn, Paris Hilton, Jay-Z, Catherine Zeta Jones, Quincy Jones, Diane Keaton, Søren Kierkegaard, David Livingstone, Jayne Mansfield, Steve Martin, James Mason, W. Somerset Maugham, Paul Merton, Bette Midler, Ed Miliband, Van Morrison, Willie Nelson, Kim Novak, Yoko Ono, Dolly Parton, Matthew Perry, Michelle Pfeiffer, Natalie Portman, Priscilla Presley, Joan Rivers, Kelly Rowland, Jenny Seagrove, George Segal, Carly Simon, Britney Spears, Johann Strauss, Verdi, Richard Wagner, Catherine Wales (Kate Middleton), Serena Williams, Neil Young, Renée Zellweger.

---

28 JANUARY 1922 ～ 15 FEBRUARY 1923   *Water Dog*

14 FEBRUARY 1934 ～ 3 FEBRUARY 1935   *Wood Dog*

2 FEBRUARY 1946 ～ 21 JANUARY 1947   *Fire Dog*

18 FEBRUARY 1958 ～ 7 FEBRUARY 1959   *Earth Dog*

6 FEBRUARY 1970 ～ 26 JANUARY 1971   *Metal Dog*

25 JANUARY 1982 ～ 12 FEBRUARY 1983   *Water Dog*

10 FEBRUARY 1994 ～ 30 JANUARY 1995   *Wood Dog*

29 JANUARY 2006 ～ 17 FEBRUARY 2007   *Fire Dog*

THE
DOG

THE PERSONALITY OF THE DOG

I have my values
and beliefs.
These are my beacon
in an ever-changing world.

The Dog is born under the signs of loyalty and anxiety. He usually holds very firm views and beliefs and is the champion of good causes. He hates any sort of injustice or unfair treatment and will do all in his power to help those less fortunate than himself. He has a strong sense of fair play and will be honourable and open in all his dealings.

The Dog is very direct and straightforward. He is never one to skirt round issues and speaks frankly and to the point. He can be stubborn, but he is prepared to listen to the views of others and will try to be as fair as possible in coming to his decisions. He will readily give advice where it is needed and will be the first to offer assistance when things go wrong.

The Dog instils confidence wherever he goes and there are many who admire him for his integrity and resolute manner. He is a very good judge of character and can often form an accurate impression of someone very shortly after meeting them. He is also very intuitive and can frequently sense how things are going to work out long in advance.

Despite his friendly and amiable manner, the Dog is not a big socializer. He dislikes having to attend large functions or parties and much prefers a quiet meal with friends or a chat by the fire. He is an excellent conversationalist and is often a marvellous raconteur of amusing stories and anecdotes.

The Dog is also quick-witted and his mind is always alert. He can keep calm in a crisis and although he does have a temper, his outbursts tend to be short-lived. He is loyal and trustworthy, but if he ever feels badly let down or rejected by someone, he will rarely forgive or forget.

The Dog usually has very set interests. He prefers to specialize and become an expert in a chosen area rather than dabble in a variety of different activities. He usually does well in jobs where he feels that he is being of service to others and is often suited to careers in the social services, the medical and legal professions and teaching. He does, however, need to feel motivated in his work. He has to have a sense of purpose and if ever this is lacking he can quite often drift through life without ever achieving very much. Once he has the motivation, however, very little can prevent him from securing his objective.

Another characteristic of the Dog is his tendency to worry and to view things rather pessimistically. Quite often his worries are totally unnecessary and are of his own making. Although it may be difficult, worrying is a habit that all Dogs should try to overcome.

The Dog is not materialistic or particularly bothered about accumulating great wealth. As long as he has the money necessary to support his family and to spend on the occasional luxury, he is more than happy. However, when he does have any spare money he tends to be rather a spendthrift and does not always put it to its best use. He is also not a very good speculator and would be advised to get professional advice before entering into any major long-term investment.

The Dog will rarely be short of admirers, but he is not an easy person to live with. His moods are changeable and his standards high, but he will be loyal and protective to his partner and will do all in his power to provide a comfortable home. He can get on extremely well with those born under the signs of the Horse, Pig, Tiger and Monkey, and can also establish a sound and stable relationship with the Rat, Ox, Rabbit, Snake and another Dog, but will find the Dragon a bit too flamboyant for his liking. He will also find it difficult to understand the imaginative Goat and is likely to be highly irritated by the candid Rooster.

The female Dog is renowned for her beauty. She has a warm and caring nature, although until she knows someone well she can be both secretive and very guarded. She is highly intelligent and despite her calm and tranquil appearance can be extremely ambitious. She enjoys sport and other outdoor activities and has a happy knack of finding bargains in the most unlikely of places. She can also get rather impatient when things do not work out as she would like.

The Dog usually has a very good way with children and can be a doting parent. He will rarely be happier than when he is helping someone or doing something that will benefit others. Providing he can cure himself of his tendency to worry, he will lead a very full and active life, and in that life he will make many friends and do a tremendous amount of good.

THE FIVE DIFFERENT TYPES
OF DOG

In addition to the 12 signs of the Chinese zodiac there are five elements and these have a strengthening or moderating influence on the signs. The effects of the five elements on the Dog are described below, together with the years in which they were exercising their influence. Therefore Dogs born in 1970 are Metal Dogs, those born in 1922 and 1982 are Water Dogs, and so on.

Metal Dog: 1970
The Metal Dog is bold, confident and forthright and sets about everything he does in a resolute and determined manner. He has great belief in his abilities and no hesitation about speaking his mind or devoting himself to some just cause. He can be rather serious at times and can become anxious and irritable when things are not going according to plan. He tends to have very specific interests and it would certainly help him if he were to broaden his outlook and become more involved in group activities. He is extremely loyal and faithful to his friends.

Water Dog: 1922, 1982
The Water Dog has a very direct and outgoing personality. He is an excellent communicator and has little trouble in

persuading others to fall in with his plans. He does, however, have a somewhat carefree nature and is not as disciplined or as thorough as he should be in certain matters. Neither does he keep as much control over his finances as he should, but he can be most generous to his family and friends and will make sure that they want for nothing. He is usually very good with children and has a wide circle of friends.

Wood Dog: 1934, 1994

This Dog is a hard and conscientious worker and will usually make a favourable impression wherever he goes. He is less independent than some of the other types of Dog and prefers to work in a group rather than on his own. He is popular, has a good sense of humour and takes a keen interest in the activities of the various members of his family. He is often attracted to the finer things in life and can obtain much pleasure from collecting items of interest, beauty or antiquity. He prefers to live in the country rather than the town.

Fire Dog: 1946, 2006

This Dog has a lively, outgoing personality and is able to establish friendships with remarkable ease. He is an honest and conscientious worker and likes to take an active part in all that is going on around him. He also likes to explore new ideas and providing he can get the necessary support and advice, he can often succeed where others have failed. He does, however, have a tendency to be stubborn.

Providing he can overcome this, he can often achieve considerable fame and fortune.

Earth Dog: 1958

The Earth Dog is very talented and astute. He is methodical and efficient and is capable of going far in his chosen profession. He tends to be rather quiet and reserved, but has a very persuasive manner and usually secures his objectives without too much opposition. He is generous and kind and always ready to lend a helping hand when it is needed. He is also held in very high esteem by his friends and colleagues and is usually most dignified in his appearance.

PROSPECTS FOR THE DOG IN 2012

The Year of the Rabbit (3 February 2011–22 January 2012) is a generally favourable one for the Dog and a lot is set to happen in the closing months.

The Dog has a loyal and true nature and throughout the Rabbit year many people will have appreciated his kind ways. Rabbit years very much favour affairs of the heart and as this one draws to a close, for the unattached there will be some excellent romantic possibilities, while for those newly in love, their relationship will often become more meaningful.

There will also be an increase in social opportunities at this time, with the Dog enjoying renewing old acquaintances and going to some interesting occasions.

This can also be a rewarding time domestically, with loved ones being supportive and some surprises or interesting family news coming late on in the year. Accommodation matters may require additional attention at this time.

During the Rabbit year there will have been opportunities for many Dogs to make progress in their work and the last few months will require some flexibility as workloads and routines are altered, but this too can be a productive time. For Dogs seeking work or desiring change, September to the end of October could see some interesting possibilities.

Overall, the Year of the Rabbit will have brought some good opportunities for the Dog and by acting on these he will have managed to gain a lot from the year.

The Year of the Dragon starts on 23 January and will be a mixed one for the Dog. Dogs are careful in their manner and like to think and plan ahead. They are not ones for acting on impulse or adapting well to sudden change, but this is the way of the Dragon year. It can be a fast-moving time and its developments will cause concern for many a Dog. However, while this may be a challenging year, it is at such times that personal qualities are tested and lessons learned.

One of the Dog's chief traits is that he is conscientious. He cares about what he does and takes his responsibilities seriously. However, because he is so caring, he can also be a worrier. In the Dragon year, if he is worried or under pressure, it is important that he talks to others. 'A worry shared is a worry halved', as the saying reminds us, and if the Dog does share his worries he will often find they can be put into perspective and support given. He should not feel he is on his own this year, for there are many he can turn to and talk to.

In his work he will often face increased pressures. Not only could his own workload suddenly become much greater but he could find bureaucracy, staff shortages or the introduction of new procedures complicating what he has to do. However, demanding though some of the year may be, the best policy for the Dog is to knuckle down and do his best. Amid the uncertainty, he will be seen as dependable and this will be appreciated.

Also, while he may not welcome some of the initiatives, the Dog can benefit from them. New positions could be created or he could be given the chance to work in another capacity. Despite his misgivings, the Dog should not be resistant to change, for it can often be to his longer-term advantage.

Although conditions may not be ideal this year, many Dogs will remain with their present employer and will have the chance to vary their role. For those who decide to move on or are seeking work, the Dragon year can be challenging. Not only will competition be fierce but openings could be limited. However, another of the Dog's qualities is his tenacity, and by keeping alert and putting himself forward, he will ultimately prevail. In addition, the year could have surprises in store. Although some Dogs may not be offered the type of work they were originally seeking, what happens this year can set their career off on an interesting new path. The tribulations of the Dragon year can have hidden benefits. March and August to October could see some interesting chances.

Financially, the Dog will need to be careful. When making major purchases he should make sure his requirements are fully met and that he checks the terms and implications. If he has any uncertainties, he should seek clarification. Similarly, when out shopping, he should give careful thought to his purchases. Without care, his spending could mount up and hurried purchases be regretted. In money matters, he needs to remain disciplined.

More positively, the Dog can get great satisfaction from his interests this year. Not only can these help take his mind off other pressures but also give him a chance to relax and enjoy something different. Whether pursuing an existing interest or taking up something new, he deserves some 'me time' this year. Any Dog who has let his interests lapse would do well to rectify this early on in the year and look for a new hobby or pursuit.

In addition, the Dog needs to give some consideration to his well-being. If he feels some changes in his diet and level of exercise could be of benefit, he should seek medical advice on the best way to proceed. With this being a demanding year, he does need to take good care of himself.

The Dog often prefers to have a small social circle and form friendships over many years. During the Dragon year he will be particularly grateful for the special way certain friends are able to advise or assist. In this sometimes challenging year, it is important that he avails himself of their help and expertise.

Certain interests or activities the Dog pursues this year can also have a pleasing social element. April, May, July and August could see the most social activity.

Where matters of the heart are concerned, this is, though, a year for care and mindfulness. For Dogs enjoying romance, especially if started in the Rabbit year, the relationship will need to be nurtured, and for any who start a new romance this year, time needs to be allowed to build mutual understanding. Rush, pressure or high expectations too early on can lead to heartache. Dogs, take note and be patient and attentive.

The Dog's home life will be generally busy this year and with his caring nature he will often find himself worrying about the activities of loved ones and attending to a great many things. Again, it is important that he does not shoulder too much on his own. Also, with some developments in his household happening quickly, there will need to be flexibility over certain plans. However, while the year will bring its pressures, there will also be much that will please the Dog and amid all the activity there will be moments he will savour.

In general, the Dog will not always feel comfortable with the pace and pressure of the Dragon year. Events can happen quickly and the year will lack the stability and order the Dog prefers. However, he can gain valuable experience and benefit from opportunities that might not have been possible before. Difficult though it may sometimes be, this is a year to go with the flow and make the best of situations *as they are.* It is also important during busy times that the Dog keeps his lifestyle in balance and preserves time for his loved ones, friends and interests. It will be a demanding year, but it will have its benefits and also prepare the Dog for the better times that await next year.

The Metal Dog

The Metal Dog's qualities will be tested in this interesting although sometimes challenging time. Dragon years can see sudden change and the Metal Dog will often be concerned by this. However, the year can also be the catalyst for new possibilities.

This is especially the case in the Metal Dog's work. Whether as a result of what is happening in his industry, new legislation or internal restructuring, he is likely to see change. Few Metal Dogs will remain untouched by the year's developments. And although the Metal Dog may foresee difficulties ahead (including problems in setting about some of his own duties), it is a case of making the best of things. Also, by accepting rather than resisting change, the Metal Dog could benefit from some of the opportunities that now become available, perhaps transferring to new duties or another section. The Dragon year will certainly create openings that can further the Metal Dog's experience.

In view of current developments, some Metal Dogs may decide to seek employment elsewhere and possibly change the nature of what they do. They may feel forced into this by the changes that have taken place, but if they give careful consideration to their options, they can see some exciting chances emerging. This is not a year for the Metal Dog to be too narrow in his thinking but be open to possibility.

This also applies to Metal Dogs seeking work. With the job market often difficult, they should widen the scope of what they are prepared to consider and remain alert for openings to pursue. By being willing to learn and adapt, many will be successful in securing work in a different capacity. For all its vexations, the Dragon year does offer opportunities. March and mid-July to the end of August could see some important developments.

With the pressures of the year it is also important that the Metal Dog gives some consideration to his well-being, including his general lifestyle and level of exercise and diet. A few changes can make a real difference.

He should also allow himself time for his personal interests. These can not only help keep his lifestyle in balance but also give him the chance to enjoy something different from his everyday activities.

With travel favourably aspected, the Metal Dog should also try to go away for a holiday during the year. The rest and change of scene can do him a lot of good. Travel opportunities could arise at short notice and to take advantage of them the Metal Dog may need to rearrange certain plans. Dragon years favour spontaneity.

In money matters the Metal Dog will need to be disciplined and budget carefully for the plans he has in mind for the year. Also, when entering into any agreement or dealing with other paperwork he should check the details and question anything which concerns him. This is a year to be thorough and vigilant and exercise good control.

The Metal Dog likes to keep his social circle relatively small, but some friends he has known for many years could offer him particularly good support and in this fast-moving year it is important that he avails himself of their help. Also, if he has opportunities to go to events that appeal to him, he should take these up. They can add balance and variety to his lifestyle. Metal Dogs who are newly in love should, though, be aware, attentive and mindful at all times. New relationships will need to be carefully nurtured if they are to endure.

In his home life, the Metal Dog will see considerable activity and there will need to be good communication and co-operation. Joint effort will pay off. For Metal Dogs who are parents, there will be the achievements of children to mark as well as the pleasure that their development can bring. In addition, shared interests, short breaks and other outings can lead to some happy times. As always, the Metal Dog will be instrumental in much that goes on and his thoughtfulness and care will be valued by his loved ones.

Overall, the Dragon year can be a demanding one for the Metal Dog. He may face pressures, often work-related, and have to adapt to change. But by being willing to rise to the challenges *and opportunities* the year will bring, he can gain valuable experience. In this respect, the Dragon year can be viewed as an important stepping-stone to the brighter and more successful times ahead.

TIP FOR THE YEAR
Give yourself some time this year – for your own interests, for recreation and to keep your lifestyle in balance. Also, be open to the possibilities the Dragon year can bring. These can have both present and future significance.

The Water Dog

This year marks the start of a new decade in the Water Dog's life and as he enters his thirties, he will not only be keen to make the most of this year but also to make progress towards his goals. As the Chinese proverb reminds us, 'With aspirations, you can go anywhere; without aspirations, you can go nowhere.' The versatile Water Dog certainly has his aspirations, but he will also realize that some of what he is hoping for is for the longer term and will not be possible this year. Dragon years can bring their obstacles but equally give the Water Dog an excellent chance to extend his experience and uncover new strengths. Rather than regard this as a particularly progressive year, he should look on it as an illuminating one. Its lessons can be far-reaching.

Many Water Dogs will have reached an interesting juncture in their career. Having now gained a good working knowledge of their industry, they will be keen to take their career to a new level. However, developments in the Dragon year can take a curious course. With many companies and organizations undergoing change, the Water Dog could find his best prospects are through a change of duties and possibly moving to another section. By being willing to do this, however, he can not only gain important new experience but also discover talents he did not know he had. What he can achieve in this fast-moving year can often be to his long-term advantage.

The majority of Water Dogs will remain with their present employer over the year, but for those keen to move elsewhere or currently seeking work, the Dragon year can have important developments in store. By widening the range of positions they are prepared to consider and keeping themselves informed, many could be offered a position which suits their talents well. The key to success this year is to be flexible and act quickly when opportunities arise. March and August to October could see some particularly interesting developments.

Progress at work will allow many Water Dogs to increase their income, but this is still a year for discipline in money matters. With his current commitments and some expensive plans, including deposits he may need to put down, the Water Dog should keep a close watch on spending. With good budgeting, however, some important plans can be realized.

Also, with travel favourably aspected and this year marking his thirtieth birthday, the Water Dog may be tempted to take a special holiday, and this can be one of the year's highlights.

With his active lifestyle, it is also important that he pays attention to his well-being. With long days and sometimes long nights he does drive himself hard, and should make sure he allows time to rest and exercise (especially if sedentary for much of the day) and has a nutritious diet. To push himself too hard could leave him susceptible to minor ailments. Water Dogs, take note and do look after yourselves.

Also, while the Water Dog's days will often be full, he should still set aside time to develop his personal interests. Not only can these sometimes give him the benefit of additional exercise but also have a pleasant social side. For Water Dogs who enjoy creative pursuits, this is an excellent year to consider promoting what they do. Dragon years favour originality and the Water Dog's many ideas and talents can open up some interesting possibilities.

The Water Dog will also value the support of his friends during the year and should aim to keep in regular contact with them. Their insights, support and news can often help and encourage him. Also, in view of the changing situations he is likely to face, he should make the most of any chances to meet others as well as take up any social invitations he receives. By remaining active, he can get much pleasure from his social life, with April, May, July and August likely to see the most activity.

However, for those in the early stages of romance, care and time are needed. To appear too preoccupied or take the feelings of another for granted could lead to difficulty and upset. Romance needs special attention this year. Water Dogs, take note.

In the Water Dog's domestic life, this can be a full and exciting year. In addition to the marking of his thirtieth birthday, he will often have various plans he is keen to proceed with. This year favours joint action and the Water Dog will do best by talking over his ideas, including the implications and costs, and being prepared to share a lot of what he does. In this way, although this will be a busy year, it can be a fulfilling one, especially as some personal and accommodation hopes are realized.

Overall, the Water Dog's thirtieth year can be a significant one. It is a time to be aware, to adapt and to make the most of current situations. What the Water Dog can learn over the year can give him a solid base on which to build in the future, especially in the following and more auspicious Snake year. He will also be encouraged by the support he receives from those around him, with his home life often being special and certain cherished ideas being realized. This will prove an interesting start to this new decade in his life – a decade which, with his aspirations, promises much.

TIP FOR THE YEAR

You are forward-looking, but in this fast-paced year be flexible too. You can gain a lot this year, but it does require an adaptable approach. Also, allow time to spend on your interests and with others. With good lifestyle balance, your thirtieth year can be meaningful and have far-reaching value.

The Wood Dog

There is a Chinese proverb which offers valuable guidance to the Wood Dog this year: 'There is no limit to learning.' No matter what the Wood Dog's present position, this can be a pivotal year for him and by making the most of his opportunities, he can do himself a lot of good.

For the many Wood Dogs in education, there will be a lot to do and some important decisions to take. The Wood Dog should be disciplined in his studying and plan how he can use his time most effectively. By keeping on top of his work and starting revision and any exam preparation early on, he can not only help ease last-minute pressures but also fare better as a result. For those with important exams to take, this is a time to remain focused and dedicated.

In addition, many Wood Dogs will have important decisions to take. These could include selecting courses for later study as well as choosing and starting at a new place of learning. For quite a few, parts of the year will be daunting, but at the same time this can mark the start of an exciting new phase for the Wood Dog. When making decisions, it is important that he discusses his options with those who have the knowledge and experience to advise. That way his choices will be made easier and better decisions can be made.

This can also be a significant year as far as work prospects are concerned. Those Wood Dogs already in a position could find the nature of their work changing. There could be new procedures to learn, changes in routine to adapt to and possibly greater responsibilities to take on. Some of what is asked of the Wood Dog will be daunting, but will nevertheless be a good opportunity for him to prove what he can do. And in the process many Wood Dogs will discover special aptitudes they will be keen to take further.

For Wood Dogs who decide to move on from where they currently work as well as those seeking a position, the Dragon year can be challenging. Obtaining a position will require considerable effort and when making applications these Wood Dogs should find out more about the work involved so they can stress any relevant skills and interests as well as indicate their willingness to learn. With extra effort, chances will be given that the Wood Dog can build on in the future. March and August to October could see some encouraging developments, but opportunities do need to be seized quickly when they arise.

Although the Dragon year will have its pressures, it will also have its pleasing aspects, and one of these will concern the Wood Dog's personal interests. Whether he prefers sport and more physical activities or something practical and creative, he will find much of what he does over the year not only satisfying but also leading on to other opportunities. With this being a year favouring the new, some Wood Dogs could be tempted by new recreational pursuits.

In addition, there could be travel opportunities and the chance to visit some interesting destinations.

With all his various plans and activities, the Wood Dog will, however, need to be careful in money matters. Too many impulse buys could result in him having to cut back on other activities. This is a year for good control over the purse strings.

The Wood Dog will value his close circle of friends over the year and often be grateful for their support and understanding. Some will have similar concerns to his own and talking these over can be of help to all. As a result of his interests, the Wood Dog will also have the chance to meet some new people this year and some will become valued friends. For a few Wood Dogs the year can also bring romance, although if it is to endure, great care and consideration will be needed. Affairs of the heart can be problematical in Dragon years.

Although the Wood Dog will often be kept busy with his own concerns, he should also involve himself in his home life. Being forthcoming and helping out when needed will not only lead to better understanding all round but also allow him to share more of the activities of the year. In addition, with this being his eighteenth year, there could be some surprises in store and the Wood Dog will often be buoyed up by the affection shown him.

Overall, the Year of the Dragon will be an important one for the Wood Dog. However, it will require effort. With discipline, commitment and a willingness to move forward, the Wood Dog can pave the way for the success that awaits in following years.

TIP FOR THE YEAR
Have self-belief. There will be some difficult moments and decisions this year, but it is worth putting in the effort now so that you can benefit from the possibilities that lie ahead. Good luck.

The Fire Dog

This is a year of important possibility for the Fire Dog. Dragon years are times of change and renewal, and over the year many Fire Dogs will be giving careful thought to their future. In their deliberations, they should draw on the support of those who are close to them. With advice and sometimes practical assistance, not only can some of their decisions be made easier, but they may be actively encouraged to go ahead with certain plans. Although some Fire Dogs do have a tendency to keep their thoughts to themselves, this is very much a year to be forthcoming.

Fire Dogs who are retired or retire this year will often have specific interests they are keen to pursue. However, they could find other interesting possibilities opening up too, including the chance to join local enthusiasts or use nearby amenities. As these Fire Dogs will quickly discover, this is no year for standing still and there will be real opportunities to advance their interests and pastimes.

Some of what the Fire Dog chooses to do this year can have a pleasing social element and it would be worth any Fire Dogs who would welcome a more active social life considering joining a local society or interest group. By making enquiries at local centres or their library, they could discover there is more going on in their area than they thought.

The Dragon year also favours travel and the Fire Dog should take up any offers that appeal to him. Over the year he could visit some particularly interesting destinations and if he is able to combine his travels with a special interest or event, this could give his time away more meaning.

However, while it can bring pleasure, the Dragon year can also bring difficulties. In particular, the Fire Dog could find himself in a bureaucratic wrangle which, while not necessarily serious, could take time and effort to resolve. To help prevent problems from arising, he does need to be thorough when dealing with paperwork. Care is also needed with financial matters. If considering a major purchase or authorizing work to be carried out, the Fire Dog does need to check what is involved. Many Fire Dogs will have additional accommodation expenses this year and some will decide this is a good time to move. Again these Fire Dogs should keep a close watch on expenses and seek advice if anything concerns them.

The Fire Dog should also take care with his well-being over the year and if involved in any strenuous pursuits, follow the recommended procedures or seek help. He could also find it of benefit to pay attention to his diet and obtain advice if feeling below par.

With all the plans and possibilities of the year, it will be a busy one domestically. However, with support and combined effort, the Fire Dog can take pleasure in the way certain plans take shape. He will also follow the activities of family members with interest and be keen to help with any problems or pressures they may have. Once again his thoughtfulness and ability to relate well to others will be appreciated. Fire Dogs who are grandparents will delight in the activities of their grandchildren and an often good bond can develop between the two generations.

There will also be good social opportunities for the Fire Dog this year, with his interests and local activities giving him more chance to go out. However, to make most of the year, the Fire Dog does need to be active and follow through his ideas. April, May, July and August could see some fine social occasions.

Overall, this can be a full and interesting year for the Fire Dog but he does need to seize the moment and act, as well as involve others in his plans. He also needs to remain aware of the Dragon year's more difficult aspects and be thorough and attentive. This is no year for risk and if he is ever in doubt or has problems, he should seek advice. This can be a satisfying year, but the Fire Dog should proceed carefully and with the support of others.

TIP FOR THE YEAR
Take an interest in what is going on around you and do not be too narrow in your approach. Dragon years are for trying out new activities and broadening what you do.

The Earth Dog
The Earth Dog is very perceptive and able to read people and situations well. And with the flurry of activity that so often characterizes Dragon years, he may well decide to keep a low profile and concentrate on priorities. He is not one who favours sudden change and will be wary of some of the developments of the year.

This particularly applies to his work situation. With the experience he has behind him and a good awareness of potential problems, he will often have misgivings over some of the proposals under consideration. However, while difficult, it will often be a case of making the best of the situation. Also, while many Earth Dogs may not be comfortable with the changes taking place, there can be benefits. New duties can provide a challenge but also a chance to gain experience in another area. Work-wise, Dragon years may be uncomfortable, but they do offer opportunities.

Many Earth Dogs will remain with their present employer over the year, but for those who decide to look for another position or are seeking work, the Dragon year can be challenging. Results and rewards do not come easily to Dogs in Dragon years and it will be very much a case of keeping alert and being persistent. Here the Earth Dog's determined nature will help, and by considering various possibilities, including possibly retraining, he may eventually secure a position that is often very different from what he has previously been doing. March and August to October could see possibilities.

However, the Dragon year can see encouraging developments in the Earth Dog's personal interests, and by building on his skills and knowledge he can derive a great deal of satisfaction from these. Some Earth Dogs could be tempted by a new activity over the year and if they are able to involve others in this and so benefit from their encouragement and company, they should do so.

In view of the pressures he may be under this year, the Earth Dog would also do well to give some consideration to his well-being. This includes making sure he has regular and appropriate exercise and a healthy, balanced diet. If he feels modifications are needed or is lacking his usual energy, he should seek advice.

With travel favourably aspected, the Earth Dog should, if possible, aim to take a holiday at some time during the year. The chance to relax and spend time with loved ones can do him a lot of good. There could also be some quickly arranged trips or weekends away, including visits to family and friends, which the Earth Dog will especially enjoy. Some parts of the Dragon year may lack the advance planning the Earth Dog prefers, but it is very much a case of making the most of the chances that arise.

In matters of finance, the Earth Dog will need to be vigilant. With some family plans and the purchases he may be keen to make, parts of the year will be expensive. Where possible, the Earth Dog should try to make early allowance for larger outgoings as well as be disciplined with everyday spending. Also when dealing with paperwork, he should take the time to check the details and question anything that is unclear. Rush or risks could lead to problems. Earth Dogs, take careful note.

The Earth Dog tends to be selective in his socializing, but in this busy year it is important that he keeps in regular contact with his friends, whether by meeting up, e-mail or phone. With some of the uncertainties he may face this year, the advice of some long-standing friends could be especially helpful. Also, going out can be another way to keep his lifestyle in balance. April, May, July and August could see the most social activity.

Matters of the heart require care and patience this year. Earth Dogs who are unattached and meet someone new during the year should allow time for a good understanding to develop rather than have high expectations of the relationship too soon.

In his home life the Earth Dog will be much in demand. There will be a lot to do and younger relations in particular will value the support the Earth Dog is able to give, especially as some may be about to leave home for education or work purposes or face other important decisions. Over the year the Earth Dog's care and astute judgement will win the gratitude of many.

However, while he will do much to assist his loved ones, it is also important that the Earth Dog gives them the chance to reciprocate. The more open and co-operative his household, the better home life can be. This will be a busy time, but there will also be some special family moments to enjoy, with mutual interests, home projects and travel all bringing pleasure.

Overall, the Dragon year will be demanding and the Earth Dog will not always be happy with its swift-moving developments. However, by being prepared to adapt as required, he can often benefit from the opportunities that will arise. This may not be an easy year but it will bring the possibility of personal growth. The Earth Dog's relations with others will be important, with mutual support leading to some enjoyable occasions.

TIP FOR THE YEAR

Tread carefully. Keep yourself informed about developments, liaise with others and be prepared to adapt as required. Despite any initial misgivings you may have about the changes taking place, there are important gains to be had. Also, preserve time for your own interests and for your loved ones. There may be a lot for you to do this year, but your efforts can reward you well and give you skills, ideas and experience to build on.

FAMOUS DOGS

King Albert II of Belgium, Brigitte Bardot, Candice Bergen, Justin Bieber, Andrea Bocelli, David Bowie, George W. Bush, Naomi Campbell, Fabio Capello, Mariah Carey, King Carl Gustaf XVI of Sweden, José Carreras, Paul Cézanne, Cher, Sir Winston Churchill, Bill Clinton, Leonard Cohen, Matt Damon, Charles Dance, Claude Debussy, Dame Judi Dench, Dakota Fanning, Joseph Fiennes, Robert Frost, Ava Gardner, Judy Garland, George Gershwin, Anne Hathaway, O. Henry, Victor Hugo, Barry Humphries, Holly Hunter, Michael Jackson, Al Jolson, Jennifer Lopez, Sophia Loren, Joanna Lumley, Shirley MacLaine, Andie McDowell, Madonna, Norman Mailer, Barry Manilow, Freddie Mercury, Liza Minelli, Simon Pegg, Sydney Pollack, Elvis Presley, Tim Robbins, Paul Robeson, Andy Roddick, Susan Sarandon, Claudia Schiffer, Dr Albert Schweitzer, Matt Smith, Sylvester Stallone, Robert Louis Stevenson, Sharon Stone, Donald Sutherland, Chris Tarrant, Mother Teresa, Uma Thurman, Donald Trump, Voltaire, Prince William, Shelley Winters.

16 FEBRUARY 1923 〜 4 FEBRUARY 1924   *Water Pig*

4 FEBRUARY 1935 〜 23 JANUARY 1936   *Wood Pig*

22 JANUARY 1947 〜 9 FEBRUARY 1948   *Fire Pig*

8 FEBRUARY 1959 〜 27 JANUARY 1960   *Earth Pig*

27 JANUARY 1971 〜 14 FEBRUARY 1972   *Metal Pig*

13 FEBRUARY 1983 〜 1 FEBRUARY 1984   *Water Pig*

31 JANUARY 1995 〜 18 FEBRUARY 1996   *Wood Pig*

18 FEBRUARY 2007 〜 6 FEBRUARY 2008   *Fire Pig*

THE
PIG

THE PERSONALITY OF THE PIG

It's the doing,
the giving,
the playing the part,
that makes life what it is.
And what it can be.

The Pig is born under the sign of honesty. He has a kind and understanding nature and is well known for his abilities as a peacemaker. He hates any sort of discord or unpleasantness and will do everything in his power to sort out differences of opinion or bring opposing factions together.

He is also an excellent conversationalist and speaks truthfully and to the point. He dislikes any form of falsehood or hypocrisy and is a firm believer in justice and the maintenance of law and order. In spite of these beliefs, however, he is reasonably tolerant and often prepared to forgive others for their wrongdoings. He rarely harbours grudges and is never vindictive.

The Pig is usually very popular. He enjoys other people's company and likes to be involved in joint or group activities. He will be a loyal member of any club or society and can be relied upon to lend a helping hand at functions. He is also an excellent fundraiser for charities and is often a great supporter of humanitarian causes.

The Pig is a hard and conscientious worker and is particularly respected for his reliability and integrity. In his early years he will try his hand at several different jobs, but he is usually happiest where he feels that he is being of service to others. He will unselfishly give up his time for the common good and is highly valued by his colleagues and employers.

The Pig has a good sense of humour and invariably has a smile, joke or some whimsical remark at the ready. He loves to entertain and please others, and there are many Pigs who have been attracted to careers in show business or who enjoy following the careers of famous stars and personalities.

There are, unfortunately, some who take advantage of the Pig's good nature and impose upon his generosity. The Pig has great difficulty in saying 'no', and although he may dislike being firm, it would be in his own interests to say occasionally, 'Enough is enough.' He can also be rather naïve and gullible; however, if at any stage in his life he feels that he has been badly let down, he will try to become self-reliant. There are many Pigs who have become entrepreneurs or forged a successful career on their own after some early disappointment in life. Although the Pig tends to spend his money quite freely, he is usually very astute in financial matters and there are many Pigs who have become wealthy.

Another characteristic of the Pig is his ability to recover from setbacks reasonably quickly. His faith and his strength of character keep him going. If he thinks that there is a job he can do or there is something that he wants to achieve, he will pursue it with dogged determination. He can also be stubborn and no matter how many may plead with him, once he has made his mind up he will rarely change his views.

Although the Pig may work hard, he also knows how to enjoy himself. He is a great pleasure-seeker and will quite happily spend his hard-earned money on a lavish holiday or an expensive meal – for the Pig is a connoisseur of good food and wine – or a variety of recreational activities. He also enjoys small social gatherings and if he is in company he likes he can very easily become the life and soul of the party. He does, however, tend to become rather withdrawn at larger functions or when among strangers.

The Pig is a creature of comfort and his home will usually be fitted with the latest in luxury appliances. Where possible, he will prefer to live in the country rather than the town and will opt to have a big garden, for the Pig is usually a keen and successful gardener.

The Pig is very popular with others and will often have numerous romances before he settles down. Once settled, however, he will be loyal to his partner and he will find that he is especially well suited to those born under the signs of the Goat, Rabbit, Dog and Tiger and also to another Pig. Due to his affable and easy-going nature he can also establish a satisfactory relationship with all the remaining signs of the Chinese zodiac, with the exception of the Snake. The Snake tends to be wily, secretive and very guarded, and this can be intensely irritating to the honest and open-hearted Pig.

The female Pig will devote all her energies to the needs of her children and her partner. She will try to ensure that they want for nothing and their pleasure is very much her pleasure. She can be a caring and conscientious parent and has very good taste in clothes. Her home will either be very clean and orderly or hopelessly untidy. Strangely, there seems to be no in between with Pigs – they either love housework or detest it! The female Pig does, however, have considerable talents as an organizer and this, combined with her friendly and open manner, enables her to secure many of her objectives.

The Pig is usually lucky in life and will rarely want for anything. Provided he does not let others take advantage of his good nature and is not afraid of asserting himself, he will go through life making friends, helping others and winning the admiration of many.

THE FIVE DIFFERENT TYPES OF PIG

In addition to the 12 signs of the Chinese zodiac there are five elements and these have a strengthening or moderating influence on the signs. The effects of the five elements on the Pig are described below, together with the years in which they were exercising their influence. Therefore Pigs born in 1971 are Metal Pigs, those born in 1923 and 1983 are Water Pigs, and so on.

Metal Pig: 1971

The Metal Pig is more ambitious and determined than some of the other types of Pig. He is strong, energetic and likes to be involved in a wide variety of different activities. He is very open and forthright in his views, although he can be a little too trusting at times and has a tendency to accept things at face value. He has a good sense of humour and loves to attend parties and other social gatherings. He has a warm, outgoing nature and usually a large circle of friends.

Water Pig: 1923, 1983

The Water Pig has a heart of gold. He is generous and loyal and tries to remain on good terms with everyone. He will do his utmost to help others, but sadly there are some who will take advantage of his kind nature and he should, in his own interests, be a little more discriminating and be prepared to stand firm against anything that he does not like. Although he prefers the quieter things in life, he has a wide range of interests. He particularly enjoys outdoor pursuits and attending parties and social occasions. He is a hard and conscientious worker and invariably does well in his chosen profession. He is also gifted in the art of communication.

Wood Pig: 1935, 1995

This Pig has a friendly, persuasive manner and is easily able to gain the confidence of others. He likes to be involved in all that is going on around him but can sometimes take on more responsibility than he can properly handle. He is loyal to his family and friends and derives much pleasure from helping those less fortunate than himself. He is usually an optimist and leads a very full, enjoyable and satisfying life. He also has a good sense of humour.

Fire Pig: 1947, 2007

The Fire Pig is both energetic and adventurous and sets about everything he does in a confident and resolute manner. He is very forthright in his views and does not mind taking risks in order to achieve his objectives. He can, however, get carried away by the excitement of the

THE PIG

moment and ought to exercise more caution in some of the
enterprises in which he gets involved. He is usually lucky
in money matters and is well known for his generosity. He
is also very caring towards the members of his family.

Earth Pig: 1959

This Pig has a kindly nature. He is sensible and realistic and
will go to great lengths in order to please his employers
and to secure his aims and ambitions. He is an excellent
organizer and is particularly astute in business and financial matters. He has a good sense of humour and a wide
circle of friends. He also likes to lead an active social life,
although he does sometimes have a tendency to eat and
drink more than is good for him.

PROSPECTS FOR THE PIG IN 2012

The Year of the Rabbit (3 February 2011–22 January 2012)
is an encouraging one for the Pig and by setting about his
activities in his usual redoubtable way, he can look forward
to some interesting results in the closing months.

At work, many Pigs will have been content to focus on
their activities and develop specific skills during the year.
Rabbit years are generally supportive of Pigs and late
August to early October can see some potentially important work developments.

The Pig's efforts in his work can lead to an increase in
income, but with some expensive purchases towards the
end of the year, he should keep a close watch on outgoings.

Also, if he has any concern over a financial or bureaucratic matter, he would do well to seek advice.

With the Pig's *joie de vivre*, he can look forward to an increasing number of social opportunities as the Rabbit year draws to a close. August, December and January could be especially busy months, with friends to meet and occasions to go to. For the unattached, someone met in a work situation or while pursuing a personal interest could add considerable sparkle to the year.

The Pig's home life will also be busy and ideally he should plan ahead rather than have a lot happening all at once. This way last-minute panics can be avoided and there will be more time to appreciate what takes place. A loved one could also have a surprise for the Pig near the end of the Rabbit year.

The Year of the Dragon starts on 23 January and will be a moderate one for the Pig. Although Pigs are hardworking and enjoy an often lively lifestyle, they will not always feel at ease with the Dragon year's heady pace. They prefer settled conditions, but the Dragon year can bring sudden change. However, while this will not necessarily be an easy time for the Pig, he can still emerge from it with some very real gains to his credit.

In his work he will need to keep his wits about him. In many a workplace change will be under way, with some industries facing restructuring and staff being affected by new initiatives. Quite a few Pigs will look askance at what is happening and will, as far as possible, aim to concentrate on their own specific tasks. However, this is no year for them to ignore what is going on around them or be too independent in approach. In Dragon years Pigs need to be aware of the wider picture, especially of any developments that might affect them. By keeping themselves informed, they will not only be better prepared to adapt to any changes but could also benefit from what arises. They need to be quick to put themselves forward when an opportunity comes their way, but this is a year of possibility. Even if they are putting in for a position that is considerably more senior than the one they currently have, by aiming high and indicating their desire to progress, they could, against considerable odds, triumph. With this being a fast-moving year, sometimes a bit of audaciousness can pay off.

Many Pigs will have the opportunity to make progress in their current place of work this year, but for those keen to make a change, as well as those seeking work, the Dragon year can open up some interesting possibilities. By keeping alert to what is available and making enquiries, many could secure a position in an often curious way. They may hear of a vacancy by chance or be offered a position despite not rating their prospects too highly, but however it comes about, in a Dragon year the Pig's actions can bear unexpected fruit. Opportunities could occur at almost any time, but April to June and November could see particularly encouraging work developments.

One of the Pig's strengths is his ability to get on well with people and over the year his talents can again reward him well. Particularly in his work situation, he should aim to liaise closely with others as well as use any chances to network. By getting himself better known, he can do his reputation a lot of good.

This also applies to other activities he may engage in. With his personal interests, the Pig would do well to go to events and meet other enthusiasts. He will often impress and establish some important new friends and contacts. Dragon years favour activity and even if the Pig may not always be comfortable with the fast pace of events, by seizing his opportunities he can benefit personally from a lot that he does during the year.

Also, the Dragon year can give rise to quite a few social occasions and the Pig will enjoy some of the lively times that take place. March, May, July, and December could see the most social activity, including, for the unattached, exciting romantic possibilities, while Pigs enjoying romance started in the previous Rabbit year are likely to find this now becoming more meaningful. For relations with others, this is a positive and pleasing year.

The Pig also attaches great importance to his home life and over the year this can again be a source of much joy. In view of some of the pressures of the year, he may regard his home as a private sanctuary. As a result, he will often immerse himself in a range of domestic activities. In many a Pig household this will be a time for tackling projects together and advancing hopes and plans. Also, at more challenging times, the help and understanding the Pig receives from his loved ones can make an appreciable difference.

Financially, many Pigs will enjoy a welcome increase in income over the year. Some may also find interests or other activities can add to their earnings. Dragon years are generally financially positive ones for the Pig. However, to benefit, he should manage his situation well and take his time when considering large purchases. Major financial decisions should not be hurried. If he is able, he should set funds aside for a holiday or break during the year. With the busy lifestyle he may be leading, a rest and change of scene can do him good.

The Dragon year will be an active one for the Pig and he may not be comfortable with its swift and sometimes unexpected developments. However, by keeping alert, he can often turn situations to his advantage. He has, after all, a talent for sensing opportunity and can put this, together with his skills and personable nature, to good use this year. This may not be the easiest of times for him, but there *will* be gains to be had, good times to enjoy and progress to be made. Overall, despite its pressures, an interesting and often personally satisfying year.

The Metal Pig

The Metal Pig will have seen a great deal happen in recent years and the Dragon year will give him the chance to build on his current situation and enjoy some pleasing success. However, while a progressive time, it will bring its pressures and the Metal Pig will need to keep alert and act quickly as situations change. The opportunities will be there, but in the Dragon year time is of the essence.

This will be particularly the case in the Metal Pig's work. Dragon years favour change and innovation, and new schemes and ways of working will often be introduced. By keeping informed of developments, the Metal Pig could see a chance to take on greater responsibilities and/or move to other duties. If so, he should be quick to express an interest. This is very much a year for quick determined action.

However, while many Metal Pigs can make good progress, the Dragon year can still present problems. Delays or equipment malfunction could cause difficulties and certain objectives may be hard to meet. However, while worrying, such challenges will give the Metal Pig the chance to show his resourcefulness and, in the process, enhance his reputation. Dragon years may not always make life easy for Metal Pigs, but they test their qualities and can present opportunities.

For Metal Pigs who decide to move on from their present employer as well as those seeking work, the Dragon year can also give rise to interesting developments. However to benefit, these Metal Pigs should not be too restrictive in the types of work they are considering. By looking at other ways in which they could use their skills and seeking advice and information, they could see some interesting possibilities emerging. Again, the moment these Metal Pigs see a vacancy that appeals to them, they should be quick to apply. Speed, enthusiasm and initiative will be important factors this year. April to early July and November can see encouraging work developments.

The progress many Metal Pigs make at work will help financially, and some could also benefit from a bonus payment or gift. However, while the Metal Pig's financial situation can improve, with family and accommodation expenses, travel and other plans, he will need to exercise good control over his spending. If tempted by too many impulse buys, he may find certain plans need to be revised. Financially, this can be an improved year, but it does require control.

With his genial nature the Metal Pig knows a great many people and his social life can be particularly pleasurable this year. Certain local amenities or events could catch his attention and his social life and recreational activities can help balance his lifestyle and do him good. March, May,

July and the last two months of the year could see the most social activity.

Also, with this being a year of possibility, if the Metal Pig sees an interest or activity that appeals to him, he should find out more. Dragon years can offer much to the willing and interested. In addition, some Metal Pigs may be tempted by a new fitness discipline or diet, and by taking advice on its suitability, could again benefit from their actions.

The Metal Pig very much values his home life and will once again devote much time and attention to family activities. Admittedly, as with any year, there will be pressures, also adjustments to be made as plans and routines change, but with co-operation and good understanding, these will not detract from the many positive family times of the year. For Metal Pigs who are parents, any additional support they can give to their children, including help with aspects of their education, can make an important difference as well as often strengthen the good rapport they enjoy.

Overall, the Year of the Dragon will require effort on the Metal Pig's part. Results will not always come easily, but by being aware, involved and willing to make that all-important effort, he can enjoy some rewarding developments. However, whenever he sees an opportunity, he does need to seize the moment otherwise it may slip by. He will be greatly helped by the support of others, with his family life being important and encouraging.

TIP FOR THE YEAR
Be adaptable. Situations can change quickly this year and to benefit you will need to act quickly too. Also, use your personal qualities well. Your ability to relate well to others

---

---

can be helpful both now and in the near future. This is a year of interesting possibility, but it requires effort and awareness.

The Water Pig

The Water Pig has a keen and generally optimistic nature and is often willing to try things out and see how they develop. This approach will serve him well this year. By being open to the opportunities that the Dragon year can present, many Water Pigs will make good headway as well as enjoy some pleasing personal developments.

One of the features of the Dragon year is that situations can change quickly and the Water Pig will need to keep alert to what is happening around him. By doing so, he will be more aware of emerging possibilities as well as situations he may need to address. All Water Pigs should keep themselves informed *and* involved.

For many there could be openings in their present place of work and by putting themselves forward they will be able to make important advances. Career-wise, this is no year for standing still, but the impetus to make that change rests firmly with the Water Pig himself. In the Dragon year he needs to be bold, quick and decisive.

For Water Pigs who would welcome change or are seeking work, the Dragon year can have interesting possibilities in store. Again, though, it is a case of remaining aware and investigating what is available. The Water Pig's willingness to try something different will stand him in excellent stead, however, and by showing enthusiasm at interview and emphasizing his desire to learn, he may well be given a significant opportunity which may also be an entry into a new type of work. April to June and November could see some interesting developments and for many Water Pigs the year will mark a new stage in their working lives.

However, while it is a year for moving forward, the Dragon year could still present its obstacles. Some undertakings or objectives may be challenging. But it is out of difficulties that reputations are born and, as many Water Pigs will find, success this year will be down to sheer hard work.

The progress the Water Pig makes at work can also help financially, but he will need to remain disciplined, budget carefully and resist impulse purchases. Any savings he can make towards his hopes and plans can help make them happen.

With his outgoing and friendly nature, the Water Pig enjoys good relations with many people and over the year will find himself much in demand. In addition to enjoying the company of existing friends, he can find work developments and the interests he pursues also leading to a widening of his social circle. On a personal level, he will be in impressive form this year. Any Water Pigs who move to a new area and would welcome new friends and/or different activities to do should take an interest in local events and amenities. They could find a social group or pursuit which particularly appeals to them. March, May, July and December could see the most social activity.

Although the Dragon year can see encouraging developments in many areas of the Water Pig's life, central to all will be his home. For Water Pigs with a partner there will be much to share and some exciting plans to move forward. This is very much a year favouring togetherness and joint ventures. Water Pigs who are parents or who become parents this year will often delight in tending to the needs of babies or young children and watching their progress. Such are the positive aspects of the year that some Water Pigs who are unattached at the start of it may have settled down with a partner by the closing months. On a personal level, Dragon years can often be special.

Overall, the Dragon year can present the Water Pig with some exciting opportunities, but to benefit he will need to keep aware of developments and act swiftly. By being prepared, he can make more of his potential and considerably help his prospects. The Dragon year can also be a time of change and, for some Water Pigs, a time when they alter the nature of their work or take up new interests. On a personal level, the Water Pig will often be encouraged by the support he receives, with his home and social life bringing considerable pleasure. A busy year and one of important possibility.

TIP FOR THE YEAR
You may be conscientious, but do not immerse yourself so fully in your current activities that you are unaware of emerging developments. *Stay informed.* Also, be open to the new. This is a year of change and it will allow you to make progress and make good use of your strengths.

The Wood Pig

The Dragon year can open up some significant opportunities for the Wood Pig. Dragon years have energy and a certain dynamism about them and many Wood Pigs will be quick to latch onto this. This can be a progressive and rewarding year with far-reaching value.

Wood Pigs in education need to remain focused and disciplined. When exams and coursework need to be prepared for, the Wood Pig should allow plenty of time, ideally setting himself a revision or work timetable. The more organized he is, the better the likely outcome. Dragon years reward commitment.

Also, as his studies progress, new opportunities can often arise for the Water Pig, including the chance to take on a new subject or learn an additional skill. By being open to such chances, as well as making good use of the facilities available to him, the Wood Pig can get much value out of the present time. 'There is no limit to learning', as the Chinese proverb reminds us, and this is a year for building on skills.

Although the Wood Pig may well be preoccupied with his current studying, it could also reward him to look ahead and consider the direction he would like to take in the future. This could include looking at courses for later study or considering the type of work he would like to enter. By thinking this over and talking to those around him, including his family and tutors, he could find some interesting ideas emerging which will give him something to work towards. The decisions and success (including qualifications) of the Dragon year can have long-term value.

The Wood Pig's personal interests can also be of value, as well as bring him much pleasure. If applicable, he should again make the most of practice or training facilities that are available locally. Dragon years favour the new, and if a different interest or activity catches the Wood Pig's attention, he should find out more. This is a year of possibility.

Throughout the year the Wood Pig should also be willing to talk over his current activities and any concerns with those around him. This way, they will be better able to assist and understand. Also, in his home life, by participating rather than keeping too much to himself, he will be able to enjoy more fully some of the activities that take place. An important message for the Wood Pig this year is to be active and involved.

The Wood Pig will also greatly value his circle of friends this year. Not only can they offer each other much mutual support, but there can be a lot of fun in sharing activities. March, May, July and December could see some particularly lively occasions as well as good opportunities to meet others. However, a word of warning does need to be given: the Wood Pig needs to be wary of gossip and rumour. Without care, he could be misled. If concerned about anything he may hear, he should check the facts himself.

Also, while the Wood Pig may keep himself active, with the pressure of all he is currently doing, including the late nights he will sometimes have, he would do well to give some consideration to his well-being and quality of diet. Without care, he could find himself susceptible to niggling ailments. Wood Pigs, take note.

For Wood Pigs in work or seeking work, the Dragon year can have some interesting developments in store. If already in work, the Wood Pig will often be encouraged to take on greater responsibilities. By showing himself keen and willing, he can make good headway and will be well supported. Whether he stays with his present employer or decides to move on, this is very much a year for building on his experience.

For Wood Pigs seeking a position, apprenticeships or positions which allow learning would be well worth considering. Significant chances can open up for many Wood Pigs over the year, and once they have their foot on the employment ladder, they will be able to build on their experience. Late March to the start of July and November could see some interesting possibilities.

The Wood Pig is enterprising and resourceful, and even though his means may be limited, he will manage well financially this year. However, as he realizes, to do all that he wants, he will need to be disciplined. Some Wood Pigs will be keen to take advantage of travel opportunities during the year and should try to make savings for this.

Overall, the Year of the Dragon will ask a lot of the Wood Pig and to do well he will need to put in the effort and remain disciplined. However, with future aspirations in mind (some of which he will decide upon this year) and the satisfaction current activities can bring, his diligence can reward him well. This will be a constructive and interesting year.

TIP FOR THE YEAR
Draw on the support of others as well as make the most of the resources available to you. By developing your skills and building on your knowledge you will be helping to open up interesting possibilities both for now and later on.

The Fire Pig
The Dragon year offers considerable scope for the Fire Pig and by acting on his ideas he will be pleased with how events develop. However, he should not be too rigid in his

planning. Events in the Dragon year can take a curious course and this is a time to be flexible, active and aware.

For Fire Pigs in work, this can be a significant year. Some will decide to retire and be keen to set about ideas they have long had in mind. Others may reduce their working commitments and again delight in the additional time they now have. However, some will decide to make more of their specialist knowledge and take on new work objectives. For many Fire Pigs, this will be a year of decision and there will often be important factors to consider. If the Fire Pig is unclear about any aspect of the options before him, especially relating to the financial implications, he should seek clarification. This will be well worth his while.

Whether the Fire Pig remains in work or retires, an interesting aspect of the year will be the support he is shown by his colleagues. By now, many Fire Pigs will be well respected and those who retire could be taken aback by the goodwill shown to them. Similarly, those who remain in work will find colleagues valuing their knowledge. Some could even take on a mentoring role. With this being an often decisive year in the Fire Pig's working life, relations with his colleagues can be both important and helpful.

Financial matters will feature significantly over the year and will require attention. Quite a few Fire Pigs will benefit from a bonus, gift or maturing policy, but while this will be welcome, the Fire Pig will need to give careful thought to how best to use it. If he does not do so, there is a risk that anything extra could be absorbed by general living expenses. Ideally, if there are any specific plans or hopes the Fire Pig has in mind, he should save up for them. Fire Pigs who retire would also find it helpful to consider the adjustments that may need to be made. Financially, the Fire Pig can fare well this year, but it does require good management.

Travel will also be on the agenda this year and if there is a particular destination the Fire Pig would like to visit or he sees a travel offer that appeals to him, he should follow this up. With the Dragon year having a degree of spontaneity about it, some Fire Pigs could also be tempted to go away for a break at short notice.

Another important aspect of the year will be the way the Fire Pig will be able to enjoy certain interests. Fire Pigs who have retired or take semi-retirement will often have ideas they will be keen to pursue, but no matter what the Fire Pig's present position, the Dragon year can open up some exciting possibilities. In addition to the pleasure he may get from existing interests, he could become intrigued by a new activity or subject and will enjoy the chance to try out something very different. This is a year to make the most of what is available, including local amenities.

Some of the Fire Pig's interests will also have a good social element to them and some important new friends and contacts can be made. March, May, July and December could see good social opportunities.

The Fire Pig's domestic life will also see a lot happen over the year, with many in his household, including himself, involved in important choices. In view of the significance of what is being considered, it is important that all involved are open and ready to talk, listen and support each other. Here the Fire Pig's ability to empathize and his considerable knowledge can be of great help, with younger relations in particular valuing his advice and practical assistance. The Fire Pig will be very much at the heart of family life this year.

He should also be fairly flexible with some of his plans. New ideas can often arise which can improve what he has in mind. By being aware and adaptable, the Fire Pig will often be pleased with how things work out for him.

Although he keeps himself occupied and active, it could also be to his advantage to give some consideration to his well-being. If he feels his diet and general level of exercise could be improved, he should seek advice on how best to proceed. This can make an important difference to his level of energy.

In general, the Year of the Dragon will be a pleasing one for the Fire Pig. By being willing to seize his opportunities and follow up his ideas, he can look forward to some pleasing developments. Throughout the year he will benefit from the support and goodwill of those around him and sharing his thoughts and activities will be to his advantage. This can be a significant and rewarding year.

TIP FOR THE YEAR
Your outgoing and curious nature can reward you well this year. Consider taking up some new interests or setting yourself some satisfying projects. Spend time in ways that you enjoy and that can potentially benefit you. So much can follow on from your actions.

The Earth Pig
The Earth Pig is both ambitious and resourceful and is set to do well this year. However, while the aspects are encour-

aging, he will need to adapt as situations change. This is no year to be inflexible or too set in his ways.

The Earth Pig's ability to relate to others will serve him well this year. Over the year he should make the most of his chances to meet others and build up contacts as well as raise his profile. The more people he knows and who know of him, the more that will open up for him.

This particularly applies to his work situation. With many organizations experiencing change, by being an active member of a team and working well with others, the Earth Pig will not only be helping his current position but also strengthening his prospects. To do well in this fast-moving year, it is very much a case of being visible, active and involved.

With the considerable experience and in-house knowledge many Earth Pigs will have built up over the years, they will now have the chance to take on a wider role. However, this may be slightly different from what these Earth Pigs were anticipating and to benefit they will need to be flexible and, in some cases, considerably extend their skills. This is a progressive year, but parts of it will be demanding and require a good deal of effort.

Most Earth Pigs will remain with their present employer over the year, but for those who feel the time is right for a change, as well as those seeking work, the Dragon year can open up some interesting possibilities. These Earth Pigs should not be too restrictive in what they are considering, and again what is offered may not always be what was envisaged, but it will offer the Earth Pig the chance to prove himself in a new way and be something he can build on in the future. Late March to early July and November could see some particularly interesting opportunities, but generally once the Earth Pig starts to explore options, developments can quickly be set in motion. This is a fast-moving year bringing change and possibility.

The progress many Earth Pigs make at work will lead to an increase in income, and some may also benefit from an additional payment or gift. However, the Earth Pig could have some large domestic outgoings as well as other plans he is keen to proceed with and he will need to be disciplined with his everyday spending and plan ahead. Also, if he can use any financial upturn to reduce certain commitments and interest payments, this can be to his advantage. Good financial management will make an important difference this year.

If possible, the Earth Pig should include travel in his planning. A change of scene can do him good and he may be able to combine a holiday with a special attraction or event. With the Dragon year favouring spontaneity, some Earth Pigs could be tempted by a last-minute travel opportunity. Again, Dragon years have surprises and possibilities in store.

This can also be an inspiring time and many Earth Pigs will be keen to take their interests in a new direction. It could be that the Earth Pig becomes interested in a different aspect of an existing hobby, sets himself a new challenge or tries out something completely different. This is very much a time when it would be worth any Earth Pigs who have let their interests lapse setting time aside to start something new.

The Earth Pig will also welcome the social opportunities the year will bring and will value the support of his close friends. Some could have experience or insights which could help at times of change. Over the year it is important the

THE PIG

Earth Pig is forthcoming and seeks the opinion of others. Through the changes that occur over the year, he will also have the chance to make some new friendships. March, May, July and December could see the most social activity.

In view of all that is happening this year, the Earth Pig will also very much appreciate times spent at home with his loved ones and the projects and plans he is able to share. Again, his talent for empathizing and involving everyone in his household will be especially appreciated. As well as assisting others with what could be important decisions, the Earth Pig could celebrate the wedding of someone close or become a grandparent. This promises to be an eventful year with special family moments to enjoy, especially in the closing stages of the Dragon year. December and January in particular could see a flurry of activity.

In view of his busy lifestyle, it is important, however, that the Earth Pig pays attention to his well-being. To skimp on exercise or a healthy diet could leave him feeling under par. Earth Pigs, take note.

The Earth Pig is determined and resourceful, and in the Dragon year his hard work and desire to make progress can lead to some excellent opportunities. Although these may not always be what he anticipated and could require some adapting to, as well as considerable effort, the Earth Pig will welcome the opportunity to move his situation forward. Also, the positive relations he enjoys with many people will not only help in a lot of what he sets out to do but also give rise to some pleasing personal times. The Dragon year can bring its surprises and unexpected twists and turns, but the Earth Pig has the qualities and strengths to fare well. And fare well he will.

TIP FOR THE YEAR

With your ambitious nature, you will be keen to achieve a lot this year. However, while your experience can stand you in good stead, do not close your mind to other ways forward. Be alert and prepared to adapt. Also, in this fast-moving year, make the most of opportunities as they arise. This can be a potentially successful and rewarding year for you.

FAMOUS PIGS

Woody Allen, Julie Andrews, Marie Antoinette, Fred Astaire, Emily Blunt, Humphrey Bogart, James Cagney, Maria Callas, Samantha Cameron, Hillary Rodham Clinton, Glenn Close, Sacha Baron Cohen, Cheryl Cole, the Duchess of Cornwall, Noël Coward, Simon Cowell, Oliver Cromwell, Billy Crystal, the Dalai Lama, Dido, Richard Dreyfuss, Ben Elton, Ralph Waldo Emerson, Henry Ford, Jonathan Franzen, Stephen Harper, Emmylou Harris, Ernest Hemingway, Henry VIII, Conrad Hilton, Alfred Hitchcock, Sir Elton John, Tommy Lee Jones, Carl Gustav Jung, Stephen King, Kevin Kline, Hugh Laurie, Nigella Lawson, David Letterman, Jerry Lee Lewis, Meat Loaf, Ewan McGregor, Ricky Martin, Johnny Mathis, Dannii Minogue, Morrissey, Wolfgang Amadeus Mozart, George Osborne, Sir Michael Parkinson, James Patterson, Luciano Pavarotti, Iggy Pop, Maurice Ravel, Ronald Reagan, Winona Ryder, Françoise Sagan, Arnold Schwarzenegger, Kevin Spacey, Steven Spielberg, Lord Sugar, David Tennant, Emma Thompson, Herman Van Rompuy, Jules Verne, David Walliams, Amy Winehouse, Michael Winner, the Duchess of York.

APPENDIX

———————◆◆◆———————

The relationships between the 12 animal signs, both on a personal level and business level, are an important aspect of Chinese horoscopes and in this appendix the compatibility between the signs is shown in the two tables that follow.

Also included are the names of the signs ruling the hours of the day and from this it is possible to find your ascendant and discover yet another aspect of your personality.

Finally, to supplement the earlier chapters on the personality and horoscope of the signs, I have included a guide on how you can get the best out of your sign and the year.

RELATIONSHIPS BETWEEN THE SIGNS

Personal Relationships

KEY

1 Excellent. Great rapport.
2 A successful relationship. Many interests in common.
3 Mutual respect and understanding. A good relationship.
4 Fair. Needs care and some willingness to compromise in order for the relationship to work.
5 Awkward. Possible difficulties in communication with few interests in common.
6 A clash of personalities. Very difficult.

	Rat	Ox	Tiger	Rabbit	Dragon	Snake	Horse	Goat	Monkey	Rooster	Dog	Pig
Rat	1											
Ox	1	3										
Tiger	4	6	5									
Rabbit	5	2	3	2								
Dragon	1	5	4	3	2							
Snake	3	1	6	2	1	5						
Horse	6	5	1	5	3	4	2					
Goat	5	5	3	1	4	3	2	2				
Monkey	1	3	6	3	1	3	5	3	1			
Rooster	5	1	5	6	2	1	2	5	5	5		
Dog	3	4	1	2	6	3	1	5	3	5	2	
Pig	2	3	2	2	2	6	3	2	2	3	1	2

APPENDIX

Business Relationships

KEY

1 Excellent. Marvellous understanding and rapport.
2 Very good. Complement each other well.
3 A good working relationship and understanding can be developed.
4 Fair, but compromise and a common objective are often needed to make this relationship work.
5 Awkward. Unlikely to work, either through lack of trust, understanding or the competitiveness of the signs.
6 Mistrust. Difficult. To be avoided.

	Rat	Ox	Tiger	Rabbit	Dragon	Snake	Horse	Goat	Monkey	Rooster	Dog	Pig
Rat	2											
Ox	1	3										
Tiger	3	6	5									
Rabbit	4	3	3	3								
Dragon	1	4	3	3	3							
Snake	3	2	6	4	1	5						
Horse	6	5	1	5	3	4	4					
Goat	5	5	3	1	4	3	3	2				
Monkey	2	3	4	5	1	5	4	4	3			
Rooster	5	1	5	5	2	1	2	5	5	6		
Dog	4	5	2	3	6	4	2	5	3	5	4	
Pig	3	3	3	2	3	5	4	2	3	4	3	1

YOUR ASCENDANT

The ascendant has a very strong influence on your personality and will help you gain an even greater insight into
your true personality according to Chinese horoscopes.

The hours of the day are named after the 12 animal
signs and the sign governing the time you were born is
your ascendant. To find your ascendant, look up the time
of your birth in the table below, bearing in mind any local
time differences in the place you were born.

11 p.m.	to	1 a.m.	The hours of the Rat
1 a.m.	to	3 a.m.	The hours of the Ox
3 a.m.	to	5 a.m.	The hours of the Tiger
5 a.m.	to	7 a.m.	The hours of the Rabbit
7 a.m.	to	9 a.m.	The hours of the Dragon
9 a.m.	to	11 a.m.	The hours of the Snake
11 a.m.	to	1 p.m.	The hours of the Horse
1 p.m.	to	3 p.m.	The hours of the Goat
3 p.m.	to	5 p.m.	The hours of the Monkey
5 p.m.	to	7 p.m.	The hours of the Rooster
7 p.m.	to	9 p.m.	The hours of the Dog
9 p.m.	to	11 p.m.	The hours of the Pig

RAT

The Rat ascendant is likely to make the sign more outgoing, sociable and careful with money. A particularly beneficial influence for those born under the signs of the
Rabbit, Horse, Monkey and Pig.

OX

The Ox ascendant has a restraining, cautionary and steadying influence that many signs will benefit from. This ascendant also promotes self-confidence and willpower and is especially good for those born under the signs of the Tiger, Rabbit and Goat.

TIGER

The Tiger ascendant is a dynamic and stirring influence that makes the sign more outgoing, action-orientated and impulsive. A generally favourable ascendant for the Ox, Tiger, Snake and Horse.

RABBIT

The Rabbit ascendant has a moderating influence, making the sign more reflective, serene and discreet. A particularly beneficial influence for the Rat, Dragon, Monkey and Rooster.

DRAGON

The Dragon ascendant gives strength, determination and ambition to the sign. A favourable influence for those born under the signs of the Rabbit, Goat, Monkey and Dog.

SNAKE

The Snake ascendant can make the sign more reflective, intuitive and self-reliant. A good influence for the Tiger, Goat and Pig.

HORSE

The Horse ascendant will make the sign more adventurous, daring and on some occasions fickle. Generally a beneficial influence for the Rabbit, Snake, Dog and Pig.

GOAT

The Goat ascendant will make the sign more tolerant, easy-going and receptive. It could also impart some creative and artistic qualities. An especially good influence for the Ox, Dragon, Snake and Rooster.

MONKEY

The Monkey ascendant is likely to impart a delicious sense of humour and fun to the sign. It will make the sign more enterprising and outgoing – a particularly good influence for the Rat, Ox, Snake and Goat.

ROOSTER

The Rooster ascendant helps to give the sign a lively, outgoing and very methodical manner. Its influence will increase efficiency and is good for the Ox, Tiger, Rabbit and Horse.

DOG

The Dog ascendant makes the sign more reasonable and fair-minded and gives an added sense of loyalty. A very good ascendant for the Tiger, Dragon and Goat.

PIG

The Pig ascendant can make the sign more sociable and self-indulgent. It is also a caring and humanitarian influence. A good ascendant for the Dragon and Monkey.

HOW TO GET THE BEST FROM YOUR CHINESE SIGN AND THE YEAR

Each of the 12 Chinese signs possesses its own unique strengths and by identifying them you can use them to your advantage. Similarly, by becoming aware of possible weaknesses you can do much to rectify them, and in this respect I hope the following sections will be useful. Also included are some tips on how you can get the best from the Year of the Dragon.

The Rat

The Rat is blessed with many fine talents, but his undoubted strength lies in his ability to get on with others. He is sociable, charming and a good judge of character. He also possesses a shrewd mind and is good at spotting opportunities.

However, to make the most of his abilities, he does need to impose some discipline upon himself. He should resist the (sometimes very great) temptation of getting involved in too many activities all at the same time and should decide upon his priorities and objectives. By concentrating his energies on specific matters he will fare much better.

YOUR CHINESE HOROSCOPE 2012

Also, given his personable manner, he should seek out positions where he can use his personal relations skills to good effect. For a career, sales and marketing could prove ideal.

The Rat is astute in dealing with finance, but while often thrifty, he can sometimes give way to moments of indulgence. Although he deserves to enjoy the money he has so carefully earned, it would sometimes be in his interests to exercise restraint when tempted to satisfy too many expensive whims!

The Rat's family and friends are important to him and while he is loyal and protective towards them, he does tend to keep his worries and concerns to himself and would be helped if he were more willing to discuss his anxieties. Others think highly of him and are prepared to do a lot to help him, but for them to do so the Rat does need to be less guarded.

With his sharp mind, keen imagination and sociable manner, he does, however, have much in his favour. When he has commitment, he can be irrepressible and, given his considerable charm, often irresistible as well! Provided he channels his energies wisely, he can make much of his life.

Advice for the Rat's Year Ahead

GENERAL PROSPECTS
Active and resourceful, the Rat can get a lot out of the Dragon year. To benefit fully, he will need to put himself forward and act quickly, but some excellent opportunities will open up for him. With belief, resolve and his persuasive personality, he can accomplish a great deal in this positive and progressive time.

CAREER PROSPECTS

This is no year for standing still and many Rats will build on their experience and make important advances in their career. Opportunities can arise quickly in the Dragon year and the Rat will need to keep alert and be swift to act.

FINANCE

The Rat can benefit from an increase in income and also be fortunate in some purchases. However, he should manage his finances well, including, if possible, making provision for the longer term. Good planning will be rewarded.

RELATIONS WITH OTHERS

Born under the sign of charm, in this active year the Rat will meet new people, make new friends, benefit from new contacts and enjoy excellent romantic possibilities. New interests and activities in particular can lead to new friendships, and the support, love and friendship of others will help and encourage the Rat.

The Ox

Strong-willed, determined and resolute, the Ox certainly has a mind of his own! He is persistent and sets about achieving his objectives with dogged determination. In addition he is reliable and tenacious and is often a source of inspiration to others. He is an achiever, and he often achieves a great deal. However, to really excel, he would do well to try and correct some of his weaknesses.

Being so resolute and having such a strong sense of purpose, the Ox can be inflexible and narrow-minded. He can be resistant to change and prefers to set about his activities in his own way rather than be dependent on others. His dislike of change can sometimes be to his detriment and if he were prepared to be more adaptable and adventurous he would find his progress easier.

The Ox would also be helped if he were to broaden his range of interests and become more relaxed in his approach. At times he can be so preoccupied with his own activities that he is not always as mindful of others as he should be, and his demeanour can sometimes be studious and serious. There are times when he would benefit from a lighter touch.

However, the Ox is true to his word and loyal to his family and friends. He is admired and respected by others and his tremendous willpower usually enables him to succeed in life.

Advice for the Ox's Year Ahead

GENERAL PROSPECTS

A mixed year, and the Ox will need to keep his wits about him and be prepared to adapt as required. This is no time to be obtuse or inflexible, particularly as the changes that happen can often allow the Ox to gain new experience as well as lay the foundations for future progress.

CAREER PROSPECTS

The Ox's skills will be tested this year, but by focusing on his objectives and taking advantage of training and other opportunities to broaden his skills, he can gain experience that will help him in the future. While a demanding year, this can also be a valuable one.

FINANCE

A year to be thorough and vigilant, especially when dealing with paperwork. The Ox should budget ahead for certain plans and requirements and, if possible, make provision for a holiday to enjoy during the year.

RELATIONS WITH OTHERS

Although some Oxen can be loners, contact with others can be very important this year. The Ox will impress many and by being forthcoming can gain support and advice. For some, new friendships and romantic prospects can turn out to be significant. One word of warning; in view of the pressures, delays and niggles of the year, the Ox should watch his temper. Words said in haste could be regretted later.

The Tiger

Lively, innovative and enterprising, the Tiger enjoys an active lifestyle. He has a wide range of interests, an alert mind and a genuine liking of others. He loves to live life to the full. However, despite his enthusiastic and well-meaning ways, he does not always make the most of his considerable potential.

Being so versatile, the Tiger does have a tendency to jump from one activity to another or dissipate his energies by trying to do too much at the same time. To make the most of himself he should try to exercise a certain amount of self-discipline. Ideally, he should decide how best he can use his abilities, give himself some objectives and then stick to them. If he can overcome his restless tendencies, he will find he will accomplish far more as a result.

Also, in spite of his sociable manner, the Tiger likes to retain a certain independence in his actions, and while few begrudge him this, he would sometimes find life easier if he were more prepared to work in conjunction with others. His reliance on his own judgement does sometimes mean that he excludes the views and advice of those around him, and this can be to his detriment. He may possess an independent spirit, but he must not let it go too far!

The Tiger does, however, have much in his favour. He is bold, original and quick-witted. If he can keep his restless nature in check, he can enjoy considerable success. In addition, with his engaging personality, he is well liked and much admired.

Advice for the Tiger's Year Ahead

GENERAL PROSPECTS

This can be a year of considerable potential, but to benefit, the Tiger will need to remain alert, act swiftly when he sees opportunities and also be careful not to push his luck too far. A positive year, but one to remain vigilant.

CAREER PROSPECTS

With his enterprise, ideas and approach, the Tiger can do well this year. With a lot happening and good possibilities arising, it is worth him making that extra effort. New skills and qualifications can substantially improve both his present situation and future prospects.

FINANCE

With spending on accommodation and some substantial purchases likely this year, finances will need good control. Careful budgeting will be helpful.

RELATIONS WITH OTHERS

In this busy year, the Tiger does need to pay close attention to his relations with others and spend quality time with those who are close to him. Being preoccupied, neglectful or, if tense, tetchy can lead to problems. This can be a good year and there will be many occasions to enjoy, but mindfulness will be so very important.

The Rabbit

The Rabbit is certainly one who appreciates the finer things in life. With his good taste, companionable nature and wide range of interests, he knows how to live well – and usually does!

However, for all his finesse and style, he does possess traits he would do well to watch. His desire for a settled lifestyle makes him err on the side of caution. He dislikes change and as a consequence can miss out on opportunities. Also, there are many Rabbits who will go to great lengths to avoid difficult and fraught situations, and again, while few may relish these, sometimes in life it is necessary to take risks or stand your ground. At times it would certainly be in the Rabbit's interests to be bolder and more assertive in going after what he desires.

The Rabbit also attaches great importance to his relations with others and while he has a happy knack of getting on with most people, he can be sensitive to criticism. Difficult though it may be, he should really try to develop a thicker skin and recognize that criticism can provide valuable learning opportunities, as can some of the problems he strives so hard to avoid.

However, with his agreeable manner, keen intellect and shrewd judgement, the Rabbit does have a lot in his favour and invariably makes much of his life – and enjoys it too!

Advice for the Rabbit's Year Ahead

GENERAL PROSPECTS

The Rabbit's abilities will be tested this year. The fast-moving Dragon year can bring its pressures and changes, but by adapting and doing his best, the Rabbit can not only learn a lot but often turn events to his advantage. This may not be an easy year, but the Rabbit's diligence can reward him well and be a contributory factor in the success he will enjoy in 2013.

CAREER PROSPECTS

Many Rabbits will find their workload increasing as changes are introduced or they take on new duties. However, this can give the Rabbit the opportunity to extend his experience and work with others. What he learns now can be good preparation for the future.

FINANCE

By nature the Rabbit is generally careful in money matters and in the Dragon year he must not lower his guard. This is no year for risk, and in all financial dealings the Rabbit needs to be thorough and check anything that is unclear. A year for increased vigilance.

RELATIONS WITH OTHERS
The genial Rabbit values his relations with others and over the year his home and social life can bring much happiness. This is a good year for joint activities, meeting others and, for some, enjoying new friendships and romance. The Rabbit's thoughtfulness, kindness and ability to relate to others will be particularly appreciated and many a Rabbit will be on impressive form.

The Dragon

Enthusiastic, enterprising and honourable, the Dragon possesses many admirable qualities and his life is often full and varied. He always gives his best and even though not all his endeavours meet with success, he is nonetheless resilient and hardy, and is much admired and respected.

However, for all his qualities, he can be blunt and forthright and, through sheer strength of character, sometimes domineering. It would certainly be in his interests to listen more closely to others rather than be so self-reliant. Also, his enthusiasm can sometimes get the better of him and he can be impulsive. To make the most of his abilities, he should give himself priorities and set about his activities in a disciplined and systematic way. More tact and diplomacy might not come amiss either!

However, with his lively and outgoing manner, the Dragon is popular and well liked. With good fortune on his side (and the Dragon is often lucky), his life is almost certain to be eventful and fulfilling. He has many talents, and if he uses them wisely he will enjoy much success.

Advice for the Dragon's Year Ahead

GENERAL PROSPECTS

Enthusiastic, determined and lucky, the Dragon will be aiming to make the most of his own year. He will need to use his time and energies wisely, deciding on priorities and making the most of opportunities, but with effort and belief, this can be a successful and personally significant year.

CAREER PROSPECTS

Great opportunities beckon and the Dragon should keep alert and actively follow up any possibilities that interest him. He should also take advantage of any chances to extend his skills. This is a time of growth and important possibility, and initiative, ideas and positive action will be rewarded.

FINANCE

The Dragon's efforts and enterprise can lead to an increase in earnings and he can also be fortunate when conducting certain transactions. However, he should resist too many impulse purchases and deal with financial paperwork promptly.

RELATIONS WITH OTHERS

The outgoing Dragon will be in excellent form this year. There will be meaningful times to enjoy with family and friends and promising romantic prospects. This is a year to be active and to enjoy the company of others and the pleasure existing or new pursuits can bring.

The Snake

The Snake is blessed with a keen intellect. He has wide interests, an enquiring mind and good judgement. He tends to be quiet and thoughtful and plan his activities with considerable care. With his fine abilities, he often does well in life, but he does possess traits which can undermine his progress.

The Snake is often guarded in his actions and sometimes loses out to those who are more action-oriented and assertive. He also likes to retain a certain independence in his actions and this too can hamper his progress. It would be in his interests to be more forthcoming and involve others more readily in his plans. The Snake has many talents and possesses a warm and rich personality, but there is a danger that this can remain concealed behind his often quiet and reserved manner. He would fare better if he were more outgoing and showed others his true worth.

However, the Snake is very much his own master. He invariably knows what he wants in life and is often prepared to journey long and hard to achieve his objectives. He does, though, have it in his power to make that journey easier. Lose some of that reticence, Snake, be more open and assertive, and don't be afraid of the occasional risk!

Advice for the Snake's Year Ahead

GENERAL PROSPECTS

Expect the unexpected. Although the Snake may like to follow carefully laid plans, Dragon years can be fast-moving and innovative. This is a year to be adaptable and make the most of opportunities *as they occur*. Importantly, what is achieved this year can often have an important bearing on the success that awaits in 2013, the Snake's own year.

CAREER PROSPECTS

An important year. While what opens up for the Snake may be different from what he was expecting, the developments of the year can give him valuable new experience, including possible entry into a new type of work. This is a year to be open to possibility. A lot can follow on from what the Snake now accomplishes.

FINANCE

With personal, accommodation and transport costs, plus other plans the Snake may have, he should manage his budget carefully and avoid too many impulse buys. He should also take extra care in looking after valuables and personal possessions.

RELATIONS WITH OTHERS

A fine year. However, the Snake does need to overcome his independent tendencies and consult others more often. This is a year to be involved and visible and not appear too retiring. Home and social life can be rewarding and many will value the Snake's thoughtfulness and judgement. A new friendship can, for some, prove significant.

The Horse

Versatile, hardworking and sociable, the Horse makes his mark wherever he goes. He has an eloquent and engaging manner and makes friends with ease. He is quick-witted, has an alert mind and is certainly not averse to taking risks or experimenting with new ideas.

He possesses a strong and likeable personality, but he does also have his weaknesses. With his wide interests he does not always finish everything he starts and he would do well to be more persevering. He has it within him to achieve considerable success, but to make the most of his talents he does need to overcome his restless tendencies. When he has made plans, he should stick with them.

The Horse loves company and values both his family and friends. However, there will have been many a time when he will have lost his temper or spoken in haste and regretted his words later. Throughout his life he needs to keep his temper in check and be diplomatic in tense situations. If not, he could risk jeopardizing the respect and good relations he so values.

However, the Horse has a multitude of talents and a lively and outgoing personality. If he can overcome his restless and volatile nature, he can lead a rich and highly fulfilling life.

Advice for the Horse's Year Ahead

GENERAL PROSPECTS

Active, strong-willed and adventurous, the Horse will find the Dragon year surprising, interesting and full of possibility. Throughout he does need to be wary of risk, as well as think through the consequences of his actions, but with awareness and a certain flexibility, he can make this a rewarding time.

CAREER PROSPECTS

Progress is indicated, but this can bring added pressure and require adjustments to be made. To do well, the Horse should rise to the challenge and seize his opportunities to learn and add to his experience. Commitment and initiative will be recognized and rewarded this year.

FINANCE

While the Horse's income may increase, this is a year to avoid risk. In money matters the Horse should be thorough and vigilant and, where possible, make advance provision for larger outgoings and travel.

RELATIONS WITH OTHERS

A promising year. Loved ones and friends will be helpful, although to benefit fully the Horse needs to listen to their views and preserve quality time for those who are close to him. For the unattached, romantic prospects are excellent, while those newly in love will often find their relationship blossoming. A personally exciting year, with the Horse's domestic and social life also busy and frequently rewarding.

The Goat

The Goat has a warm, friendly and understanding manner and gets on well with most people. He is generally easy-going, has a fond appreciation of the finer things in life and possesses a rich imagination. He is often artistic and enjoys the creative arts and outdoor activities.

However, despite his engaging manner, there lurks beneath his skin a sometimes tense and pessimistic nature. The Goat can be a worrier and without the support and encouragement of others can feel insecure and be hesitant in his actions.

To make the most of himself he should aim to become more assertive and decisive as well as more at ease with himself. He has much in his favour, but he really does need to promote himself more and be bolder. He would also be helped by sorting out his priorities and setting about his activities in an organized and disciplined manner. There are some Goats who tend to be haphazard in the way they go about things and this can hamper their progress.

Although the Goat will always value the support of others, it would also be in his interests to become more independent and not be so reticent about striking out on his own. He does, after all, possess many talents, as well as a sincere and likeable personality, and by always giving his best he can make his life rich, rewarding and enjoyable.

Advice for the Goat's Year Ahead

GENERAL PROSPECTS

Hold tight! A busy, volatile year ahead. However, while it will have its uncomfortable moments, there will also be the chance to learn. If the Goat rises to the challenge this fast-moving year will present, its benefits can be considerable.

CAREER PROSPECTS
There will be important developments this year which will give the Goat a good chance to extend his skills as well as take on new and sometimes unfamiliar duties. This may be a demanding time, but by being willing and adaptable the Goat can help both his present and future situation.

FINANCE
To do all he wants this year, the Goat will need to take careful control of his budget and make advance provision for more major outgoings. Some Goats may find personal interests supplementing their income.

RELATIONS WITH OTHERS
The Goat's sincere and genial nature can win him new friends and much support this year. There could also be good romantic opportunities. However, when under pressure or facing decisions, the Goat should consult those around him. His positive relations with many will stand him in good stead this year as well as bringing pleasure, fun and encouragement.

The Monkey
Lively, enterprising and innovative, the Monkey certainly knows how to impress. He has wide interests, a good sense of fun and relates well to others. He also possesses a shrewd mind and often has a happy knack of turning events to his advantage.

However, despite his versatility and considerable gifts, he does have his weaknesses. He often lacks persistence, can get distracted easily and also relies tremendously on his own judgement. While his belief in himself is a commendable asset, it would certainly be in his interests to be more mindful of the views of others. Also, while he likes to keep tabs on all that is going on around him, he can be evasive and secretive with regard to his own feelings and activities, and again a more forthcoming attitude would be to his advantage.

In his desire to succeed, the Monkey can also be tempted to cut corners or be crafty and he should recognize that such actions can rebound on him!

However, he is resourceful and his sheer strength of character will ensure that he has an interesting and varied life. If he can channel his considerable energies wisely and overcome his sometimes restless tendencies, his life can be crowned with success. And with his amiable personality, he will have many friends.

Advice for the Monkey's Year Ahead

GENERAL PROSPECTS

The Monkey will enjoy the activity of the Dragon year and by keeping alert and adapting as required, he can gain a great deal from it. This is a time of considerable scope and possibility, with his initiative rewarding him well.

CAREER PROSPECTS

Change is in the air and the Monkey will often be well placed to take on new challenges. This is a year to move forward, to act smartly when opportunities arise and to add to skills and experience. The Monkey's resourcefulness, quick wits and good working relations with many will serve him well this year.

FINANCE

Income may improve, but the Monkey should remain disciplined and control his spending.

RELATIONS WITH OTHERS

The Monkey will find himself in demand, with family, friends and colleagues valuing his many abilities. There will be an excellent chance to add to his social circle and, for some, to enjoy romance. However throughout the year the Monkey should act in consultation with others. With help, support and encouragement, he can get to do – and enjoy – far more.

The Rooster

With his considerable bearing and incisive and resolute manner, the Rooster cuts an impressive figure. He has a sharp mind, is well informed on many matters and expresses himself clearly and convincingly. He is meticulous and efficient in his undertakings and commands a great deal of respect. He also has a genuine and caring interest in others.

There is much in his favour, but there are some aspects of his character that can tell against him. He can be candid in his views and over-zealous in his actions, and sometimes he can say or do things he later regrets. His high standards also make him fussy, even pedantic, and he can get diverted into relatively minor matters when in truth he could be occupying his time more profitably. This is something all Roosters would do well to watch. Also, while the Rooster is a great planner, he can sometimes be unrealistic in his expectations. In making plans – indeed, in most of his activities – he would do well to consult others. He would benefit greatly from their input.

The Rooster has many talents as well as commendable drive and commitment, but to make the most of himself he does need to channel his energies wisely and watch his candid and sometimes volatile nature. With care, however, he can make a success of his life, and with his wide interests and outgoing personality, he will enjoy the friendship and respect of many.

Advice for the Rooster's Year Ahead

GENERAL PROSPECTS
This is a positive and progressive year and the Rooster should act determinedly and make the most of it. With his skills, style and personal strengths, he has a lot in his favour, but in order to carry through his plans he does need to make that all-important effort.

CAREER PROSPECTS
Excellent chances await. If already established at work, the Rooster can take his career to a new level, and if currently unfulfilled or seeking work, he can gain an important new position with potential for the future. This is a year for keeping alert, taking action and making headway.

FINANCE

Earnings can increase and some Roosters can also benefit from some money luck this year. However, accommodation and other plans could involve considerable cost and the Rooster does need to manage his money well, including budgeting ahead for more major outlay.

RELATIONS WITH OTHERS

A busy and pleasing year, with the Rooster's home and social life both seeing a lot of activity. This is a time favouring joint undertakings and the Rooster should regularly consult those around him as well as involve them in his various activities. Friends and contacts made at work can be helpful while, for the unattached, romance can beckon. The Dragon year can be pleasing and often special.

The Dog

Loyal, dependable and with a good understanding of human nature, the Dog is well placed to win respect and admiration. He is a no-nonsense sort of person and hates any sort of hypocrisy and falsehood. With the Dog you know where you stand and, given his direct manner, where he stands on any issue. He also has a strong humanitarian nature and often champions good causes.

The Dog has many fine attributes, although there are certain traits that can prevent him from either enjoying or making the most of his life. He is a great worrier and can get anxious over all manner of things. Although it may not always be easy, he should try to rid himself of the 'worry habit'. Whenever he is tense or concerned, he should be prepared to speak to others rather than shoulder his worries all by himself. In some cases, they could even be of his own making! Also, he has a tendency to look on the pessimistic side and he would certainly be helped if he were to view his undertakings more optimistically. He does, after all, possess many skills and should have faith in his abilities. Another weakness is his tendency to be stubborn over certain issues. If he is not careful, at times this could undermine his position.

If the Dog can reduce the pessimistic side of his nature, he will not only enjoy life more but also achieve more. He possesses a truly admirable character and his loyalty, reliability and sincerity are appreciated by all he meets. In his life he will do much good and befriend many people, and he owes it to himself to enjoy life too. Sometimes it might help him to recall the words of another Dog, Sir Winston Churchill: 'When I look back on all these worries I remember the story of the old man who said on his deathbed that he had had a lot of trouble in his life, most of which never happened.'

Advice for the Dog's Year Ahead

GENERAL PROSPECTS
The Dragon year will not always make the Dog's situation easy. However, he must not always assume the worst. Despite the pressures and volatility of the year, interesting possibilities can emerge. 'Every cloud has a silver lining', as they say, and this also applies to the Dragon year.

CAREER PROSPECTS

Events can happen quickly and the Dog will need to keep his wits about him. He will do best by keeping himself informed and adapting as situations require. What he is able to accomplish this year can often add considerably to his skills and may even set him off on an interesting new career path.

FINANCE

The Dog should be thorough with paperwork and keep careful control over spending. Lapses and hasty purchases could come to be regretted or work to the Dog's disadvantage. If anything concerns him at any time, it would be worth him seeking advice.

RELATIONS WITH OTHERS

The Dog may sometimes keep his thoughts to himself, but with this a busy and demanding year, he does need to be prepared to consult others and act jointly. The best results will come from combined effort. With this being a good year for travel, holidays and other trips with loved ones can be much appreciated, but new romances need special care and attention.

The Pig

Genial, sincere and trusting, the Pig gets on well with most people. He has a kind and caring nature, a dislike of discord and often a good sense of humour. In addition, he has a fondness for socializing and enjoying the good life!

The Pig also possesses a shrewd mind, is particularly adept at dealing with business and financial matters and has a robust and resilient nature. He is tenacious and will often rise up and succeed after experiencing setbacks and difficulties. In his often active and varied life he can accomplish a great deal, although there are certain aspects of his character that can tell against him. If he can modify these or keep them in check then his life will certainly be easier and possibly even more successful.

The Pig can sometimes over-commit himself, and while he does not want to disappoint, he would certainly be helped if he were to set about his activities in an organized and systematic manner and give himself priorities at busy times. He should also not allow others to take advantage of his good nature and it would be in his interests to be more discerning. There will be times when he proves gullible and naïve; fortunately, though, he quickly learns from his mistakes. However, he possesses a stubborn streak and if new situations do not fit in with his line of thinking, he can be inflexible. Such an attitude may not always be to his advantage.

The Pig is a great pleasure-seeker and while he should enjoy the fruits of his labours, he can sometimes be self-indulgent and extravagant. This is also something he would do well to watch.

However, though the Pig may possess some faults, those who come into contact with him are invariably impressed by his integrity, amiable manner and intelligence. If he uses his talents wisely, his life can be crowned with considerable achievement and he will also be loved and respected by many.

Advice for the Pig's Year Ahead

GENERAL PROSPECTS

This will be a busy year and the Pig may be concerned by the pace of developments, but there will be opportunities aplenty. The Pig should keep alert and informed and be prepared to adapt as required. With effort, he can achieve a great deal.

CAREER PROSPECTS

Change will affect many Pigs, but while there will be some uncomfortable moments and demanding situations, there will also be good opportunities for the Pig to use and demonstrate his strengths and move forward. With willingness and perseverance, he can gain a lot from the year.

FINANCE

Income may improve and many Pigs enjoy some financial good fortune, but the Dragon year can bring its temptations and the Pig should be wary of too many impulse purchases, particularly in view of the plans he will be keen to proceed with. A year for discipline and good budgeting.

RELATIONS WITH OTHERS

By being active and seizing any chances to meet others and get himself better known, the Pig can help his situation and prospects as well as have a lot of fun. At work he will enjoy a lot of support, with new contacts proving helpful, while his personal interests can also lead to social opportunities. His home life will see much activity and some exciting times. This will be a busy year, with the Pig on often impressive form.